Grace Charlotte Vulliamy

Wearing a medal ribbon

Also by Katherine Storr

Facing East (England's Eastern Counties Welcome Belgian Refugees 1914 – 1919) 2018 (ISBN:-10: 1985409844 ISBN-13: 978 1985409842)

Excluded from the Record: Women, Refugees and Relief, 1914 – 1929 (Peter Lang. 2010. ISBN 978-3-03911-855-7)

'Education for Peace and Equality 1914 – 1930) in *Woman Education and Agency*. Ed. Dr Sarah Aiston, Jean Spence & Dr Meikle (Routledge 2009)

Lincolnshire Home Front in WWI – South Holland website:
www.southhollandllife.com/dr-katherinne-storr.archive/

ISBN: 10: 1986435350
ISBN-13: 978-1986435352:

27.12.18

Dear Bill
Some light reading
Regards Jock
(Jonathan Vulliamy)

Shining
While the Lamps were Out

The life of Grace Charlotte Vulliamy, CBE

1878-1957

"The lamps are going out all over Europe,
we shall not see them lit again in our life-time".

British Foreign Secretary Sir Edward Grey
on the eve of the United Kingdom's entry into the First World War

KATHERINE STORR

CONTENTS

PHOTOGRAPHS and FIGURES

PREFACE

Grace Vulliamy came to my attention when I was working on my PhD thesis and the resultant book *Excluded from the Record*[1] in which I studied the relief work carried out among European civilians by the Society of Friends, known as Quakers, during the First World War. She was impossible to research further because references to her were quite brief and there was no clue as to what her next or previous step was and the Internet as a tool of research was not then well developed. In addition, Grace herself was very cautious about recording anything that could be regarded as contentious, compromising or personal and this tended to make tracking her even more difficult. On 24 July 1918 she had an interview with Agnes Conway, Honorary Secretary of the Imperial War Museum's Women's Sub-committee. Conway recorded: 'Miss Vulliamy is most anxious to keep her work private and never writes anything if she can help it.' This is one important reason why she is so little known and why my searches produced no further information.

Apparently with no further archive material to help me, I wondered "What does a woman have to do to be remembered by posterity?" It became evident that women who deserve to be kept in the public eye must have a 'champion' who will frequently write or talk about them. If this does not happen, it is almost certain the woman will be forgotten, especially within patriarchal societies. Such women also need to leave archive material available for later researchers! However, as Dr Elsie Inglis of Edinburgh exemplifies, women can be re-discovered. Although Dr Inglis was famous during the Great War with her work of the Scottish Women's Hospitals, her name was almost forgotten, and Edinburgh has only recently been persuaded to erect a statue in her honour. It would be wonderful if Ipswich, where Grace was born on 12 September 1878, would do the same for her.

I was delighted when in 2014 the Vulliamy family told me they held Grace's archive material and asked me if I would like to see it. Overall, it gives information about her early life, her training as a nurse, her work in Europe among refugees during the Great War, her work as Representative of the Society of Friends, of the YMCA, the Red Cross and the British Prisoners of War Department at The Hague, and her life of relief work afterwards in various countries, ending in South Africa where she settled in 1937. Post-

---

[1] Storr, Katherine. *Excluded from the Record. Women, Refugees and Relief. 1914 – 1929.* Peter Lang. 2010.

war Grace became Assistant Commissioner to Lady Paget's Mission to Czechoslovakia for a few months. Following this, seeing the suffering caused by the Russian Revolution and resultant famines, she founded the Committee for Relief in Poland. When the necessity for that work ceased, she became the founder of The Cape Flats Distress Association (CAFDA) in South Africa where she died in 1957. She was also an active life Vice-President of Save the Children Fund. I found that several people started to write about Grace Vulliamy's work while she was alive but none of it was completed or published.

With the Anniversary of the Armistice in 1918 looming I decided to concentrate on her work during the Great War. This book therefore represents to some extent an unfinished work using Grace's papers. They show how the outbreak of the Great War shifted the question of women's role in a patriarchal society. Grace was already at a crossroads in her career and was asking herself how to conduct herself when her country was suddenly at war with another nation. By her actions over the four years of war and for the even longer period after it, she gave answers to this question: 'use your skills,' 'alleviate the suffering, clear up the mess,' and 'see to it that women and children are valued.' She told her adopted son that the greatest happiness was to be found in thinking of others and it is evident that she spent her life doing exactly this.

It was decided to use the papers, if possible, as a basis for a biography. There are two 80 litre plastic boxes containing Grace's papers and photographs as well as one other smaller box, so it appeared there should be enough material to draw on. However, it was immediately obvious that in Grace's mind it was her work that was important, not Grace Vulliamy herself. She was not unique in this: Rachel Crowdy, a member of the Secretariat of the League of Nations felt the same, devoting herself to League business rather than women's emancipation. In addition, the contents of the boxes are neither organised nor listed, making it difficult to return to a particular document to check it if necessary. I felt I had the choice of either organising everything first and then writing, or using it as it is, and I chose the latter due to time factors and my own age-related physical limitations. We know that everything passed through Grace's hands but on examination these documents exemplify what Conway recorded about her – she was very private and never gave anything away. Therefore, it is hoped that by finding out what was important to Grace it might be possible to get glimpses into her thinking and character, to find the "real Grace." However, there was another problem – how to refer to her. When she was alive, life was more formal and she was always referred to as 'Miss Vulliamy,' but I have got to know her very well (and also some members of her family) and tended to refer to her just as Grace. I did not want to refer to her just by her patronymic so mostly use just her first name.

In order to do this it is necessary to look at her family background and this I do in Chapter 1. I also use many of the photographs without editing, showing them as she put them into albums.

In order to contextualize her life I have used notes I took in my earlier studies; I also referred to a small amount of extremely relevant other material, such as the Friends House Library records and to published works such as *In Ruhleben, Letters from a Prisoner to his Mother,* edited by Douglas Brooke Wheelton Sladen and *the Life and Times of RNAS Bomber Pilot* Donald E Harkness.

My thanks go to Daniel Vulliamy for contacting me about Grace's papers, to Nicolette Vulliamy for allowing me to keep them while I worked on them and wrote this book and to Mark Vulliamy for his input; also to Chris Morrell and Maryrose Hughes Finally to my husband Dave who shouldered the task of supporting me in all possible ways while I was writing.

CHAPTER 1

INTRODUCTION
MEETING THE VULLIAMY FAMILY

Grace Charlotte Vulliamy

The name Grace Charlotte Vulliamy is not one which many people recognise today, yet in her lifetime she was famous; her contemporaries compared her to Florence Nightingale and Edith Cavell because she had a caring and brave nature like these better-known women and had unique wartime experiences. The newly-discovered archive material used here shows that Grace Vulliamy was a highly intelligent initiator and organiser like Florence Nightingale. Like her, Grace was a pioneer in nursing, but in mental rather than corporeal nursing. In the light of the fact that the Great War saw so much mental suffering on the part of the soldiers, it seems surprising that Grace Vulliamy is not better known in this connection. However, she was not a member of any of the official nursing services such as Queen Alexandra's Imperial Military Nursing Service (QAIMNS) nor was she a member of a Voluntary Aid Detachment and historians have therefore missed her. In addition, shellshock was not recognised at first as a mental wound but thought to be psychological weakness. Grace was compared to Edith Cavell because, disregarding her own safety, she rescued prisoners-of-war and helped them escape, smuggling men onto ships about to cross the Channel.

So, who was Grace Vulliamy and what kind of person was she? Grace was a member of 'a large English family of the higher middle class' but needed to earn her own living. She led a life of unconventional and devoted service to others, mostly people who were marginalized such as those suffering from mental illness, refugees, prisoners-of-war and black people. She was a forerunner in some of the tasks that it was considered inappropriate for women to do. For example, she ran her own nursing homes and was not subordinate to doctors. She was a woman who pushed at boundaries, did not suffer fools gladly, could be caustic and reduce inefficient workers to a 'quivering jelly.' She was an extremely efficient organiser and administrator and did not take no as an answer. However, she was greatly loved, because she expressed love for others, not in a sentimental manner, but in one which restored their self-respect. At the end of her life she was referred to as a war heroine who showed self-sacrifice, kindness, and sympathy.

Grace was very independent and in some respects a maverick, one of the often-denigrated New Women who smoked and were liberated socially and economically. Grace very seldom wrote about herself. Her multitude of photographs answer some questions but raise far more. For example, there are photos of her roof garden, but we do not know precisely when she used it. It was evidently a place she and her friends enjoyed; it had a home-made phone from the garden to a room below in the form of a pipe for speaking into. Who were the friends who relaxed in this way with her?

Plate 1.1 Grace Charlotte Vulliamy

We know that she crossed the Channel to return to England many times during the First World War and many of these journeys were to accompany sick prisoners, some of whom may have been escapees from behind German lines. What we are uncertain about is how many journeys were for personal reasons and if so what those reasons were. She kept pictures of topical events such as riots following the sinking of the Lusitania on 5 May by German U-boats, and the damage done to such boats by torpedoes but as she left few personal papers and no diaries, she makes no comments about these events. However, there are indications that she was gathering information that she passed to the British authorities and was therefore spying. Cavell's fate showed that Germany would not show Grace Vulliamy any mercy if she were caught.

So who was Grace Vulliamy? Born in 1878, Grace's address in the 1881 census, when she was four years old, was Spring Road, Oakstead, Ipswich, Suffolk, where she lived with her parents and brothers and sisters. Grace's family background, her schooling, and early career years show her to be something of a rebel, not cowed by authority. They indicate the social class from which she came and give clues as to her character and its formation; a piece of her imaginative early writing is included for this purpose.

Plate 1.2. The roof garden at 42 Great Russell Street, right opposite the British Museum.

It was important to attempt to determine Grace's views on and relationship with the suffrage campaign which was so significant at that period. Unless new information becomes available we must conclude that Grace was not herself a member of one of the suffrage societies but she was undoubtedly sympathetic to the cause. On the declaration of the Great War she enrolled with the Women's Emergency Corps which was formed by suffragettes who became her closest and lifelong friends. In the Corps she was able to use her many skills to help the refugees then pouring into Britain. Thereafter her career was unusual for a woman at that time. For example, she became a member of the Government Commission for the Transportation of Belgian Refugees to England and worked in Flushing. Holland, for the purpose, becoming Representative of the Local Government Board. At the same time, she helped the Quakers in their work with Refugees in camps in Holland and became Representative of the Friends War Victims Relief Committee. She was also a Representative of the Consul General for the Netherlands, Ernest

Maxse, for the purpose of meeting on the Dutch frontier British returned civilians from Germany and accompanying them to the UK. During these war years she was also representative of the British Red Cross and YMCA in Holland assisting civilian and military prisoners-of-war as they were exchanged. These were all very unusual positions for a woman to hold. She organised the first temporary Hospital for sick or wounded p.o.w.'s, the first batch arriving in Rotterdam on 29 December 1917. She was awarded a CBE for this work and received other honours, so it was important to study and write about these years in considerable detail, augmenting them to a limited extent by using my previous research into relief work by the Quakers among civilian refugee camps in Europe during the Great War.

Grace's girlhood and education were not very happy. Described by one of her sisters as 'Ahead of her time', a rebel, a born leader and full of energy, she was not understood by her parents or by the boarding schools to which she was sent, rejecting the restrictive double standards imposed on young Victorian women. Being at a boarding school left some girls with a memory of being 'dumped by unfeeling parents'[2] and of a closed, authoritarian regime. Jane Eyre's deeply unhappy experience at Lowood School described by Charlotte Brontë, was a fictional boarding school experience but has the ring of experience throughout. Charlotte Despard, founder of the Women's Freedom League, sister of Sir John French and campaigner for women's rights, did not enjoy her experiences at boarding-school in the 1850s. She wrote:

> I was continually seeking to find expression for the force that was in me, trying to learn, asking to serve with my life in my hand ready to offer, and no one wanting it. I must not, I was told, pursue certain studies - they were for boys - I must not be so downright, it was unladylike.[3]

As with Despard, the curriculum may not have been sufficient to keep Grace occupied and interested. The concern to develop a more distinctive girls' curriculum with a focus on domestic science, cooking, laundry and needlework came after 1870 and especially in the 1880s and 1890s when

---

[2] Lambert, Angela (1990) *No Talking After Lights, Black Swan* http://www.independent.co.uk/news/obituaries/angela-lambert-403739.html

[3] This notion is hard to dislodge. The writer experienced this when growing up in the 1950s.

Grace would have been at school. Helena Swanwick who was a League of Nations delegate in the 1920s explained the difficulty:

> Girls' education was suffering from a shortage of well-educated and trained teachers, and secondly, the effort to make the girls' curriculum the same as that of boys' schools. 'The present generation has no conception of what a mass of prejudice had to be overcome before women could be free to say they did not choose to go in for certain examinations because these did not suit their aims. At that time it was almost universally believed that if girls did not take certain subjects it was because they could not.[4]

In the latter part of the 19th century there were no games at girls' schools and no outlet such as the Girl Guides. Men were believed to dislike 'blue-stockings', so parents thought the serious education of their daughters superfluous: deportment, music and a little French would see them through. Consequently, probably out of boredom, Grace led other children into various pranks. The one example that has survived shows her to have an enquiring mind and able to find ways of satisfying it, albeit unconventionally and with little regard for propriety. When she was a boarder at the Church School in the Cathedral Close, Gloucester, pyjamas had come into fashion. The children wondered whether the old Canons were still wearing night shirts or had changed into the more fashionable night attire. So Grace got several of the girls together late one night and they went out and shouted 'fire' and although they stayed out long enough to satisfy their curiosity, they weren't seen, and by the time it was realised there was no fire they were all in their beds apparently sound asleep. This kind of prank made her popular with the children, but not with those in authority. Hence the first two schools she attended suggested she would probably do better somewhere else and she was expelled from both.

One of the schools to which she was sent was St Katharine's at Wantage, in Oxfordshire, England, an Anglican church school run by English nuns of the Community of St Mary the Virgin. This Order was founded in 1848 by the Reverend William John Butler, vicar of Wantage and is one of the oldest surviving religious communities in the Church of England. St Katharine's School is named for St Catherine of Alexandria, despite the different spelling. After her father had suffered a financial set-back one of her elder sisters, Eva, took up teaching. Thinking that the elder sister could keep an

---

[4] Swanwick, Helena. *I have Been Young,* Gollancz. Chapter IV.Adolescence. 1878-1882

eye on the younger, her parents sent Grace to the same school, where she had to live with her sister and the principal. The arrangement was naturally a failure. When Grace arrived her reputation had gone before her and the other scholars had been forbidden to associate with her!'[5] Nevertheless, one of the nuns, Sister Isabel, understood her better and she stayed there until her schooling days were over. School, however, was a preparation for women's inferior role in society.

It seems that Grace was not deflated by the results of her pranks or cowed by being expelled because years later she told her sister-in-law Constance[6] about these events for her amusement. On 5 September 1954, after Grace had a stroke and was in financial distress, Constance sent her a cheque and wrote:

> I was delighted to get the translation of the article about you and will read it to Mother and Beano, I mean Gerald. ... It is lovely, and I surely learned a lot about you I did not know. ... I recall you telling us some of the school episodes when we were children but I always thought you made them up!'

Children, animals and those who were suffering were instantly attracted to Miss Vulliamy, who seemed to have a knack for changing people's lives for the better. There is enough information in the Vulliamy papers and photographs to realise that this was the pattern of Grace's life. But who were the Vulliamys and where did they originate?

The Vulliamy Family

Grace's father was a solicitor in Ipswich and was a descendant of one of the families who escaped from France at the revocation of the Edict of Nantes by Louis XIV in October 1685. This Huguenot ancestor, Francis Justin Vulliamy, (1718-1797) found refuge in Switzerland and took up watch making. Vulliamy watches and clocks became well known, and more than 200 years later, at the time of the First World War, one of their clocks was still in Buckingham Palace. Another member of the family, George Vulliamy, was architect to the Metropolitan Board of Works at the time when the Thames embankment was being constructed. He submitted a design for a lamp with pairs of dolphins curling around the base. This was adapted from the Fontana del Nettuno in Rome and the visual impact was perceived as enhancing London's status. In 1874, Vulliamy designed benches that featured Sphinx and Camel shaped armrests, anticipating the

[5] Vulliamy Papers. A Woman of Action

[6] Born 1876, left New Orleans arrival Bristol 37 February 1915.

arrival of Cleopatra's Needle, installed in 1878. These have all become iconic symbols of London and the Vulliamy family are rightly proud of them. This background of France and Switzerland caused a degree of confusion outside the immediate family leading to some discussion in newspapers. One article stated the 'Vulliamy family was Swiss, with a little English blood but not a drop of French.' However, they were originally French protestants, some of whom, with many others, migrated to London or Geneva to escape persecution.[7] From the nineteenth century, this branch of the Vulliamy family was central to the life of Ipswich. At a mid-century election for County Coroner the candidates were Mr Arthur Frederick Vulliamy, Grace's father, and Mr Chaston. At that time, candidates could provide voters with refreshment and pay their expenses; in many places this gave rise to malpractice. The voting took place at the Corn Hall in Ipswich. The hall was packed and when the show of hands was taken not another could be got in. However, Mr Vulliamy lost by 300. Shortly afterwards the other Coroner died and this time when Mr Vulliamy offered himself there was no opposition and he was elected *pro forma.* This raises questions concerning the honesty of the previous election. Arthur Fredrick Vulliamy attended various Poor Law Conferences, including the Central one in London. He was a staunch Liberal, acting as agent in several Parliamentary elections in the area, including for Hugh Edward Adair in 1847.

Grace's Mother - Anna Museur Vulliamy On 21 July 1864, Arthur Frederick married Anna Museur, who was of Irish descent on her mother's side, but through her father was a native of Brussels, Belgium. There is no information on how they met but there was a scattering of Belgian people in England at that time usually clustered around a Catholic church. Both Ireland and Belgium were strongly Roman Catholic but Grace's mother did not appear to follow this religion. Marriage meant she soon had a large family to care for, so it could be anticipated that she would not have much time available for charitable works. This would be incorrect; Anna Vulliamy devoted a good deal of her time to the activities of St Lawrence's Church, including the Mothers' Union and the Girls' Friendly Society. St Lawrence's was built on Dial Lane in the heart of present-day Ipswich. Uniquely, the Victorian restorers left the church with no central aisle, in an attempt to defeat the introduction of High Church practices.[8] We might correctly deduce from this that the Vulliamy parents were not 'high church'.

[7] Signed Eustace A Stedman, Old House Tisbury, Wilts.
[8] http://www.suffolkchurches.co.uk/stlawrenceipswich.htm
Accessed 28/11/2015

The Girls' Friendly Society,[9] with which Mrs Anna Vulliamy was also involved, was an organization founded in 1875 in England by Mary Elizabeth Townsend, the first organization for women in the Church of England, and therefore forward looking. Its purpose was to provide a place for girls who were not married and who had been sent to the city by their families to work in textile mills. Through the Society they could experience friendship and recreation in a fellowship of Christian love and service. As this new organization was a place for finding comfort and friendship, the name Girl's Friendly Society was decided upon. This was one of the organisations with which the Women's Emergency Corps co-operated when the war began. Grace was extremely active in the Corps for the first months of the war.

Grace's father - Arthur Frederick Vulliamy

Mr Vulliamy's church allegiance was different from his wife's, although still Anglican. He was Sunday School Superintendent at St John's Church for 50 years. St John's was an Evangelical Anglican fellowship church located in the east of Ipswich, a 'lower church' than St Lawrence's, built as were so many churches in the 1870s to encourage the population to attend. Their comparatively slight religious difference helps to explain why Arthur Frederick and Anna Museur worshiped in separate churches. Arthur Frederick was also a member of the Church of England Temperance Society. He became deeply involved in social work and started the Town Relief Association. There was no Welfare State at this time therefore charity was an important issue and depended on wealthier members of society helping the poorer. There was no taxation system to cover the cost as there is today. It was realised that people with money had a duty to help the poor and those in trouble but one dilemma was that the receipt of charity created dependence. There were attempts to control the amount of money needing to be raised partly by determining those who were 'worthy' recipients and those considered not worthy. Nonetheless the number of people needing help appeared to be increasing and this placed a growing burden on those who were charity givers. Although money could be raised for special purposes, there was little money for ordinary relief so the Town Relief became instead part of the Charity Organization Society; Mr Vulliamy was a Member of the Executive Committee.

The Ipswich Poor Law Union was formed on 9th September 1835 before Arthur Frederick was born. Arthur Frederick Vulliamy was appointed Clerk

---

[9] Storr, Katherine. *Excluded from the Record. Women, Refugees and Relief. 1914 – 1929.* Peter Lang. 2010. 25

to the Ipswich Guardians in 1877. He retired from that position in 1904 but nevertheless continued to take a great interest in everything concerning the Poor Law. He was vice-chairman of the movement for securing pensions for Poor Law officers and was still secretary for the Eastern District Poor-law Conference at the time of his Golden Wedding. He was clerk of Ipswich Union responsible for the administration of such places as workhouses and hospitals. In 1905 at the Central Poor Law Conference he read a paper on the treatment of tramps, making the distinction between those who trudged the streets towards some place where they hoped to find work, and vagrants who were aimlessly wandering about the country.[10] He was concerned to prevent tramps becoming vagrants who were regarded, with vagabonds and beggars, as the 'lazy' or ‘unworthy’ poor. Grace’s father was present at a Poor Law Conference at the London Guildhall on 22 February 1910, when he read a Minority Report concerned with work of the Royal Commission on those on parish relief.

The Ipswich Poor Law Union workhouse for pauper children became the St John's Children's Home. Mr Vulliamy had some responsibility for the home. This was not an unusual kind of institution in more urban areas, but it was the only one of its kind in Suffolk, and as such seems to have been the place where poor orphans from all over the county ended up. Built in 1879, the year after Grace’s birth, it had room for 130 children. It eventually closed in 1930. Also in the parish was one of the last workhouses ever built in England. Replacing the aging one at Whip Street in the centre of town, the Ipswich Union Workhouse was constructed in the late 1890s on heathland on the corner of Woodbridge Road and Heath Road. It became known as the Heathfields Poor Law Institution. Hospital blocks were added to it, and these soon became the greater part of its operation.[11] So the family was greatly concerned with the importance of social and political issues, having a strong sense of social responsibility - an example of ‘faith in action’; these attitudes would undoubtedly have informed Grace Vulliamy’s outlook and opinions as she was growing up. She would also have been convinced of the necessity of sticking to her principles.

But how did Arthur Frederick Vulliamy earn his living and support his family? Or was he a gentleman who did not need to work? In the Ipswich County Directory of 1901 he is listed as being of the firm Vulliamy & Son, 20 Upper Brook Street and 19 Tower Street, Ipswich, the former being close

---

[10] *The Times.* 23.02.1905

[11] http://www.suffolkchurches.co.uk/stjbaptipswich.htm Accessed 27.11.2015

to his home in Northgate Street. By 1891 when Grace was age fourteen, the family had moved to Upper Brook Street. Ipswich was a town where several members of the family made their homes. Frederick, Grace's grandfather, a retired bank manager, lived in a house in Bolton Lane, within walking distance. He had four children: two girls and two boys, the youngest of whom was Rose, born 1846 although it is uncertain whether her mother was Charlotte (formerly Clark) or Anna Frampton. Grace wrote copiously about her work in Poland to her Auntie Rose and appears to have been closer to her than she was to her parents. There was, therefore, through Grace's parents, a concern for the sick and those in less fortunate circumstances than themselves but in addition a connection with refugees.

Family and Women's Suffrage

By the time Grace was born, many women had become increasingly dissatisfied with their subordinate and restricted position in society and were seeking emancipation through being able to vote for parliamentary candidates. Fifteen Ipswich women signed the petition raised by the London Women's Suffrage Petition Committee that was formed in 1866.[12] By then, Ipswich was a thriving town, permeated by a strong nonconformist influence. In May 1869 an Ipswich women's suffrage petition was presented in Parliament. Two years later[13] a suffrage meeting was held in the Ipswich Lecture Hall, at which the main speaker was Rhoda Garrett; her cousin Millicent Fawcett, founder of the National Union of Women's Suffrage Societies, was also present. This influenced the formation in 1871 of the Ipswich Committee of the National Society for Women's Suffrage. There was, however, little activity from this Society until the meeting in the Council Chamber in the Town Hall on 16 April 1874 when Grace's father, Arthur Vulliamy was present, as he was again in 1876. By 1907 he was a vice-president of the Ipswich Women's Suffrage Society – one of eleven, many of whom did not pay their subscriptions on time![14]

In addition, the family were involved with women's rights through a Mrs Vulliamy who lived in Cambridge. No initials are given in any reference to her so it is difficult to be absolutely certain of her identity. She was a prominent member of the constitutional, non-militant National Union of Women Suffragists, the NUWSS. This was formed in 1897 when seventeen

---

[12] Elizabeth Crawford. *The Women's Suffrage Movement in Britain and Ireland: a Regional Survey.* Routledge. 2006. 1, 85

[13] On 12 April 1871

[14] Joy Bounds. *A Song of their Own. The Fight for Votes for Women in Ipswich.* History Press. 2014. p30

local groups joined together under Millicent Garrett Fawcett.[15] The Union was supported by many influential men including the philosopher John Stuart Mill, Henry Nevinson, the campaigning journalist, and Israel Zangwill, the Zionist author, among others. It was certainly not necessary to be militant to support or be active in the NUWSS, rather the reverse. The NUWSS abhorred violence. NUWSS Members campaigned on behalf of parliamentary candidates who professed support for women's suffrage by introducing Parliamentary Bills. They held public meetings, organised petitions, wrote letters to politicians, published newspapers and distributed free literature: all considered very daring things for women to do at the time, but fully 'constitutional'. They were determined to achieve their purpose of votes for women, but they never resorted to violence although individual members might hold different views from the leaders. Many WSPU members, known as suffrag*ettes* – distinguishing themselves from the constitutional suffrag*ists* – were doubtful about violence and the Pankhurst's autocratic rule over the WSPU, and left it, returning in many instances to the NUWSS; many women were simultaneously members of both organizations. Bertrand Russell believed the WSPU's tactics would delay women's enfranchisement by 20 years, and in many ways he was right. Women were not given the vote on the same terms as men until 1928. The 1918 enfranchisement was to a limited group of women only.

When Asquith's Liberal Party came to power in 1906, the hopes of women were raised because the Liberal Party was seen as the party that would pioneer women's political rights in Britain. Instead, it was ruthless in its opposition. Suffragettes were imprisoned, many went on hunger strike and were forcibly fed, having to be temporarily discharged early on health grounds. The government sought to deal with this problem with the 1913 Prisoners (Temporary Discharge for Ill-Health) Act, commonly known as the Cat and Mouse Act. This allowed for the early release of prisoners who were so weakened by hunger striking and force feeding that they were at risk of death. They were recalled to prison once their health recovered, where the process would begin again. There were suffragettes in Ipswich jail.

Mrs Vulliamy was on the Provincial Council of the NUWSS before World War I. Three months after war was declared, on 12 November 1914, she took part in a NUWSS Provincial Council Meeting in Wallasey. There was a discussion on the 'General Position of the Woman Suffrage Movement.' Mrs Vulliamy said that what suffragists were opposed to was the substitution

[15] A statue to Millicent Fawcett bearing a banner with the words *Courage calls to Courage,* was unveiled in Parliament Square, London on 24.4.2018

of physical force for Government, from which we can deduce she did not approve of the Government's policy of force-feeding suffragette prisoners or the militant tactics of Mrs Pankurst's Women's Social and Political Union, the WSPU, formed in Manchester in 1903. This is confirmed by the fact that after war was declared, Mrs Vulliamy became a member of the Women's International League. Members were those who wanted to work for peace as well as campaigning for equality.

So one member of the Vulliamy family at least was active in promoting women's suffrage and Grace's father Arthur Vulliamy was publicly supportive. There is no clear evidence as to the position of other members of the Vulliamy family. Although apparently not a member of one of the better-known suffrage groups, Grace was at the least not averse to women's campaigns for equality – although probably she did not approve of militancy. However, two of her greatest, life-long friendships - with Lena Ashwell and Beatrice Harraden, formed during the war - were with active suffragists, at least one of whom did not eschew militancy. Other members of the Writers Suffrage League such as Cicely Hamilton were on the committee of her post-war British Committee for Relief in Poland.

On 12 February 1913 Mrs Emmeline Pankhurst visited Ipswich for the second time, when the talk was of the escalation of violence against property belonging to establishment figures and the state until the vote was won.[16] It should perhaps be emphasised that militancy as practised by members of the WSPU did not intend harm to any person, only to property such as windows, burning letterboxes and gaining publicity by chaining themselves to railings. These events took place not long before Grace's return to Ipswich in 1914; she could not be unaware of them.

Pressure for women's equality began before the nineteenth century. At the time of the French Revolution there were discussions about what rights, if any, women should have, and in *A Vindication of the Rights of Woman: with Strictures on Political and Moral Subjects* (1792), British feminist Mary Wollstonecraft argued that, like men, women should have an education commensurate with their social position in society. In 1866 a group of women from the Kensington Society organised a petition that demanded equal rights (not just the vote) for men and women. They realised that having the vote should help them achieve other aims – control of their own money, being legally responsible for their own bodies, having rights over their children, and so on. The women took their petition to Henry Fawcett (the blind MP who married Millicent Garrett Anderson) and John Stuart Mill,

[16] Bounds. *Song.* 88

two MPs who supported the idea of universal suffrage – i.e. votes for everyone, regardless of sex. Mill added an amendment to the Reform Act that would give women the same political rights as men, but it was defeated by 196 votes to 73. Disappointed members of the Kensington Society decided to form the London Society for Women's Suffrage, which still exists today as the Fawcett Society. This was the background to women's position in society when Grace Vulliamy was growing up, and there is no doubt that there was an active concern in Grace's family for women's emancipation and for social issues. In fact, women's position as nurses, of which Grace was one, typified many of the problems.

Nursing

Nurses were often not members of the suffrage organisations – instead they focussed on the single issue of nurses' status and professionalization. It is likely that during her nursing training Grace Vulliamy's interest would have been in the autonomy and professionalization of nursing and countering its subordination to doctors.

As well as having an interest in suffrage, Mrs Vulliamy of Cambridge seems to have shared a common interest in nursing with Grace Vulliamy. She *w*as Chairman of a Committee formed to promote the candidature of independent women as Members of Parliament; this was reported in the *British Medical Journal* of 7 December 1918, emphasizing the family concern with medicine, nursing and politics.[17] Mrs Vulliamy considered that 'any reforms which Societies exist to promote or any subject on which women's opinions are organized would gain immensely by having an independent M.P.' She reported how attitudes were changing. She told the NUWSS meeting that two nurses had been returned to the Canadian House of Representatives and said that a nurse would be a popular candidate in England just then - the first post-war general election in England was held on 14 December 1918. The most likely member of the family to be this Mrs Vulliamy was Katherine J F Tite, born in Brixham (1876 – 1965), whose father was Arthur Tite, a scholar, and whose mother was Elizabeth F K Tite. Katherine married Edward Owen Vulliamy, (1876 – 1962) a watercolour artist and honorary Keeper of Art at the Fitzwilliam Museum, Cambridge. They had three children who at the 1911 census are listed as: Justin 8, Margaret 5, Adrian 4.

It was difficult for pre-war employers of nurses to conceive of them other than as high-grade domestic servants whose professional aspirations were out of keeping with their social status. Dickens' image of the grotesque

[17] *The British Journal of Nursing*

Sairey Gamp was hard to dislodge. Nurses wanted to reconstruct nursing as a free profession which controlled its own fees and conditions of work; the definition of who was a nurse was key to this and registration was central. However, the Government set severe limitations to the freedom of the nursing sector to becoming like medicine or the law, the gender hierarchy had to be maintained[18] and conform to the separate spheres theory in which a doctor had skill, a nurse virtue. Proposed registration challenged the theoretical foundations of the gender order in health care; opponents emphasized the subordinate status of nursing. It was thought that registered nurses would have an inflated view of their position. Sydney Holland, Viscount Knutsford, who was Chairman of Poplar Hospital in 1891, and who contacted Miss Vulliamy in 1918 about shell shocked soldiers, said in those earlier days: 'we want to stop nurses thinking they are anything more than they are, namely the faithful carriers-out of the Doctor's orders'.[19] By 1918 he recognised that at least one nurse, Grace Vulliamy, was considerably more than that.

Doctors' testimonials to Grace, written before she left for her visit to America in 1914, although complimentary, reflect the required subordinate position of nurses by stating that the work was carried out 'under my personal observation'. Nevertheless, one tribute in particular reveals the proficiencies and qualities she was to display so effectively later in her life. Dr Blake wrote on 9 April 1914 'I cannot commend her too highly for any post where highly skilled training in medical surgical nursing is required and where experience and management is essential; for apart from her knowledge of all medical and surgical operations, she has extraordinarily good business capabilities.'[20]

Was she a feminist? Oldfield says of her *Women Humanitarians,* of which Grace Vulliamy is one, 'The huge majority were on the left/liberal side of the political spectrum. All women were *de facto* feminists who transgressed psychological and societal gender constraints in order to speak and act in the public world.'[21] It is evident that she fitted into this category. She was not subservient to men and acted as though she expected to be treated as an equal which she usually was - and was evidently respected by most, if not all of

[18] Robert Dingwall, Anne Marie Rafferty, Charles Webster. *An Introduction to The Social History of Nursing.* Routledge, 1988. 78, 86, 88

[19] HMSO 1904: 37

[20] P.L.Blake, RCP., M.R.C.S., of 70 Shoot-up-hill, Cricklewood, London

[21] Sybil Oldfield. *Women Humanitarians: A Biographical Dictionary of British Women Active between 1900 and 1950. 'Doers of the Word'.* Continuum, London, SE1 7NX. 2001

them. Nevertheless, some of the newspaper extracts she kept amongst her papers show that she was interested in women's issues. For example, she kept a page of *Het Leven* of 18 May 1915 showing a picture of the women's march in London, passing Dickens & Jones, headed by a women's band.

Her work was acknowledged by different countries and organisations. After the War it was suggested that she was given the Freedom of Ipswich, but this was not carried out. Instead it was given to a man.

CHAPTER 2

GRACE VULLIAMY, SAILING HOME TO A TROUBLED WORLD

JOURNEY

In July 1914 Grace Charlotte Vulliamy, spinster, aged nearly 36, crossed the Atlantic on her way back to England from America. She had gone there in April to visit family members, including her niece Constance who lived in Parkville, Missouri. Grace Vulliamy, an experienced mental nurse, also wanted to see whether it would be more possible there to open and run simultaneously several homes for the mentally sick, needing more trained, reliable and experienced nursing staff than she had been able to find in Britain. She was not successful. Nursing was struggling to become a recognised and respectable profession, especially for middle class women, and mental nursing, the newest form, was finding gaining acceptance a particularly knotty problem.

Grace Vulliamy made this return journey to England 'via Bremen'. We do not know why she came this way, or why it was important to mention it. As with so many things concerning Grace, it has to be a matter of conjecture. Since the 1830s, ships sailed regularly between Bremen and the United States, so this was nothing special. There is, however, a tenuous link with Grace's visit to Bremen and her family's connection with the city through table tennis. The Vulliamy name was given to a bat patented by Mr Vulliamy, a solicitor in Ipswich (probably Grace's father) on behalf of another family, the Woottons, who, like the Vulliamys, lived in Ipswich. Table Tennis championships were held in Bremen and the International Table Tennis Federation Museum is located there. However, there is another more likely reason for Grace to choose a ship going by this route. Money. In this family money was tight and economies were necessary. There were immigrant ships on this route, with a cheaper passage than on a more direct trans-Atlantic liner. Three years earlier Grace had travelled this way from Montreal to Glasgow and after the war she travelled back from Poland to Britain on free-passage cargo ships,[22] showing that she needed to be financially very careful and did not mind 'roughing it'.

As she made this cross-Atlantic journey eastwards the world was in a state of tension, teetering towards the worst war mankind had so far devised. What was she thinking as the ship made its way across the ocean? Did she have

[22] 24 July 1911

any kind of premonition that before long Germany and England would be at war and even crossing the English Channel would be extremely dangerous due to German submarines and British mines? She returned to a country in turmoil. Women were being imprisoned and force fed for vehemently and, many thought presumptuously, asking to be considered as citizens and allowed to vote in parliamentary elections! There was industrial unrest including strikes, and in addition Ireland was on the verge of civil war. The shift from agricultural to industrial economy was causing financial and mental stress to both men and women and workhouses and asylums were filling as fast as they could be built. As a mental nurse, Grace would not struggle to find patients. The problem was for her to make a respectable living at it and one that fulfilled her considerable potential for administration.

She knew that she was at a cross-roads in her life, and almost certainly mulled over what had so far occurred and wondered about her future role. Although she left many papers and letters about her work, she left few hints about herself. There are, for instance, no personal diaries recording her daily activities and thoughts. Nevertheless, undoubtedly one of the most important reasons she had for coming home precisely at that time was to attend her parents' Golden Wedding Anniversary in August 1914.

Grace Vulliamy – A Woman of her Times

In family photos taken at the Anniversary, Grace is shown as having a long face and a strong family resemblance to her siblings. She was 5ft 6in tall and had brown eyes. Her long hair, as required for Edwardian women, was swept up into a bushy style, and parted on the right. She wore high collars, long sleeves, and in some pre-war photographs was tightly corseted so that her waist became tiny, possibly as small as 18" (46 cm) or less, as propriety demanded. One sister, presumably Janet, Mrs Collard, wore a fox fur – a sign of increased wealth and fashion consciousness. Grace has left so little information about herself except for photographs, which do not often identify the people in them, that it is difficult to know who she was close to in this large family. However, studio photos and family snaps show her with Eva, recognisable by her nun's robes, while snaps taken in a garden show Grace with her brother Lionel's children, David, the eldest, Poppy, and Chlöe. Chloe Armorel and Hope (Poppy) Museur were deeply involved in Basque refugee work during the Spanish Civil War, working there with Grace who influenced them to become drawn into this rescue work. Lionel, who visited Grace while she was in Holland working under the Government, and also when she was in Poland, was in partnership with his father and was the Coroner for the Lowestoft division of Suffolk. He and his wife were 'unavoidably absent' from the Anniversary party. He acted as accountant for Grace's financial affairs. Although we are told that Grace needed to be careful with money, her 'poverty' was relative. At different times in her life she owned a house in London and another in the countryside. The house in London was at 42 Great Russell Street, opposite the British Museum.

Plate 2.1 42 Great Russell Street, London

After the Russian Revolution when she established workshops for the refugees in Poland, she opened a shop in the ground floor flat for Slavonic Handicrafts where she sold their work. The other floors were for accommodation, some of which were let out and some Grace used. Peter, who became Poppy's husband, was in one of them. Grace was instrumental in introducing the couple. She spent many Christmases at Cauldwell Hall where Lionel lived, and where years later Poppy was the prime entertainer with her various pets: a monkey, ferrets, and a border terrier with which they used to go ratting. Grace asked if she could bring Peter as he knew no one in London and that is how he met Poppy. When the two of them wanted to spend a weekend together Grace said they could do so and could always say that Poppy was staying with her! This is another example of the New Woman in Grace. The 1914 to 1918 War shifted many values including relationships between the sexes.

In snaps taken during and after the war Grace is either in groups of people, or has a child or an animal, usually a dog, on her lap. Just after the war, in 1922, her Polish passport photo showed her hair as brown; she wore a coat with a fur collar, and a fur hat, definitely needed for the cold Polish winters which she endured for several post-war years. In 1934, when she had a British passport, her hair was grey. Records show that the Vulliamys were great travellers and Grace was perhaps to become the greatest of them all, especially after the First World War.

Plate 2.2. Grace with Leon, a child refugee

Party

A celebratory Anniversary party was held at her parents' home in Northgate House, Northgate Street, Ipswich, and among the guests were Canon J Owen of Norwich and the solicitor Charles Steward, who had been best man at her father Arthur Vulliamy's wedding. Five of their six daughters were at the party: Blanche, a pottery designer who lived in Bloomsbury; Fanny, until recently a missionary in China, one of the two girls who had taken up the religious life. Also present was Janet who had 'married well', her husband, Tom Collard, being a member of the Corporation of London, was typical of the current imbalance in demographics, which became worse after the slaughter of men in WWI.[23] Another sister was the absent daughter Eva, who was a nun in South Africa, reputedly 'after the shock of the

[23] The 1911 Census showed 17,445,608 men and 18,624,884 females out of a total population of 3,070,492 people.

organist playing the organ in a church exposed himself to her when she had dropped into pray.' She then joined the Community of the Resurrection.[24] She penned a very brief biography about her sister at a time when Grace was evidently thinking of getting her experiences written up and published because there are several similar attempts written by different people. Lastly there was Violet, a medical gymnast practising in London. Violet seems to have been especially close to Grace, joining her in Holland, helping in the refugee camps organized by the Religious Society of Friends, the Quakers as they were known. The other daughters remained single. As mentioned, by the time of this pre-war party Grace, who came between Justin and Violet, had chosen a new and unusual career for women of her class – that of mental nursing. Of the sons, the youngest, Bertram who had been engaged in scholastic work in Finland and Russia, acting as English tutor to Tolstoy's grandson, returned from Moscow in time for this Anniversary, the only son present at the celebration. In 1910 Grace accompanied by Miss Winifred Ball, had travelled to Russia. She kept her passport – an early one on a single sheet of paper – bearing Russian stamps and handwriting, showing it had been used. The passport was issued on 5 July 1910 when Grace was 31 years of age. Perhaps she had gone to visit her brother? And perhaps Miss Ball was her maid? There are no clues.

Plate 2.3 Grace Vulliamy playing with puppy at The Hague

[24] Letter from Poppy to Daniel, 27.10.1989

Plate 2.4 The Vulliamys at the Golden Wedding Party.
Grace stands behind her father.

Arthur Frederick Vulliamy was born in Kensington, London in 1838 and moved to Ipswich in 1853, becoming a student at Ipswich School. On leaving he was articled to Charles Steward, a solicitor, and once qualified also began practising as a solicitor. Two years later, on 21 July 1864, he married Anna Marie Museur. We know little of Grace's mother, except that, three years earlier, Anna was listed in the 1861 census as being a visitor to the household of Frederick, Arthur Frederick's father. After her marriage Anna Marie Museur Vulliamy became the mother of thirteen children. There is a family story that Anna allegedly continued with an interrupted card game of rummy immediately after giving birth to one child. Her 'pee'd on' chair was bequeathed to David's wife (Daniel's mother,) Lisel as a Pidon chair. Anna's thirteen children were comprised of six girls and seven boys of whom the eighth child was Lionel, born in 1875, and the eleventh was Grace Charlotte, born in 1878.[25] At the time of the parents' Golden Wedding, ten of the children

[25] Email from Daniel to the writer and Nicki, 17 January 2015, 16:27

were still alive.[26] Cecil had died in the Boer or South African War, Fred died in 1913, and another son died in infancy. In 1914, the Golden Wedding year, two of the sons were abroad: Justin was an estate agent in Winnipeg while the oldest sibling, Hugh Francis Vulliamy (1865 - 1939), who lived in Louisiana, spent much of his life in the military in Canada and the USA and became 'Veterinary Surgeon to His Majesty's Forces in World War I'. He had been banished in disgrace to the States when it was found he was having an affair with a shop girl, but this transformed his life – 'he trained as a veterinary surgeon and spent the Great War bringing shiploads of mules to England for the army.'[27] He married Constance Marion Gardner, a naturalised American, in 1905, but lived in England between 1915 and 1920. It was this family Grace had bidden farewell to just before the First World War. Despite the importance of the Golden Wedding occasion it was therefore impossible for the whole family to be together. In one newspaper article Grace was described as 'of New Orleans' which is where she had been living before returning to England for the Anniversary.

The Golden Wedding party was to be one of the last occasions on which the family gathered. On 29 March 1915, Grace's father Arthur Frederick Vulliamy died, aged 76. Condolences were sent by many local institutions such as the Ipswich Board of Guardians, and the Infants School and Boys Sunday School.[28] He was buried in the family grave space. Flowers were sent by the widow, and members of each following generation. It is likely that Grace had come across from Holland to spend some time with her father when he was gravely ill but whether she was able to attend the funeral is not known.[29]

---

[26] Next came Fanny Selina (1866 -1918), then Blanche Georgina (1869-1923), Frederick Arthur (1870-1912), Lionel Hastings (1875-1956). Lionel, who lived at Cauldwell Hall, Ipswich, was a solicitor and Coroner for a northern district of east Suffolk. Janet Anna (1876-1919), Eva Katherine (1872-1960), Alfred Herbert (1873-1923), Cecil Paliser (1874-1906), Justin Drayton (1876-?), Violet Norah (1880-1942), and finally Bertram (1883-1964). Grace was born between Justin and Violet in 1878. (Photos: Children of Arthur Frederick 3.1)

[27] Letter from Poppy to Daniel, 27.10.1989

[28] The Ipswich Institute, the Chess Club, Felixstowe Chess Club, Ipswich Education Committee, the Ipswich Parliament of which Mr Vulliamy was Deputy-Speaker, St Andrew's Mission Hall, the St John's Girls National School

[29] Hugh and Connie, Janet, Tom and their son; Lionel and Nellie; Chloe, Poppie and David; Auntie Rose (Miss R C Vulliamy) and many others.

As we have seen, the Vulliamy family was a typical Victorian one: concerned for the well-being of those less fortunate than themselves and having involvement in local and current affairs. Grace's father, Arthur Frederick, was a director of the Local Government Guarantee Society. This was a kind of insurance scheme providing limited liability to contributors; it was backed by Act of Parliament. The local Society sent congratulations to the couple on their Golden Wedding, as did the St John's Girls' Council School. There were presents, bouquets, telegrams and letters. Imaginary telegrams were read by Bertram during dinner, including one 'from' the King and Queen apologising for their absence saying: 'our regrets at being unable to grace your festive board'. There was one 'from' the Archbishop of Canterbury and another 'from' Lloyd George who at this time was Chancellor of the Exchequer. They reflected the social tensions of the time. One from John Redmond, an Irish Nationalist leader, said: 'Can hardly think that anyone can disbelieve in Home Rule after your unique experience. Your family would greatly increase our Nationalist Volunteers,' a tongue-in-cheek comparison between the size of this family and the number of Volunteers. As Anna Vulliamy was partly Irish it is to be expected that the family would closely follow the debate around Home Rule.

Plate 2.5 Auntie Rose and Uncle Theo, Ware, Herts. 1923

Women's rights were referred to. One telegram purported to be written by the militant suffragette, Mrs Emmeline Pankhurst, founder of the Women's Social and Political Union. 'She' wrote: 'Awfully sorry that I cannot persuade Mr McKenna to let me out [of prison] in time to be with you. I am convinced however, that Mr Asquith will not be able to appreciate your continued efforts for the state's welfare until women have the vote.' While there is no evidence that Grace was a member of one of the women's suffrage societies, it is clear that the family were sympathetic to the cause and at least one Vulliamy was active in it.

Who invented these pretend telegrams for the Vulliamy's anniversary party is not known, but the social and political issues of the day were fore-grounded by them in a manner that entertained the guests; evidently as a family they were not afraid of discussing contentious issues and shared a lively sense of humour. Tea and a reception were held in the garden where the company were further 'entertained by a novel amusement' - a pair of alligators, brought from the United States some time previously by Grace.[30] It is not explained whether these creatures were roaming free or were penned up in an enclosure!

---

[30] Unidentified newspaper cutting.

CHAPTER 3

FROM GOVERNESS TO NURSE

GOVERNESS

Some years before the Golden Wedding celebration Grace's father had suffered a financial set-back so it was necessary for the girls as well as the boys to find ways to support themselves. Society always assumed men and women wanted to marry and there were enough bachelors to marry the number of spinsters available but with two million more women in the country than men it was inevitable that many women needed to be able to support themselves. Grace's parents therefore had two reasons for finding a suitable way for her to earn her living when she finished her schooling: demographic trends and family finances.

Plate 3.1 The Vulliamy Family. Children of Arthur Frederick and Anna Museur Vulliamy

Her sister Eva explained the particular choice: 'Being considered a somewhat unruly child, she had been sent to Germany and to France for a year each as a preparation for becoming a private governess.' It appears probable, however, that the year in France was actually spent in Belgium. Misnaming of Belgium was common at the time, there being considerable confusion because Belgium had only existed as a separate state since 1830, and French was one of the main languages, the other being Flemish, which was based on Dutch. Among Grace's testimonials is this letter from Spa, which is in the Walloon region of Belgium, about 80 miles distant from Brussels where Anna Museur's family originated:

> Je certifie que Mademoiselle Villiamy (sic) a suivi pendant un an et demi les cours de français et d'allemand dans mon établissement que pendant ce laps de temps elle s'est distinguée par son application et sa bonne conduite.
>
> Mademoiselle Villiamy (sic) peut enseigner ces deux langues avec succès.[31]
>
> (signed) H.Lecoq de Theusy. Directrice de l'Institut Supérieur
>
> Spa. Avril 97

This gives her an affinity with the area and informs her concern and ability to assist the Belgian refugees who arrived in England in August 1914.

Eva, the elder sister who became a nun, recognized that being a governess was an unsuitable employment for Grace, but to be fair to her parents, the choices for impoverished middle-class women were extremely limited. Becoming a governess was almost the only means of earning a living for women of gentle birth. In 1851, there were some 25,000 governesses in England but they had no proper training and often an education barely above the accomplishments, such as music and drawing. In addition, as is well known, being a governess placed such women in an ambiguous situation – above the servants but not one of the family. We can see this depicted in Plate 3.2 where Grace is shown as a prim Victorian Miss seated on the steps of the Chateau St Marie near Diedenhofen in Lorraine, then in Germany, at Christmas 1898. She is with Baron von Wedel and his family, holding Tan the dog on her lap; this was during the 'governess' period between school and starting her nursing training. She is seated above the children but below the family. Charlotte Bronte described this as Jane Eyre's position when a governess at Thornfield Hall. Another woman who will come into this story who also initially trained to become a governess was Edith Cavell and yet another was a close friend of Grace – Lena Ashwell. Yet another photo dated 30 June 1899 shows her at the Chateau St Mark, Diedenhofen, Lorraine.

---

[31] I certify that Mlle Villiamy (sic) has followed for a year and a half French and German courses in my establishment during which time she distinguished herself by her application and good conduct.
Mlle Villiamy (sic) is able to teach these two languages with success.

There may be another reason why Grace Vulliamy was not happy in this employment. She wrote a story about a young woman who, while staying with a Baron and Baroness and their family, became embroiled in their financial difficulties. In the version given below the narrator is at the end of her school career, staying with a school-friend whose parents had insufficient money to pay their bills. They decided to sell some of the family silver and sent the young woman to pawn it at the nearest town. The story was sufficiently important to her to write two versions of it. In the second version she was employed as a governess, but on her way to the pawnbrokers she was arrested and accused of stealing the silver. Was this a fiction from Grace's imagination, or fiction based on a real experience? The version given here begins as if it is describing Grace's own experience including the reasons for her boredom at school. It then places her in Lorraine as a guest.

Victorian girl

The Victorian Girl and the German Nobility

The spectre of Education had at last been laid, after an ineffective career, due to successive retirements, voluntary or otherwise, from the scene of its activities. The Norman period seemed to dog my footsteps from school to school in a most trying manner, but no sooner had the year 1135 or thereabouts been reached, than disaster befell. At least from the parental point of view. Finally, Germany was selected as a spot from which running away would present greater, and it was hoped, insuperable difficulties. There the kings of England, early or late, were mercifully ignored, only however to be replaced by the equally dull doings of Frederick the Great.

But now the trying period of youth was over. Birthday Number 17 had dawned and died, seeing my hair go up and my skirts come down. Grown-upness was the one salient fact of life, and beyond it lay dreams: rainbow hued and fantastic, none of them however quite so wild as the reality was to prove. For in 19-- a European war had not entered even into the nightmares of politicians, while for me the one important event ahead was a visit with one of my German schoolfellows to her father's chateau in Lorraine.

"What are you going to do with your life, Ursula?' I demanded as the train flashed through the summer green of the countryside. Seriousness seemed called for, having regard to our promotion to womanhood.

"Do, why, stay-at-home of course and go to dances and parties – at least I hope there'll be some until I get married. What else can one do?"

"Lots of things. That's stupid, and behind the times too. In England" vaingloriously, "women have 'careers.' I think I shall write books."

"What can you write about?" Demanded the practical damsel beside me. "You only know about schools and teachers, and I shouldn't think anyone wanted to hear about them."

"Of course they wouldn't, but now we are grown-up we are going to see life, as my sister Janet is always saying about herself. I hope" I added anxiously "we shall be allowed to come down to dinner, and all that kind of thing, with your people?"

"I should hope so indeed. They could hardly have the face to poke us away in the schoolroom any longer." Then she added, somewhat irrelevantly as it seemed at the time, "you know our château is quite French – the furniture and everything I mean. It was given to my grandfather by the Kaiser in 1870 and he just settled down in it as it was. Father hasn't altered anything either. It sounds rather un-patriotic doesn't it? But then, you see, we haven't much money".

This seemed rather a remarkable trait in a Baron, but its literal truth only dawned upon me, when we marched in state into the lofty dining room, where ancient paintings of slim, beruffled and belaced henchmen looked down from the panelled walls upon the tall Baron and his petite Baronin.

The table gleamed with silver and crystal, which to a ravenous schoolgirl suggested a corresponding luxury and plenty beneath the heavy covers. Alas! The staple dish proved to be roast chestnuts!

"Never mind," whispered Ursula, "we can go and have a feed in the orchard afterwards."

This was the invariable habit of the family and though the trees had long been unacquainted with a pruning knife, the Raspberry canes had become a thicket and the gooseberry bushes were rapidly degenerating into a state of Nature. Yet to healthy young animals even a rather acid fruitarian diet did not come at all amiss.

But trouble started the next morning when my hostess politely enquired over our meagre breakfast. "I hope you slept well my dear?"

"Oh yes thank you" I answered cheerfully 'except that Herr Seidwitz and Gretchen kept waking me up with laughing such a lot in the next room."

A deathly silence greeted this unwitting betrayal of the love affair of the tutor and the lady's maid. How his pupil giggled. Seidwitz became scarlet, Valentine pink, the Baronin pale, and the Baron purple.

"Dismiss her," growled the latter, when he had finished an attempt at wordless annihilation of the guilty young man.

The Baronin cheered up at once. "Certainly" she agreed and added enigmatically "it will be very convenient. Her wages are due in a day or two." Time brought enlightenment as to the meaning of this comment, when during a lunch of which potatoes formed the chief item, my hostess observed in terms of distress, "my dear, the cook has been here nearly 2 months.'

"Has she indeed?" snapped her spouse.

"I hate to trouble you with these trifles," she pursued, "but really she was quite offensive this morning – about her money you understand."

"Impudent Jade!" He shouted roused to action by this presumptuous conduct. "Ring the bell at once, Hans" and when the butler had duly appeared "send the cook up here at once" he thundered.

Presently the great folding doors open slowly and reluctantly, and a large, unwieldy head appeared between them.

The baron seized a potato from the dish of unoffending potatoes, and I for one, watched with regret its rapid passage through the air though forced to corroborate Hans' "Good shot!" The aged Baron's aim was surprisingly accurate.

"You call these things cooked!" He shouted. "Get out of my house this instant!"

With a yell of mingled fear and resentment the Cook fled and we saw her no more. Personally, I felt delightfully conscious of acquiring a wider "knowledge of the world" than even Janet could boast. In England one never saw a maid dismissed in this dramatic fashion.

"I'll try Hamburg tomorrow" remarked the Baronin complacently, when the butler had at last cleared up the mess and withdrawn. "They don't know us there," then mystified me still further by adding "it's very advantageous to have a good address, and fortunately the German Empire is very extensive".

Despite the grownupness, it took me quite a long time to grasp the idea that X... Château in Lorraine plus a large slice of Europe as a hunting ground, enabled the family to obtain gratuitous service. Fares were always "to be paid on arrival," and needless to say, were not forthcoming. Forbearing and trusting servitors sometimes remained for as long as two months, but in cases promising any truculence on the subject of payment, three or four weeks was the average before the devastating wrath of the Baron caused them to take the line of Safety First.

It was only on these occasions that this lofty personage was ever called upon to interfere in domestic matters, but the Baronin found them too exhausting, also her belief in the divine right of Barons was not as reliable at crucial moments as that of her *hoch geborenen* husband. In him, nothing ever caused it the faintest tremor, until perhaps 1915.

But to return to the sins of Herr Adolf Seidwitz. When the momentous breakfast was over, Valentina, Ursula's elder sister caught me just as we were making for a supplementary one in the orchard and Ursula basely deserted me. "You little fool!" She snapped angrily. "How could you say an embarrassing thing like that? You ought to be ashamed of yourself."

"But they did make an awful noise" I protested

Val stamped her foot impatiently

"that was no reason for announcing in public that they had spent the night together. Why couldn't you have said it quietly to Mother afterwards instead of blurting it out like that and making everyone hot and uncomfortable?"

"I don't see why it should make people uncomfortable" I retorted assailed by a sense of undeserved injury. Victoria stared and then threw up her hands. "Liebe Himmel!" she ejaculated, and turning on her heel left me to the reflection that after all, growing up to be less easy in fact than in anticipation.

There are various mix-ups in this story. For example, Valentina becomes Victoria, and Grace Vulliamy's sister Janet is included. Her remarks about going to see life, and 'knowledge of the world' could be exactly what an older sister would say while the narrator's criticism about 'that ridiculous Bertram Kingston' (below) would be typical of a younger sister. Comment about a large family might be from personal experience as also the Mother's despairing cry which follows:

> It was true Mother had always been in the habit of saying, "Child, child, will you never grow up, never ceased to be an enfant terrible?' and Janet who was 22 and therefore quite ancient, was always shoving me into silence especially when that ridiculous Bertram Kingston she was going to marry, was anywhere about. But no one ever subjected her to a similar humiliation. Grown-ups can say whatever they chose it had seemed but now –
>
> I stalked rather disconsolately out of the room and went in pursuit of Ursula to drown my sorrows and perplexities in unripe plums. But the next day the Baroness restored my damaged self-confidence to its pristine glory.
>
> "Dearest child," she began, flinging her arms around me and kissing me so vigorously that I inadvertently swallowed a large plum stone, "dearest child you know I feel towards you as to one of my daughters!"
>
> .... "Yes indeed," she asserted. "You may be surprised but I took you into my heart the moment I saw you." This was certainly gratifying, not that the proceeding had been mutual – she had struck me as tainted with German 'sloppiness' – but because it was the first time anyone had openly succumbed to my charms. In a large family these are always liable to be discounted and subjected to a ruthless criticism, particularly galling at the 16 – 17 stage when one naturally craves approval ...
>
> The next words of the Baroness supplied this in a manner most acceptable at the moment, though losing its flavour later from continuous repetition. "Oh by the way my dear" she cooed. "I wonder if you have any small change? So tiresome – a little Bill has just come in and I never like to disturb the Baron at his studies (the nature of these proved, on later

discovery, to be a surprising variation of the term as hitherto understood) “I have nothing less than 1000 mark note and the stupid messenger cannot give me change for that.” Actually old enough to be borrowed from! The thought was intoxicating. Yesterday’s disaster faded into insignificance. ‘oh yes,” I cried eagerly. “I have 100 marks mother has just sent me, I always get my pocket money on the first of the month you know but I had extra this time for my birthday. Will that be enough?”

“Plenty darling. Of course I will let you have it back tomorrow.” But these tomorrows only existed in the brain of the Baroness and the inadvertent confession of the arrival date of my small allowance, led to its being regularly requisitioned, always on a variation of the same plea of temporary – merely temporary – embarrassment. “So far from the town, and inconvenient to go in today!” “So risky to have money forwarded by post from the Dresdener Bank (the account there was mythical) Mogendorf is full of thieves you know and naturally letters to the Château always possibly contain money,” and so on and so on.

“In England,” I ventured once sympathetically “things are much better. People hardly ever get their letters stolen in the post.” The Baroness threw up her plump little hands. “Ah your dear, safe England!” She ejaculated.

Under her able tuition my education in the art of growing up progressed apace, so that it did not seem surprising when she came to me one day, armed with a small suitcase and a wholly new type of request. “Liebchen,’ she began. “I wonder if you would do something very special for me,” and received a ready acquiescence, for faith in the ultimate return of my various relays of pocket money was not yet wholly quenched. “It is like this,” she continued. “I have had a good many extra expenses lately in one way or another and so have run short of ready money. I never speak to the Baron of money if it can possibly be avoided. He thinks the mere mention of it undignified and debasing. So I have just thought of a little scheme which will save him annoyance, and only you can help me to carry it out, for unfortunately Victoria shares her father’s feelings on the matter. It shall be a little secret between me and you whom I love as one of my own daughters."

"How exciting!" I exclaimed more moved by the mark of confidence and equality between us than by the affection formula which had staled from frequent use. "we will collect some of the silver – only things that the Baron will not miss, you understand – and pack it in this suitcase. Then you shall take it in the dogcart to Mogendorf and pawn it for me." Pawning had not yet arisen on my horizon, but the Baroness explained it airily as just a simple method of borrowing in use among the higher classes of society when they did not wish to bother their family lawyers.

Having allowed that it seemed quite clear and simple we set about the task of selection. "If Victoria or anyone else comes, shut that case at once. This must be entirely between ourselves." To 17 this provided a delightful conspiratorial thrill particularly as Gustav the sour faced Butler, opened the door just as the Baroness was holding up a heavy *epergne*. "Gustav" she said with commendable presence of mind. I am just looking through some of the silver. Now this' with a scowl at the *epergne*, "has been disgracefully neglected. Kindly take it away and clean it at once." When the door had closed behind the indignantly muttering Gustav, she sighed, "that was tiresome. It would have fetched quite a lot. However it can't be helped. I think we have enough now. You had better put the horse in the dogcart yourself and then bring it round to the front and we will smuggle in the case. Johann is working in the garden so that the coast will be quite clear."

The huge stables of the Château were empty save for two good horses and the dogcart aforementioned, but the awkwardness of this was always lightly passed over when distinguished visitors had to be met. "You should be back by dinnertime," said the Baroness as I sprang to the seat and seized the reins. "I'm sorry to send you so far, but in Megan Dorf you might be recognised as coming from here. Of course you won't mention our name. Ask for 1000 marks as the pawnbroker is sure to offer less. Try to get 800 marks."

That gentleman seemed a little surprised, both at me and the German which betrayed my land of origin and the contents of the suitcase. Certainly it must have seemed odd that a young English Fraulein should travel about encumbered with family plate. However he said nothing, probably supposing it to be stolen goods, and anxious to prove my business capabilities I haggled brazenly over the price, finally securing 900 marks.

The horse was a bit fat, and as we jogged slowly homewards, I reflected with considerable self-satisfaction upon the achievement. Pawning was assuredly a most grown and probably unusual proceeding; even Mother perhaps never done such a thing. She would naturally leave it to Father who didn't share the Baron's opinions as to the disgrace attached to money. It was mortifying to discover on my return home that though the surmise as to Mother's acquaintance with Pawning was correct yet the deed itself was regarded as but another and most disgraceful addition to the long score of Peter Pan-isms credited to my account. However for the time being my pride remained undimmed, for the Baroness was delighted at the result of the campaign. "You are a darling," she declared, "and now we will all go to Mogendorf and have a feast at the Gastof there. Run and tell the others to get ready and I'll fetch the Baron." Accordingly we all set off in the highest spirits, travelled first class, and ordered a sumptuous meal to which we did a justice that would have shocked an English waiter but left our German one unmoved. Even the German appetite is a thing to marvel at but when it has been whetted by forced abstinence….!

It must be confessed that the brain of the Baroness was fertile in the extreme along its own particular line. Her schemes for acquiring ready cash were as varied as they were numerous. On one occasion the deepest consternation reined in the Château owing to the proposed visit of some dignitary when the family finances were at their lowest ebb. "I must think of something" cried the distracted Baronin as she walked up and down the morning room. "Liebe Gott! How unfortunate!"

Ursula and I, feeling unable to throw light on the situation left her to her cogitations, and retired as usual to the Orchard. For the letter announcing this unexpected visit had arrived at breakfast and the Baron had as usual, dismissed the matter of finance with a wave of his hand. "Arrange it as you will, but spare me these financial dissertations, I beg of you,

Albertina. They try me excessively." And Albertina "arranged" it, after some reflection. "Get on your hat, dearest" she begged some half-hour later. I want you to drive me into S..... I have a scheme." This she unfolded as we bumped along in the rickety dogcart. "My dear, a really splendid idea came to me just as I was almost in despair. I am going to make my Will."

The connection between making a Will and providing an adequate meal was not at first apparent, but she rattled on "you see S... is only a small town and I shall call upon the lawyer there, tell him I have heard good reports of his discretion and that therefore I wish him to make my Will. I shall explain that for family reasons I prefer not to disclose the contents to my own legal advisers."

"But Baronin," I objected. 'what about dinner tonight?'

"He will pay for it" she announced cheerfully

"Oh I see. I suppose he's a friend of yours." The Baroness bridled. "Certainly not. he is merely a pettifogging little country lawyer. Therefore he will be immensely flattered that I shall come to him. And this will pave the way to borrowing some money from him. I shall have meant to do some shopping in S... And unfortunately, in the preoccupation over my Will have left my purse behind. You will see, it will work admirably."

And so indeed it did. The dignitaries were lavishly entertained and departed full of congratulations to the hostess upon the pleasant little visit they had just enjoyed. And the lawyer fed upon the condescension bestowed upon him.[32]

The mention of the European war implies that this was written after it began. However this may not be the case. Many people expected the war because of the arms race between nations and although it was a shock when it began it was not necessarily a surprise.

---

[32] It has been typed to indicate the kind of display shown in the handwritten version.

BECOMING A MENTAL NURSE

Holloway Sanatorium

As in the above story, Governesses were connected with impecunious middle-class backgrounds. Their social status was compromised by the need to earn their own living, but birth made it inappropriate to treat them as servants. Unsurprisingly, Grace was not happy and when a friend suggested she should go to Holloway Sanatorium, Virginia Water, to train as a mental nurse she welcomed the idea. In many ways this was a surprising suggestion and response, nursing being considered an unsuitable occupation for an upper-middle-class lady, somewhat as Nightingale found when she began her nursing career. Further, as we have seen, nursing was struggling with the issues of registration and training, at the back of which were gender issues concerned with patriarchal control. However, in this respect mental nursing was in advance of corporeal and the sector was considered the more militant. Holloway was also ahead in its employment of female medical attendants. This would have suited Grace's independent, indeed rebellious nature. Despite its problems, there were advantages to this career. It provided a salary, a roof over her head and a possible career for life. In this respect Grace, like Florence Nightingale, was part of a social movement. Nightingale, who drew her inspiration from Kaisersworth, Dusseldorf,[33] avoided the stigma of being paid by receiving an allowance from her father and established a regime modelled on the management of sickness in a large household. Whether Grace had a similar parental allowance is uncertain, although she talked during the war of using 'her own money' but this might have been rent from her home, let while she was in Holland. In contrast to the myth of the 'Lady with the Lamp', Nightingale was not a deliverer of care but an organizer of others' labour and this is what Grace became. So nursing could be taken up by women from economically marginal middle-class backgrounds without threatening their social status. They were often widows and daughters of clergy, military etc.[34] As the daughter of a solicitor, Grace fitted into this category. The early asylums for mental patients were basically prisons for the insane, not offering treatment but incarceration and restraint. Patients who were violent to themselves or to others, or destroyed property, were caged, shackled or put into strait jackets. However, new ideas about the treatment of the mentally ill were introduced in the mid-19th century - restraints were viewed as cruel and unnecessary - and conditions for the patients began to improve. Over time,

[33] *British Journal of Nursing.* 14 September, 1912. 210

[34] Robert Dingwall, Anne Marie Rafferty, Charles Webster. *An Introduction to The Social History of Nursing.* Routledge, 1988. 40, 47

diagnosis became more accurate and the range of treatments expanded. Most of the patients Grace Vulliamy nursed would have come in with complaints such as melancholia, self-harming, anorexia, mania or hysteria; some may have been suicidal. Here Grace did very well, even as a probationer on the worst wards. By this time moral therapy was the new form of treatment that recognized the fact that boredom caused illness, and ensured that patients were entertained and occupied. This was an indictment of middle-class society's practice of reducing the amount of activities and work available to women, turning them into nothing other than ornaments who displayed their husbands' status. We can be sure that Miss Vulliamy would not have approved of the treatment advocated by Dr S. Weir Mitchell, in 1886 the country's leading specialist in nervous disorders, whose treatment in such cases was a "rest cure" of forced inactivity.[35] This was described vividly by Charlotte Perkins Gilman's *Yellow Wallpaper* when boredom literally drove the patient mad. Relief through employment became Grace's maxim.

Holloway Sanatorium, Virginia Water, was ahead in some of the new developments in the mental health field, including the use of chemicals, Turkish baths and the use of occupational therapy for recovering patients, who were encouraged to work according to their social status. Patients who were voluntary boarders, that is, uncertified by a doctor, were often more troublesome. Wealthier ones often brought their own servants with them, who looked down on the sanatorium staff and nurses. So gentility was especially necessary in those who looked after women patients. Rees Phillips, the first superintendent, wanted lady nurses of good social position and by the time of Grace's arrival the staff ratio was one nurse to two patients. By 1900 a senior female attendant at Holloway earned between £4.0.0 and £45.0.0 p.a. The work was arduous and potentially dangerous, with long hours, isolation, and workers prone to institutionalization. To make it more unpalatable, workers' lives were subject to close scrutiny. In the early years of the sanatorium, nurses and domestic staff lived on the premises. In 1901 the superintendent was Dr William David Meares, and there were 384 patients and 210 resident staff.

---

[35] Charlotte Perkins Gilman. *The Yellow Wallpaper.* In 1886, early in her first marriage and not long after the birth of her daughter, Charlotte Perkins Stetson (as she was then known) was stricken with a severe case of depression.

Plate 3.2 Grace Vulliamy with the von Wedel family at Chateau St Marie near Diedenhofen in Lorraine, then in Germany, Christmas 1898.

However, Holloway was created to help middle-class patients and was run something like a hotel, with entertainments and outings as part of the healing process. There was a *table d'hôte* dinner with tea and music. The tennis courts were flooded in winter to provide facilities for skating; there was a swimming pool and other pastimes were provided indoors. There were sea-side trips, dances, theatricals and lectures, an athletics sports day and competitions with other hospitals. Teams were often made up of staff and patients together and local people were invited to watch Exhibitions were held of patients' work in oils, watercolours, drawing, photography and needlework. It was also one of the first hospitals to include photographs of patients with their case notes. Assuming that Grace took a large proportion of the photographs in her archive, she became an avid photographer and her earliest surviving photographs were taken at the Sanatorium. She seems to have had several cameras at different times in her life, using different sizes of film and also glass plates for negatives. However, she left no photographs between this period at the Sanatorium and her work in Holland, but throughout the war she photographed colleagues, refugees, returning prisoners of war; some of her photos were published in newspapers. Some were used by the Save the Children Fund as a means of publicising what the Allied blockade had done to children and in order to raise money.

Plate 3.3 Grace in London 1910

Holloway Sanatorium expanded in time by buying other properties. Two houses were purchased in 1890 - The Poplars and Red House - from Sir G.M. Holloway, the Red House becoming the residence for the chaplain. In June 1891 a large house in Brighton - Hove Villa - was purchased for £1,500 as a convalescent home.

In the early years of the 20th century nursing was struggling with the issues of registration and training. Nurse registration was a source of conflict between those who wished to maintain the supremacy of the organizational interests of the hospital and those who wanted to reconstruct nursing as a free profession which controlled its own fees and conditions of work. The discord revolved around a complex mixture of economic interests and gender rivalries. There was no nationally recognized examination or certification of general nurses until 1925. Until then, each institution awarded its own certificates, whose value reflected the status of the hospital or infirmary. But mental nursing was ahead of the game. The reputation of the hospital and its training certificate underwrote the quality of the nurses and Holloway's management were enthusiastic about training their staff. Attendants and nurses took the Medico-Psychological Association examination

Plate 3.4 Holloway Sanatorium on a garden party day.
These photographs probably taken by Grace herself

Plate 3.5 One of GV's Nursing Homes. Virginia Water

The Certificate of Proficiency in Mental Nursing was founded at the Medico Psychological Association Annual Meeting in 1890. The Medico Psychological Association announced in the *British Medical Journal* that the Committee had unanimously recommended a system of training. This included a period of three months' probation, a period of two years' training and service in the asylum before the attendant should be allowed to become a candidate for examination. The training was to include study of prescribed textbooks, various exercises under supervision, clinical instruction by medical officers, lectures or demonstrations given by medical staff at least twelve of which were to be attended by the candidate during the two years' training, and periodical examination to test progress. Until 1921 this Certificate was the only recognised qualification in mental nursing.[36] This began the process of turning the job into a profession, but

[36] Dingwall, et al. *The Social History of Nursing.* 60-62, 78

once people had passed the preliminary exams, they often thought themselves qualified and left to seek better pay and conditions elsewhere. 'To combat this, in 1901 the sanatorium established a new scheme, whereby silver medals were awarded to [those] who served over five years in addition to gaining the certificate in mental nursing.' Grace was at the Holloway Sanatorium from 20 August 1900 to 8 November 1902. One testimonial gives the leaving date as 5 January 1903, which appears to add three months to the required two years' training and may be a misunderstanding on the part of the writer, since the probation was expected to be included in the two years required for her to become an examination candidate.[37] Grace passed the Medico Psychological Association nursing examination and, according to W D Warne, MD, Medical Superintendent at Holloway Sanatorium, Virginia Water, she gained her certificate and medal which implies five years' work.

In 1910 new regulations were drawn up for the Medico Psychological Association exam. The examination entry required that all nurses must be trained in a recognized institution for not less than twelve months before presenting themselves for the primary exam; they had to attend a course of twelve lectures with demonstrations on First Aid, which included dealing with fractures, dislocations, poisons and other emergencies. They had to learn about elementary anatomy, physiology, and hygiene and could only take the exam after three years in one of the recognized asylums. The exam was partly written and partly *viva-voce.*[38] This was the situation when Grace took the exam. It is important to recognise that the training involved physical nursing, including surgery, and was not a form of psycho-analysis and mental therapy alone.

On leaving Holloway 'on her own resignation', Grace Vulliamy took up private cases and for a time she had three houses for her patients at different stages in their recovery, but she found it too difficult to get trained and responsible women to be left in charge of the other two houses while she was visiting the third, so she gave them up and worked for doctors in London. She never had a failure in curing any one of her cases and in this way she saved many from the stigma of having been to a mental hospital because she nursed her cases in their own homes. In this career she secured the high opinion of others.

[37] Testimonials from Anne Coornaby at Holloway. Another one gives 20 August to 24 November 1902

[38] *British Journal of Nursing*. 30.7.1910. 87

Plate 3.6 Nursing Home. Virginia Water

At one time during this period she worked at Camberwell House Lunatic Asylum, a Metropolitan Licensed House which opened in January 1846 with the surgeon Mr John Hayball Paul (1816-1899) as the Medical Superintendent. The Asylum consisted of three substantial houses built in 1790. The grounds of the Asylum consisted of 20 acres, laid out in a park-like manner. A small market garden within them provided produce for the inmates. By 1859 the Asylum contained 318 inmates - some 247 paupers and 71 private patients - who were kept occupied by work in the grounds (unusually for the times, both sexes were allowed to mix together in the garden). Each year a house by the seaside was hired for use as a holiday home. Grace adopted this idea for the children in her Polish orphanages. By 1878 Camberwell was the second largest asylum in London, licensed to accommodate 362 inmates (the largest was Grove Hall in Bow, with 443 patients). By this time the Asylum consisted of the original buildings and several detached houses and cottages in which patients were accommodated according to their illness and social status.[39]

Grace worked at this Asylum at a time when Dr Francis Henry Edwards was the Medical Superintendent and it had become known simply as Camberwell House. Sports were encouraged and the facilities for the patients included tennis courts and a putting green. The Recreation Hall contained a badminton court. There was also a Chapel. On 6 April 1914 Dr Francis Edwards wrote a glowing testimonial for her that gives some idea not only of her abilities, but also of the work she had been doing since leaving Holloway.

---

[39] http://ezitis.myzen.co.uk/camberwellhouse.html Accessed 02/09/2015 18:54

'She has, under my supervision, had charge of several patients ... successfully conducted nursing homes and taken sole charge of cases requiring a staff of nurses and I have come to regard her as a woman with exceptional gifts of organisation and general ability.'[40]

Changes were also happening in the care of the insane due to the ideas of the Austrian neurologist, Sigmund Freud. He was attempting to find effective treatments for patients with neurosis or hysteria. As such treatments became available for mental patients, Camberwell House offered prolonged immersion baths, action-therapy, shock treatment and modified insulin treatment. Occupational therapy and callisthenics were also encouraged.[41] Most patients would have been skilled in a trade, and work was encouraged in the asylum, where a routine was implemented comparable to one that they would have experienced outside it. The patients' labour also contributed to the self-sufficiency of the asylum, reducing costs. The work was segregated by gender: men worked on the asylum farm or market garden, in the workshops or helped to maintain the fabric of the institution, while women worked in the laundry, the kitchens, the sewing rooms or did cleaning. Later this changed and women were also allowed to work outdoors.

For some years Grace Vulliamy was in charge of some of Netterville Barron's patients. Barron was physician in Ordinary to Their Royal Highnesses Prince and Princess Christian. Princess Helena was the fifth child and third daughter of Queen Victoria and Prince Albert. They made their home at Frogmore House in the grounds of Windsor Castle and had five children; Princess Marie Louise, born on 12 August 1872, was the fourth. This contact may have assisted Miss Vulliamy's approach to Royalty on behalf of prisoners of war in 1918.

One of her private patients was so grateful for his recovery that he gave her a car and another paid for her to have a holiday in Ceylon. Mortimer Singer wrote to her from Cannes where possibly Grace had been nursing his wife. He sent her a piano, music and croquet set saying 'if you don't like it, change it. I want you to be as happy as you can considering and I am very grateful for your kindness to my poor little wife.'[42] This, and especially the underlining, may suggest some unhappiness in Grace Vulliamy's life of

[40] Camberwell House. 6 April 1914

[41] Lost Hospitals of London. http://www.ezitis.myzen.co.uk/holloway.html 10 September 2015

[42] Mortimer Singer, from Hotel Metropole, Cannes. Undated.

which we are unaware, but which he knew about. Later from Brighton he wrote: I hope the New Year will bring you the beginning of the reward you deserve.'[43] Mary Scharlieb, who was one of the early women doctors, had a high opinion of Grace Vulliamy. Dr Scharlieb had an illustrious career in India running a full medical degree course for women so that they could treat Indian women's everyday ailments and also when in childbirth.[44] White women were able to enter medicine in India far more easily than they could in England where severe obstacles to training were put in their path. Scharlieb was made CBE in 1917. She was therefore very influential in the medical world and was in touch with Grace Vulliamy at least until May 1916. We do not know, however, whether Grace kept in touch with other nurses and doctors, although it is recognized that she had a full social life.

Nonetheless, mental nursing did not have, and still does not have the status of physical nursing and there are historical reasons for this. Mental nursing has not received the attention from medical or women historians that physical nursing has been given; even the focus on 'shell-shock' experienced by men during the war has not altered this inequality. Mental nurses remain in the shadows. Further, Holloway's records are incomplete. Although annual data was collected from opening in 1885 until 1905, when the asylum closed in 1981 much was lost or destroyed. Further, the extant records focus on Holloway's construction and the patients; the staff are marginalised.

Grace Vulliamy's career, like that of so many others, was radically altered by the First World War and she never resumed her mental nursing, although it stood her in good stead for the rest of her life. She was in England in time for the declaration of war on Germany by the British Government on 4 August 1914.

---

[43] Mortimer Singer, from Norfolk Hotel, Brighton. 31.12.1914.

[44] Catriona Blake. *The Charge of The Parasols: Women's Entry to the medical profession in Britain.* Women's Press 1990. 175-177.

CHAPTER 4

WAR BEGINS

WOMEN'S EMERGENCY CORPS

START OF WORK IN HOLLAND

Grace Vulliamy Joins the Women's Emergency Corps

Among the various personal papers that Grace Vulliamy started to write is one that describes her reaction to the start of the First World War. She said:

> The first feeling that swept through the world on that never-to-be-forgotten 4th of August in 1914 was one of over-whelming horror, temporarily stunning the mind, but after the first shock of realization had passed everyone became feverishly active in the intensity of the desire to serve – to be of use to his or her country in its hour of desperate need. Within a few days of the declaration of War, a centre called 'The Women's Emergency Corps' was formed by the suffragist actress Decima Moore, who in private life was Lady Guggisberg and had personal experience of commissariat[45] organization work in West Africa. She arrived at the actress Lena Ashwell's home at 36 Grosvenor Street, London, with a list of the work that the women of the country would be required to do because men were mobilising for the armed services.

So began the Women's Emergency Corps. Grace Charlotte Vulliamy was one of the earliest members. She joined shortly after having arrived back in England, and after her parents' Anniversary Party. Perhaps she saw the advertisement inviting women to register at the Corps' temporary office at Robert Street, London.[46] The Women's Emergency Corps records are almost non-existent and give no clue. In private life Lena Ashwell, mentioned above, was the wife of an eminent surgeon, Henry Simson, whose work at the Hospital for Women in Soho brought the couple into contact with the Royal Family. Princess Christian (Princess Helena), the daughter of Queen Victoria, took an active interest in the hospital and in disabled

[45] Department for the supply of food and equipment

[46] *The Times.* 8.8.1914

soldiers and sailors.[47] This interest made an important overlap with Grace Vulliamy's work later in the war and the relationship with Grace became personal. The Princess wrote a letter on 27 March 1921, from Windsor Castle, thanking Grace for a parcel and letter and offering condolences on a death, probably of her Auntie Rose who died on 16 March 1921, age 95. Theodore Vulliamy, aged 86 died shortly after - on 16 April 1921 both in Ware, Hertfordshire. The Princess begged:

> 'Dear Miss Vulliamy' to 'accept my heartfelt sympathy … Sincerely yours, Helena'

The Women's Emergency Corps was founded to relieve the distress of middle class British women workers such as clerks, typists and needlewomen thrown out of work because offices and small factories were closing due to the war emergency. It aimed also to organize and prevent the overlapping of volunteer aid and to assist refugees of the 'better classes'. It became the first organized body to protest publicly against flooding the market with amateur, unpaid workers wanting to do their bit but thereby risking the employment of paid workers. It was also the first to assist people from Belgium, and Grace Vulliamy had a large part to play in this.

Like Grace Vulliamy, Lena Ashwell had originally been educated to be a governess and when asked why she had gone on the stage instead, she responded: 'I think you must see that I would not probably have been much of a success as a governess, and I do like to get on in whatever I take up.'[29] Lena and Grace became close, life-long friends. With her husband Henry, Lena had been to stay with Her Highness Princess Marie Louise at Frogmore.[48] The Princess gave her support to the Women's Emergency Corps and she is the most likely contact that enabled Grace to approach the King and Queen on behalf of prisoners of war in 1918. Friendships with suffragists Lena Ashwell and the writer Beatrice Harraden, who wrote the Corps' first appeal,[49] were important for the rest of Grace's life, both women visiting her when she worked in Holland and later being on the Committee that supported her relief work in Poland.

The actress friends showed their list of work to men who could help, but instead of assisting, they were horrified and contemptuous thinking it

---

[47] Ashwell, Lena. (1936) *Myself a Player.* (London:Michael Joseph). P.187. Lady Randolph Churchill, (ed) *Women's War Work.* *http://bobrowen.com/nymas/jenniechurchill.html*. 08/02/2016

[48] Ashwell, Lena. *Myself a Player.* p.186-7. Ashwell was also trained to be a governess.

[49] WEC Half-Yearly Report, August 1914 – 31.1.1915. p.3.

ridiculous that women could organise or undertake 'men's work', even if, as in this case, they were supportive of women's fight for the vote. So the women advertised in newspapers for others who wanted to help the war effort, where their various capacities could be placed to most advantage, to register at the offices of the Actresses' Franchise League at 2 Robert Street, Adelphi, London.[50] Immediately, many hundreds of women offered their services. Lena Ashwell described how Grace:

> dashed into our office, offering to help. Asked what she could do, she replied that she had but one doubtful asset, 'perhaps some languages'.[51]

Clearly, Grace was modest, since in addition to her nursing training and administrative experience, she spoke three languages fluently. Later events show she could speak German like a native and picked up languages easily. This ability and her mental nursing experience were vital in the War. She was among the first, if not *the* first qualified mental nurse to take care of military patients abroad and certainly the first to help civilian prisoners. Her languages and administrative abilities were put to good use.

Lena Ashwell was a member of the Actresses' Franchise League whose members co-operated in the formation of the Women's Emergency Corps. Grace's other friend, the writer Beatrice Harraden, was a 'pronounced suffragist', influenced by the work of Shelley and Ibsen. She subscribed to the Women's Social and Political Union in 1906 and became one of the vice-presidents of the Women Writers' Suffrage League which was formed in 1908. On 9 February 1912, the Women Writers Suffrage League had given a morning performance at the Prince's Theatre which included a pageant of Shakespeare's heroines. The words were chosen by Beatrice Harraden, and Lena Ashwell was among those who appeared; Laurence Housman designed a *tableau* symbolising women's struggle for freedom.[52]

Harraden and Ashwell were also members of the Tax Resisters' League which queried why women should pay taxes if they were not citizens and could not vote. These women's friendships were founded on the female ideal of women as equal citizens with men but also through their relationship

---

[50] *The Times.* 8.8.1914. The League neither condemned nor supported militancy. Crawford. *The Women's Suffrage Movement.* 4

[15] Ashwell, Lena. *Myself a Player.* 224

[52] "The Theatres." *Times* [London, England] 29 Jan. 1912: 10. *The Times Digital Archive*. Web. 5 May 2015.

to power and the public sphere.[53] Having visited America, Harraden noted how much more sympathetic to suffragists were the journalists there. They were both therefore to a greater or lesser extent 'militant' suffragettes.[54]

Nevertheless, not everyone, however sympathetic, was willing to help. When Lena asked Sidney and Beatrice Webb for assistance in training women for agriculture, they assured her that the war would be over by Christmas so all this effort was unnecessary.[55] However, Millicent Garrett Fawcett of the NUWSS saw things differently. It was recognized that there would be shortages and that some people, especially the poor, or those who suffered as a result of the war, might go hungry. 'We . . . very early arrived at the conclusion,' she recalled, 'that the care of infant life, saving the children, and protecting their welfare was as true a service to the country as that which men were rendering by going into the armies to serve in the field.' The age-old cultural associations of men with war and women with home and children had virtually no resistance from feminists; indeed, they were often fostered by their rhetoric. For suffragists, the war meant the suspension of much of their political campaigning for the vote; relief work was to be a disguised and alternative campaign for enfranchisement. It was also 'genuinely humanitarian'.[56]

Many women who were not suffragists were involved with the Women's Emergency Corps, but the Executive included some women prominent in the movement, including Mrs Pethick Lawrence; Eva Moore, Decima's sister who was also an actress and charity worker;[57] Mary Macarthur, the Independent Labour Party activist, and Caroline Spurgeon, Professor of English Literature at Bedford College to which place the Corps moved in October when they started working with the Local Government Board (LGB), dealing with the arrival of refugees. Miss Maud Bell, an Executive member of the Church League for Women's Suffrage worked with the Emergency Corps from its inception. The Emergency Corps' seventeen

---

[53] *A Passion For Friendship* – Janice Raymond

[54] She left the WSPU after Olive Beamish and Lilian Lenten had been re-arrested due to WSPU mismanagement. During the First World War she was librarian at the military hospital run by Dr Flora Murray and Dr Louisa Garrett Anderson at Endell Street, London. Elizabeth Crawford. *The Women's Suffrage Movement: A Reference Guide, 1866 – 1928.* First published UCL Press. Routledge 2001. 276

[55] Ashwell. *Myself a Player.* 183-4

[56] Fawcett, M.G. (1924). *What I Remember.* Fisher Unwin. 924: 218

[57] Eva Moore's house in Brighton has recently been restored. BBC TV News. 12/04/2016 08:19

vice-presidents included women who were well known in their own right, and who quickly became concerned with helping the refugees who came to Britain. The need for hostels for educated women thrown out of employment by the war was early recognized by the Conservative and Unionist Women's Franchise Association whose President was the Countess of Selborne. A house in South Kensington was opened to help ladies in distress such as the many governesses who were stranded owing to the war; this might have happened to Grace had she adopted that line of work. Guests included fashion artists, literary women, teachers, buyers in drapery establishments, actresses, vocalists, and a host of others whose incomes suddenly disappeared. To these women the hostel was of real assistance. They were admitted temporarily and helped to find work or make other plans. Finding work was a prime task. Lena Ashwell and other members of the Actresses' Franchise League arranged concerts and entertainments to give work to actors, actresses, concert artistes, and variety artistes who had been thrown out of employment. On 5 November 1914 Ashwell contributed to a programme raising funds for the relief of members of the artistic professions in distress and took part in many other such entertainments thereafter. Ashwell was one of the first to suggest artists be gainfully employed to boost troop morale by providing entertainment. After initial official resistance to the idea, she was thrilled that:

> on one never-to-be-forgotten day, when I had quite lost hope of the drama and music of the country being regarded as anything but useless, Lady Rodney called on behalf of the Women's Auxiliary Committee of the YMCA. She had returned from France, and came from Her Highness Princess Helena Victoria, Committee Chairman, to ask if it was possible for a concert party to go to Havre.'

Twice a week the Actresses' Franchise League gave entertainments in the Church Army Hut in Hyde Park. Jennie Churchill wrote of the League that 'It organized its offices and the work of its committee so that its relief work should not overlap' indicating how closely connected the Emergency Corps' philosophy was with that of the Actresses' League. Lena Ashwell was President of the Women's Emergency Corps' Advisory Board and part of her job was to appeal for funds. Despite being an actress, she was very nervous when making these speeches. Women were not supposed to speak in public, nor put themselves forward in any way.

Women's Emergency Corps volunteers and their families contributed to the funds to keep the Corps afloat. Grace Vulliamy's wider family were an example, contributions mentioned in the First Annual Report dated 1914 – 1916 include:

Mrs Vulliamy, 10s. Miss Vulliamy, £85.3.6., Miss K Vulliamy 5s.

Such women got on with their own lives and other commitments while helping the Emergency Corps. They were often involved in organizing more than one charitable enterprise at a time – multi-tasking before the term was invented. Beatrice Harraden continued with her writing; Lena Ashwell and Eva Moore with their theatre work.[58] According to one source, during the First World War, Beatrice Harraden visited refugee camps under the auspices of the American-founded Commission for Relief in Belgium. She also visited some camps where the Society of Friends operated. Grace Vulliamy's collection of photographs include some of Harraden with Grace in camps where Vulliamy worked in Holland. Grace Vulliamy had thought to continue with her mental nursing, but this was not to be – at any rate, not in the same way as previously.

Food

The Corps described itself as having two sections: Voluntary Work and Paid Work. It had at least eleven departments including Interpreting and Hospitality. Three were concerned with food - Cooking and Catering, Kitchens, French Canteens. Food is a weapon of war and Britain was vulnerable due to its reliance on imports. The Corps' Kitchen Committee headed by Lady Aberconway organised dinners, and had a 'band of helpers to deal with food for the Food Fund.'[59] Following the fall of Antwerp in October, 100,000 Belgian refugees, and 6,000 wounded were helped in Folkestone where the Belgian Refugees' Relief Committee was supplied by the National Food Fund up to 1916 at least, probably longer. Hostels, including the one in South Kensington for distressed professional gentlewomen, were also supplied.

In early August, the War Refugees Committee in London contacted the Emergency Corps to say: 'We are offered shelter for 100 Belgians arriving to-morrow. Can you feed any of them?' Miss Carey, described as the Emergency Corps housekeeper, answered: 'Ring me up at such an hour and I will tell you.' Then she went out to the Metropolitan markets for food to feed the refugees. When she returned, her answer was that all could be fed - even when told that 300 refugees were being sent. The food was supplied free by traders in Covent Garden, Smithfield and Billingsgate. In

[58] IWM. Women's War Work. VOL 1.1.16. *Cambria Daily Leader.* 3.4.15

[59] IWM VOL. Vol 1.1/6 *Ladies Pictorial.* Lady Aberconway's report.

large part it was food which in the usual course would have been thrown away or turned into manure.[60] As well as food, Miss Carey was also remarkably successful at getting in necessary money and when she had sufficient and a large enough staff of helpers she separated from the Women's Emergency Corps and formally opened the National Food Fund at premises lent to her cost free at 1a Dover Street, Piccadilly, formerly the Grosvenor Club. Despite this auspicious beginning, Miss Carey got into difficulties and was expelled from her own National Food Fund in October. However, Carey's departure did not immediately solve the Food Fund's problems. An important part of its work was education regarding economy in the use of food, avoiding waste. On 13 September 1915 Lady Chance complained to Mr Algernon Maudslay,[61] who was also Honorary Secretary of the War Refugees Committee, that the Executive Committee was repudiating the Educational work. Grace Vulliamy had contact with Maudslay in the post-war years concerning relief work in Poland.

Since these events took place in September and October, 1914, when Grace was in charge of the Interpreting Department and then the Organising Secretary of the Corps, it is almost certain that she knew Carey and about the questionable events that surrounded her.

THE CORPS STARTS WORK

War conditions created new openings for women to use traditionally-constituted female domestic skills, considered a 'natural' part of the private function of women whose ability to provide care was consequently brought firmly into the public arena. The women starting the Emergency Corps got to work very quickly and by 22 August were able to announce in the *Daily Mail* that 'Fifteen societies are affiliated already'.[62] On 28 August the *Morning Post* reported that the Corps had held two public meetings, with only a few men present. In this article Decima Moore was correctly credited with the idea of the Corps' inception. The writer reported: 'War has already caused a great deal of suffering among women.' Their Register now had 5,000 names classified according to qualifications, including women who could drive buses. Some hundreds of women motor-cyclists and motorists who ran their own cars and were capable of doing running repairs, registered in the Motor Department. 'These cars rendered

---

[60] *Morning Post.* 28.8.14

[61] Hon. Organising Secretary Lady Chance (Education Campaign), Lady Emmott, Mrs Eustace Miles. Included Sir Wm Chance and Algernon Maudslay.

[62] IWM. VOL 1.1/3 *Daily Mail,* 22.8.14

invaluable service in the early days of the war, meeting trains of refugees, and they have also led the War Refugee Committee, private hospitals, officers, and various societies.'[63] The Honorary Secretary, Mrs Haverfield, organising this branch, caused much amusement by telling how one official declined an offer of a motorist's help by saying the duty might require her going out at night! Mrs Haverfield assured the audience that the Corps' motorists were ready and capable for duty night or day. Lists were compiled of cooks, crèche and mother carers, stores' distributors, clothing collectors, carers of horses and riders, motor drivers and 'all women trained in any capacity' including interpreters. Within three weeks a crowded meeting of women at the Queen's Theatre was informed that the Corps had 10,000 offers of help.[64] Lists were circulated to institutions, councils, mayors and government departments.[65] The fact they had the prescience to send lists to the government was to have a profound effect on Grace Vulliamy's life.

Government Invitation to the Belgians

On 9 September, after the retreat from Mons, the President of the Local Government Board (LGB), the Rt Hon. Herbert Samuel announced in Parliament that the Government had formally invited the Belgians to come to the UK to receive the hospitality of the nation. Women were, of course, the traditional distributors of charity and the Government officially encouraged women to provide succour and called on their organizations to help. The boundaries of women's gender role within the separate spheres ideology therefore became blurred and permeable. Upper- and middle-class women were traditionally the dispensers of charity that had by this time become a status symbol for both giver and recipient, but women did not count as citizens, being unfranchised. Legally, they were not part of 'the nation' giving hospitality.

When the influx of refugees was reputed to amount to 20,000 in one week alone, it was obviously a task that could not continue to be undertaken entirely by voluntary organisations, so the Local Government Board took over financial control and part responsibility, working closely with the War Refugees Committee in London. Some of the work Grace Vulliamy did with refugees was directly under the auspices of the Local Government Board (LGB). This was a supervisory body overseeing local administration in England and Wales; it took over all the work of the Poor

[63] Lady Churchill. *Women's War Work.* 1916.

[64] *The Times.* 4.9.1914

[65] WEC. Half Yearly Report. ..3

Law Board and was responsible for public health to which refugees were thought to be a threat.

The War Refugees Committee, which became financially supported by the Government, was divided into a number of Departments. Its Health Department set up hostels as maternity homes for refugees along class lines; even newly-born babies therefore were categorized by conceptions of social class, often connected to whether the mother spoke French or Flemish. The Women's Emergency Corps sometimes supplied trained midwives to help in these maternity homes.[66]

On 8 September there was a meeting between Herbert Samuel and a deputation from the War Refugees Committee, where division of responsibility between the LGB and the War Refugees Committee was decided. The arrangements really meant volunteers doing most of the work for the War Refugees Committee with limited financial aid from the LGB. When Antwerp fell on 9 October contemporary estimates were of a quarter to a half a million refugees. In total throughout the war, about 250,000 came to Britain, most were women and children.[67]

Work of the Corps

On 20 September, the Government opened a Labour Exchange on the Corps' premises and a number of professional women were found temporary or permanent work. In the first months the Corps found paid employment for 460 women and themselves employed 196 workers such as typists.[68] Yet this was completely insufficient to meet the need. On 1 January 1915, shortly after Grace Vulliamy had gone to Holland and they were still on the formal terms of addressing each other as 'Miss Vulliamy' and 'Miss Harraden,' Beatrice Harraden wrote to her 'can you tell me whether there is any Fund whatsoever for professional women in distress?' The writer Cicely Hamilton, who would eventually become Honorary Treasurer for Grace's British Committee for Relief in Poland, undertook some of the publicity, writing in the *Evening Standard* on 26 August 1914 that the Corps was 'perhaps the largest of all the Women's Organizations for the relief of war distress. In one week it became too big for its temporary office and migrated to the Little Theatre which was lent by Miss Gertrude Kingston' and became the HQ of the Corps.'[69] Miss Vulliamy's

[66] IWM. VOL 1.1/29. Women's Emergency Corps. First annual report, 1914-15.

[67] Cahalan. *Belgian Refugee Relief*, 92

[68] WEC Half-Yearly Report, August 1914 – 31.1.1915. .11, 20

[69] Cicely Hamilton writing in *Evening Standard*, 26.8.14

organisational abilities were soon recognised and she had as her office one of the theatre's boxes used by Countess Benckendorff, daughter of the Russian Ambassador.[70] The Little Theatre was not only used for administration, but for women making hospital requirements. The Corps provided carefully compiled lists of hotels, boarding houses, and lodgings of all kinds, and investigated and arranged accommodation. 'In those early days before the Belgian Relief centre in Kingsway (Aldwych) was opened, many hundreds of refugees would have fared very badly without the help of this able band.'[71]

Again the Corps outgrew its accommodation and the Duchess of Marlborough, who was the Honorary Treasurer, lent the premises of Old Bedford College in Baker Street. Here 'chaos reigned as masses of women were sorted out.'[72] An office was established which was crowded with Belgians coming for help and advice. Hospitality was found for them in private houses. Other houses were furnished through the kindness of private people and Belgian families were re-established there. In the first few months thirty to forty workers enrolled, nearly all voluntary.

When the Emergency Corps moved to Bedford College in October 1914 Grace Vulliamy was appointed Organising Secretary. Therefore, as head of administration and in charge of publicity it is reasonable to surmise that she would have close contact with the heads of all departments and with the Executive. Further, Grace also initiated and organized certain Corps' activities and was not confined to the office which she would not have liked. By the time of its first Annual Report, the Emergency Corps listed nearly 30 societies taking part in its work. Half of these were directly related to the fight for women's equality and others, such as the National Society of Day Nurseries, were concerned with women's welfare and work. On 25 October the *Mid Sussex Times* reported that although only a few weeks old, the WEC 'was already a beacon of light for many'.

Women and Work

A vast army of young women workers in shops, restaurants, factories, and offices, who were thrown out of employment, were assisted by the Corps

---

Lady Randolph Churchill (Ed.) (1916) *Women's War Work.* (London:Pearson) http://bobrowen.com/nymas/jenniechurchill.html - prepared by Kay Larson's.mht. Accessed 29.3.2009

[70] Vulliamy Papers. Summary of War Work Record of GCV.

[71] Percy Alden. 'The Florence Nightingales of War: Interview with Mrs Lloyd George'. Unattributed newspaper article. 8.11.1915

[72] Ashwell. *Myself a Player.* 183

at Old Bedford College, where toy-making workrooms were opened and at first twelve girls were employed. In September 1914, Grace Vulliamy took over the Toy-Making department. This worked on a co-operative basis and profits were used to train workers and increase their wages. This was the principle that Grace used when working with refugees in Poland. The WEC toys were all marked with the trademark of the Emergency Corps - a lion's claw. A selection of toys was sent to Buckingham Palace and Queen Alexandra and Princess Victoria visited the York Place workrooms. Toys were sold locally. There were branches of the Women's Emergency Corps all over the country including Southampton. Many years later on 1 December 1983 one of the workers in Southampton was interviewed by Jean Berry. Then aged 83, the worker told the interviewer that she left school at 14 years old and her first job was making toys at the HQ of Women's Emergency Corps in Hanover Buildings, Southampton.[73] This is the only record found concerning the Southampton Branch, the existence of which would otherwise not have been known.[74] Branches sent their toys to HQ, who sold them to some of the big London firms – Marshall & Snelgrove, Army & Navy, Harrods. Demand was so great they disposed of all the toys to trade but hoped at some stage to be able to supply wholesalers.

Some of the largest London firms, besides two in Natal and Cape Town, where Grace Vulliamy was eventually to live, gave important orders for toys.[75] The work soon outgrew the accommodation at head-quarters, and Lord Portman lent them a disused chapel on his estate where the girls worked. Ten branches of this big undertaking were established in different parts of the country, and on 13 November Lady Londonderry opened a Women Workers Shop at 180 Oxford Street as a London outlet for the work.[76] Letters of appreciation to the Corps showed how highly they were thought of. For example, Sir William Ward's letter of recommendation says: 'In order to find something, even if not well paid, at once, I should advise your applying, if possible in person, to the office of the ladies of the Emergency Corps – Old Bedford College, Baker Street, London. I believe these ladies would best be able and willing to advise you and help you.'[77] By November 1915, the need for women as munition workers had forced the government to insist that employers make provision for them to be

[73] Records held in the Southampton Archive: W0029

[74] Horsham LSE. 7MGF/E/4/03.

[75] *The Times.* (London, England) 3.10.1914

[76] *The Times.* (London, England) 14.11.1914

[77] Vulliamy files. Folder of Extracts From Letters of Appreciation to the W.E.C.

employed in this 'men's work' and 20,000 women applied, including those in the Corps' Toy Department. By November 1915 the Toy Department was almost closed. The war impacted quickly on what women were able to do.[78]

In the Emergency Corps, Grace Vulliamy was now in an environment where suffrage and women's emancipation was in the atmosphere, and the conviction amongst such women was that once women got the vote, war would cease - a theory that would have been attractive to her. On 24 November 1916 a letter to *The Times* on woman suffrage was signed by many women that Grace Vulliamy potentially knew because of their connection to the Emergency Corps. These included Laura Aberconway who joined the Women's Emergency Corps about mid-August having received a letter from Miss Ashwell asking her to join the Executive Committee.[79] Grace Vulliamy's hospitable nature is shown by a note from Aberconway accepting Miss Vulliamy's invitation to a Christmas Tree party on Saturday week, New Year's Eve, 31 December 1914. Grace was happy to count suffragists among her closest friends.

Arrival of Refugees

When war was declared, various organisations sent women to railway stations to meet refugees but there was 'not much doing until after August 15'.[80] The fall of 'invincible' Namur on 22 August began the influx and from 26 August an ever-increasing stream of refugees arrived. Press propaganda constructed the Belgians as heroes and emphasized the 'debt' owed to Belgium and also to Serbia.

As the Germans swept across Belgium, refugees arrived in England in waves, numbers swelling during August, reaching tens of thousands through September and October. The military 'race to the sea' in September and October 1914 changed what happened on the other side of the Channel so that refugees were directed first to Ostend, later to Calais, and then to Flushing. From these ports they boarded ships and ferries sent by the British to bring refugees across the Channel. The ordinary cross-Channel services between Dover and Calais or Ostend were suspended immediately war was declared, but some boats were chartered especially for refugees. Boats ran six days a week from Antwerp to Tilbury from 10 to 25 September, then numbers fell off, and the service reduced to three times a week until Wednesday 7 October. There were no steamers from

[78] Percy Alden. 'The Florence Nightingales of War'. 8.11.1915

[79] IWM. VOL 1.1/6 *Lady's Pictorial*, 14.1.15

[80] IWM. BEL 9.1/2

Antwerp, but after the fall of the city on 9 October, refugees poured in from Ostend. On Sunday 11 October about 1,500 refugees came from Rotterdam, and 2,000 from Ostend.[81] During the great exodus, between 7 and 14 October, no less than 26,000 fugitives were landed in Folkestone harbour. A large number arrived at Tilbury also, and on the 14th of October hundreds of fugitives who had embarked upon fishing-boats arrived at Ramsgate and other small harbours of the south-east coast. Finally, England received the surplus of the Dutch immigration. In October, Francesca Wilson, an author and later a relief worker with the Society of Friends, who knew Grace Vulliamy, went to Tilbury where she found the first refugees she had ever seen. 'Few of them knew on what shores they had arrived.' Because she could speak French she went each day until a 'young man wearing an armlet told me I was a nuisance and that refugees were the concern of officials.'[82]

By 21 November the British Government decided to begin the transport of a considerable number of Belgian refugees from Holland.[83] But there were problems. The President of the Local Government Board, the Rt Hon. Herbert Samuel, requested a representative from Scotland Yard, Aliens Officers and Belgian police in Flushing to sift the refugees for spies. The Dutch shipping companies were swamped by the numbers and the Netherlands Steamship Co. was unwilling to take them to England free. In a telegram dated 9 October, Sir A. Johnstone at The Hague, asked if British ships could be sent, and such was the urgency, asked 'Please send reply *en clair.*'[84] Ports notified the Women's Emergency Corps of the number of refugees arriving so that lodgings and transport could be provided accordingly. Soon Folkestone became the only port available for cross-Channel traffic from Flushing, Ostend, Boulogne and Dieppe.

Through the centuries, the poor had to be seen as 'worthy' of being helped, and sometimes harsh judgements were made. The 1914 Aliens Act controlled entry to foreigners by facilitating 'sifting', that is examination of people's physical condition, ethnicity and finances, and thereby acceptance or rejection. This process, carried out in Holland, was agreed by the Belgian authorities, and enabled categorization of people as 'deserving' because they had private means, (which was taken to imply the necessary good character and class) or were from devastated areas; if their homes

[81] IWM. BEL 1/20 Cd7763

[82] Wilson, F.M. *In the Margins of Chaos, Recollections of Relief Work in and Between Three Wars.* John Murray. 1944. 1

[83] *Jus Suffragii* 1.12.1914, 212.

[84] HO 45 10737 No 7, 10.10.14

were still in safe areas it was considered that they should not come, but stay in their own land. Before being allowed to cross the Channel refugees without private means or who were not from devastated areas were subjected to medical examination through a Board of Trade Committee run by Mr Nicholas Reyntiens, a Board of Trade officer lent to the Local Government Board, a major concern being the importation of diseases.[85] With the ports of Ostend and Zeebrugge falling on 15 October the chaos increased. Reyntiens and Dr Farrar, the Board's Medical Inspector, were unable to inspect all the refugees.[86] Working with the Local Government Board Grace Vulliamy helped weed out undesirable refugees at Gravesend where one 'benevolent-looking old gentleman' was seized by police as a bank robber. We are not told what techniques were used to identify such unwelcome refugees! However, her ability and efficiency undoubtedly impressed the LGB officials.

At the ports and in London interpreters were needed, and Grace Vulliamy, whose mother, Anna Museur, was Belgian, was given the task of forming the Emergency Corps' Interpreting Department prior to any such Department being started by the British Government. 'they organised from the beginning a large company of interpreters, most of them conversant with several languages of which the most useful proved to be Flemish.'[87] One of the first tasks which this department took in hand was the handling of the Belgian Refugees as they arrived in England. Over 600 interpreters were enrolled in first few weeks and five languages spoken, and in the early months there were 30 – 40 workers, nearly all voluntary.[88] Despite the incomplete Corps records, we discover when Grace Vulliamy started and finished working with the Emergency Corps through the 1917 work of Agnes Conway at the new Imperial War Museum. Conway started gathering information about the work women had undertaken during the War. She tried to make a complete record but it was impossible – there was simply too much. Mrs Morton Evans, who answered the questionnaire in February 1920 on behalf of the Women's Emergency Corps, wrote that the Interpreting Department started on 6 August and closed officially on 13 April 1916. She herself, had worked in the Department from 14 October 1914 and was Head of that Department from June 1915, after Grace

[85] Report of the Work Undertaken by The British Government in The Reception and Care of the Belgian Refugees. 1920. HMSO.

[86] Peter Cahalan. 1982. *Belgian Refugee Relief In England During The Great War,* New York: Garland Publishing, Inc. 95

[87] Harraden, Beatrice. *British Women and the War.* SUP 60.109

[88] WEC Half-Yearly Report, August 1914 – 31.1.1915 p.13

resigned, to April 1916. So Grace Vulliamy started on 6 August 1914 and left in June the following year.[89]

One of the Emergency Corps' first activities was to help the earliest Belgian refugees, meeting them at stations, providing suitable hospitality, food and clothes, even prior to the Government's invitation in September 1914. Interpreters were needed and Grace Vulliamy organised volunteers to carry out this task. Refugees were put on special refugee trains laid on by the Government at Folkestone. Grace organised volunteers to meet them at London's main railway Stations: Charing Cross, Victoria, Fenchurch Street, and also at ships at the various docks. 'This work became a stupendous labour, increasing in proportion as the devastation of Belgium deepened and widened.'[90] Grace organised women to serve milk, cocoa and food, and help carry babies, and bundles. Trains usually arrived late at night, those expected at Charing Cross might instead be sent to Victoria[91] necessitating long and sometimes fruitless periods spent waiting for their arrival. Refugees were sorted into those who had money but needed information, and those who required full hospitality. 'Those who had money were recommended hotels and other places of lodging corresponding to their means, those who were without resources were accommodated temporarily in the Committee's hostels, and these were drafted as promptly as circumstances permitted to the homes which had been offered to them.' The Corps saw the refugees safely to various destinations, providing suitable hospitality, food and clothes, and in the weeks that followed helped them find jobs, dealing chiefly with the 'better class' – it was the LGBs responsibility to deal with poorer people. Some had friends to go to, including as far away as Lincolnshire, and needed directions as to how to cross London and find the appropriate transport.

The Interpreting Department under Grace's direction worked closely with the Hospitality Department. For those refugees who had friends or relatives already in England or Scotland, temporary accommodation was needed while contact was made to find out if the relevant local refugee committee or individuals caring for refugees could provide extra accommodation for the new arrivals. They also aided stranded British women, that is, English refugees. The Women's Emergency Corps was one of several groups to report distress among English refugees. Their Miss Burke described cases of English men and women in business in Europe who had lost everything,

---

[89] IWM. BEL 5/4

[90] Harraden, Beatrice. SUP 60.109

[91] IWM 86/48/1

were out of touch with England, having no friends or relatives here. The Corps provided for them as far as possible in hostels, but the problem became an increasingly difficult one. While there was no difficulty in getting help for the Belgian refugees, the same assistance was not available for English refugees because the need was unrecognized. Eventually, on 3 March, 1915 the *Morning Post* advertised for helpers to investigate cases of distress and hospitality for English refugees, but such a request did not compare with the amount of much earlier requests and information about the 'brave Belgians'. On 1 October Sir Francis Villiers, British ambassador to Belgium, reported that there were still British residents in Antwerp, and wanted a vessel chartered to take about 500 home.[92]

Clothing, employment, missing relatives, lost luggage, and free education were dealt with. Some refugees were taught English in classes and also individually; free medical and dental advice was given, hospitals and convalescent Homes visited, letters were distributed, and assistance was given in the registration of wounded Belgian soldiers. These tasks, plus assistance in finding jobs, includes virtually the full range of assistance given to the refugees all around the country.

Few people spoke French and even fewer understood Dutch or Flemish so anyone who spoke a foreign language was extremely useful in these traumatic days. In the first half of December, coming from Yorkshire, a Mr van Doonen arrived for the first time in London with little money and no lodging. He met a lady, a member of the Women's Emergency Corps, who directed him to Baker Street and promised to help him find cheap accommodation. A month later he wrote a letter of thanks from his 'digs' in Hallam Street. He now lived there with his wife and wanted to thank 'noble Great Britain' for their hospitality to him and 'the other hundred and thousand helpless refugees coming every day from Holland.' He did not know the name of the lady who helped him but hoped his thanks could be passed on to her. Under his signature is 'Interpreting Department'.[93] So he got a job, paid or unpaid, with the Emergency Corps as well as receiving help! An undated printed document entitled 'War Service at Home'[94] quotes from a private letter addressed to the head of the Guides and Interpreters' Department, giving further insights into the help that the Interpreting Department was able to give these 'brave Belgians'.

[92] TNA. FO 369 /671. Belgium Files 35554-36871

[93] Vulliamy Papers.

[94] *War Service at Home.* (Vol LXXVI, No 453) p.1116-8 No publisher, no date.

'The Emergency Corps [was] ready to give the help which so surprised and touched the Belgians. Trains in those days of disorganised sea and land service arrived at all sorts of hours. If too late to take the refugees to hotels or lodgings, there were addresses, on those wonderful lists, of private houses in London where emergency hospitality was available. The ladies of the Corps had cause to know there was not an hour on the clock-face that would be called an inconvenient one for opening certain doors to those unhappy travellers – many with nerves horribly shaken by days of bombardment; others quite stupefied with grief. One train brought a woman who had given birth to a dead child on the way. Another woman died on the journey. One man had slept four nights in the trenches among the dead.[95]

Emergency Corps interpreters worked at Police Courts and Hospitals, as well as at what the Report described as the Belgian Refugees Society, presumably the War Refugees Committee – people were often imprecise in their use of such titles. The War Refugees Committee was another voluntary organisation started by a woman but soon taken over by high-ranking men, including Lord Gladstone, and then made responsible by the Government for all refugees of any social class. Most who applied to the Corps for help were educated people, and 618 families were helped. They traced relatives that refugees lost *en route* for England, arranged hospitality at Universities for Belgian professors and found textbooks for a Belgian soldier interned in Holland who wanted to teach himself English. The Military Superintendent of the London Hospital was helped by the Interpreting Department in the registration of hundreds of Belgian soldiers. *The Soldiers' First Aid to French,* or *German,* was published by the Emergency Corps and included in the 400 words or phrases were military and camp terms.

The Hospitality Department and the Belgian Department of the Emergency Corps were in same room, and on examination it seems that the 'Belgian Department' was probably the same as the 'Interpreting Department.' The Head of the Belgian Department interviewed families, 'having a good knowledge of Belgian life, conditions and language. She could judge social class and therefore the type of hospitality required could be matched with what was offered.' Grace Vulliamy was more than capable of doing this necessary work so it might be describing her. Details of the family were entered on a form and passed to the Hospitality Department who returned a list of possibles. The Hospitality Department carried out 'colossal work for Belgian and French refugees in supplying both homes and clothing to those

[95] VOL 1.1/28. Printed document War Service at Home 1116-118

who were homeless and destitute.'[96] As most Belgian families consisted of at least six people this represented some 3,700 men, women and children, of which 2,000 were found homes and 1,675 clothed. The family had the final choice about where to go. Most middle and upper class people wanted to live in a big town and there were problems of fitting people into the right size accommodation so as not to waste space. Some large families refused to be separated, so it was necessary to fit as many as 14, 16, or even 27 people into one lodging at midnight. However, a family of six, for example, was never put into a space for eight. Next morning an Emergency Corps interpreter visited and took the head of the family to Aldwych to be registered with the War Refugees Committee and have their papers regularised. It was arranged for families to call at Emergency Corps' HQ if hospitality or help was required. Interviewing began 9 am and finished at 7 pm.

Many refugees arrived with nothing but the clothes they were wearing and these were usually dirty and in poor condition due to the privations of their flight. The Emergency Corps were able to supply some clothes but most refugees needing clothes were sent to the War Refugees Committee's store at Aldwych, where there was a big clothing store of garments donated by the public. Some families would go from one clothing store to another to get more than their share, or to pawn or sell, so preventative measures were adopted and only with written authority from Aldwych were clothes given. The Corps sent clothing to the refugees at Calais and Holland and for wounded soldiers and those on active service who were interned in Holland. This included when Grace Vulliamy was in Flushing.

In December 1914, a Miss Ethel Walton wrote to Grace Vulliamy from 29 Bramham Gardens, London, knowing that she was a member of the Emergency Corps. Miss Walton had received some clothing from South Africa and wanted Grace's help in distributing it for the Belgian refugees. She was Head Mistress of the Girls Government High School in Durban, Natal and while she was in England the staff and pupils had made up 232 garments of various kinds, in each of which 6d (six pence) had been sewn up as a small Christmas gift. She had also received from her school a case of worn clothing to be given to the refugees. Miss Walter then introduced herself as 'a cousin of Miss Jessie Ball, late of Pretoria, with whom I believe you are acquainted.'[97] Neither Miss Ball, nor Miss Walter appear again in

[96] Churchill. *Women's War Work.* 1916.

[97] Vulliamy Papers. Ethel Walton to GCV. 10.12.14

the Vulliamy Papers, but nonetheless this shows the value of acquaintance and networking in humanitarian aid.

Registration of refugees was undertaken with great care by those involved so that the recorded identity of each individual enabled families to be reunited and properly repatriated in due course. Records were sent to the War Refugees Committee and refugees were guided there when searching for members of their families.[98] When the Local Government Board took over responsibility for this type of record-keeping, they used a simplified registration questionnaire but still employed some of the same women as registrars.[99] Emergency Corps members were also present at the huge refuge at Alexandra Palace where 4,000 refugees were given temporary accommodation when it was opened in September[100]; the Corps provided suitable hospitality, paid and unpaid, and also food and clothes.

Education

Although its focus was on civilians and it was not a military organisation, the Corps did not ignore the military.[101] Grace realised that men were being sent to France and Belgium without any idea of how to speak the language, so she set up classes for them. On 7 September the Corps became the first organisation to start teaching elementary French and German to the soldiers in training. Classes were held in nearly fifty military centres.[102] The numbers increased so rapidly that it was impossible to meet the whole demand. Lena Ashwell wrote:

> Applying to the Government to take over the classes, we met with a curt refusal, followed up presently by the visit of an official personage, irritated and even a little hurt at our interference with the concerns of Proper Authority.[103]

This is an example of what Sarah MacNaughtan (1915: 81-2), had in mind when she wrote:

---

[98] *Times.* 28.1.15, 5e.

[99] *Englishwoman*, Oct-Dec, 1914. 54

[100] IWM BEL 5/7

[101] Lucy Noakes. 'Women's Military Service in the First World War.' http://www.gale.cengage.com/pdf/whitepapers/gdc/WomensMilitary.pdf

[102] WEC. Half-Yearly Report, August 1914 – 31.1.1915. 14

[103] Ashwell. *Myself a Player.* 224.

> 'the Voice of Authority abrogates command to itself. ... Initiative which had the courage to launch schemes becomes hidebound and even penalized. Workers are dismissed, or put in their proper place.'

A large proportion of the refugees were children and parents were concerned that their schooling should not suffer, so schools needed to be found. Women's Emergency Corps records state that the 'Interpreter was a Catholic and quite successful in finding schools to take children free, or at small charge.' The Corps gave help on any subject: infant care, buying school outfits, shopping, and transport.

Widows

The widows of soldiers and sailors became another concern – immediately they heard of the death of their husband, their separation allowances were stopped, because they no longer fell into the category of 'wife.' They then only received 5s. (five shillings) and 1s. (one shilling) per week for each child. In October the Women's Emergency Corps realised that was a matter they would have to consider and put before the 'proper authorities'.[104]

Medical Matters

The Women's Emergency Corps had a nursing department but as far as can be ascertained Grace Vulliamy was not directly involved in its work: her skills as organiser and administrator were better used elsewhere at this time. The Corps received offers of help from women anxious to use their nursing skills in the emergency from all over the world, including two from Zululand. Girls were placed as probationers in hospitals, partially trained women were found work in private hospitals and VAD Units, and several women dispensers were placed, some paid, some voluntary. Untrained nurses were found work in War Clubs and one was placed in the War Refugees Committee's Poland Street Refuge where Jews (always a separate category) were given refuge.

When war was declared and troops arrived from the Empire, there was a moral panic over the likelihood of an increase in VD through prostitution.[105] British soldiers' wives' separation allowances were stopped if their husbands were found to have VD, the wives themselves being placed under surveillance. An amendment to the Defence of the Realm Act, Regulation 40D, had the implication that women were not to have intercourse with their own husbands – from whom they might have caught VD in the first place!

---

[104] *Mid Sussex Times 27*.10.1914 Page 6

[105] K.Storr, 'Belgian Refugee Relief: an example of "Caring Power" in the Great War', *Women's History Magazine,* Issue 41, June 2002, 16-19

But there was another alarm even more directly connected with refugees. Cases of VD among men were discovered at the War Refugees Committee's Sheffield Street clinic in London, giving rise to concern. Sexual danger was linked with foreigners and since women were held to be responsible, necessitated control of women's bodies, brought about fear of refugees and a panic over the increase of Venereal Disease.[106]

A worried contributor wrote to *Common Cause* about:

> 'the serious condition of things existing at our railway stations on the arrival of the Belgian refugees. Well-dressed ladies select the young women they want and take them for the White Slave trade.'

It was thirty years previously that William Alex Coote, with some prominent suffragists involved, had founded the National Vigilance Association in response to the revelation of the frequency with which apparently respectable ladies were able to abduct young women, especially at railway stations, and later dispatch them to France and Belgium, particularly Brussels and Antwerp, as white slaves.[107] The social purity movement and the obsession with male vice led to repressive public policies. Commenting on the enforcement of the White Slavery Act of 1912, Sylvia Pankhurst remarked, 'It is a strange thing that the latest Criminal Amendment Act, which was passed ostensibly to protect women, is being used almost exclusively to punish women.' As late as 1914, first-wave feminists were rediscovering that the state 'protection' of young women usually led to coercive and repressive measures against those same women.[108]

There were undoubtedly visual similarities between those events and the way in which middle-class refugees were now met by British women. Mr

---

[106] K. Storr. 'Belgian Refugee Relief: an example of "Caring Power" in the Great War.' *Women's History Network Magazine*, June 2002

[107] Holton, Sandra S. 1994. '"To Educate Women into Rebellion," Elizabeth Cady Stanton and the Creation of a Transatlantic Network of Radical Suffragists.' *The American Historical Review, 99 (4)*
W.T.Stead. 'Maiden Tribute.' Pall Mall Gazette, 6.7.1885. No 6336. Vol XLII.

[108] Judith R. Walkowitz, "Male Vice and Female Virtue: Feminism and the Politics of Prostitution in Nineteenth Century Britain", in Powers of Desire: The Politics of Sexuality, ed. Ann Snitow et al. (New York: The Monthly Review Press, 1983).

Coote reassuringly responded: 'We have about 100 ladies on duty at the different railway stations,' and

> 'We have had the advantage of the help of ladies from the Women's Emergency Corps,' and others.[109]

This was another facet of the work which Grace Vulliamy was involved in organising.

Dr Mary Scharlieb, whom Grace knew pre-war, was an Emergency Corps Executive Committee member. One of the early women doctors, she was a member of the Royal Commission on Venereal Diseases from 1913–1916 and a member of the National Council for Combating Venereal Diseases. Amongst Grace's papers are several copies of a letter from the National Council dated 17 June, 1916 concerning the possibility of arranging a conference for women teachers to consider the problem of VD in relation to educational questions in Girls' Secondary Schools. Grace Vulliamy would have been intending to distribute these among women delegates.

The Crisis Ends

Before long the Corps needed more of everything in order to keep going. More money was needed for such things as rail fares for destitute refugees, working capital for the Toy Department, more materials for workers, more clothing. Toy samples needed to be made in January so that delivery of orders could be made at Midsummer.

The long hours and heavy work caused by the crisis lasted until early in December when the Emergency Corps was again short of funds and advertised in *The Times* for help.[110] This was a problem many voluntary organizations found themselves dealing with four months after the war began – in many people's minds the war was supposed to be over by Christmas and they could not continue donating funds any longer. But that same month the Corps was appointed by the Government to cooperate with the Local Government Board in dealing with the 29,000 refugees in Holland and Grace Vulliamy went to Flushing to assist. Beatrice Harraden wrote that she 'missed GCV when she left England for Holland to work for the LGB.'

---

[109] *Common Cause* No 284: September 18th 1914, 439

[110] Source Citation: VIOLET VANBRUGH. "Women's Emergency Corps." *Times* [London, England] 13 Jan. 1915: 9. *The Times Digital Archive*. Web. 14 Dec. 2014.

In January 1915 the Secretary of WEC enquired of the Commission whether and when Miss Vulliamy would return to London. They were told:

> Miss V is still with us and is doing very useful and indeed indispensable work in connection with the Transportation of Belgian Refugees to the UK. Her personal qualifications are so exactly what we require and her experience in this special work is by now so considerable that I hope you will be able to spare her services to us for some weeks further. We expect to be continuing the work to about the first or second week in March, yours very truly (no signature)

By January 1915 the emergency in England was over and the *raison d'être* of the Corps' Belgian Department came to an end, most of the work being done by the Central Authorities at Aldwych to whom all papers were finally handed over when the Corps Department shut a few weeks later. In all, some 4000 Belgians were dealt with and hospitality found for 335 families.[111]

Once the War Refugees Committee was given responsibility for the refugees, the Corps no longer had full responsibility but the Government often called for help and their first annual report stated that 'Interpreting work is not now so necessary.'[112] Indeed, 'The Corps itself, which started as women's work, was largely taken over by men.'[113] This fact, plus the comparatively short life of the Corps may help to explain why its work has received so little attention from historians, who tend to focus on women doing men's work such as making munitions, rather than humanitarian relief. As far as Grace Vulliamy is concerned, she was only with the Corps for a few months and by the time their first Half-Yearly Report was written she was already with the Local Government Board in Flushing. Her work is discussed in the Emergency Corps Report, but her name is not mentioned.

Grace Vulliamy resigned from the Corps in March 1915. On 13 March 1915 the Quakers underlined her importance to their work in Holland when Philip Burtt of the Friends War Victims Relief Committee sent a telegram to the WEC Secretary asking for Miss Vulliamy to be released to help at

---

[111] IWM. BEL 5/7 Report Women's Emergency Corps Belgian Department 1914. Signed E G Merston, Hon Sec Belgian Department, WEC, October 1914 – Jan 1915.

[112] IWM. VOL 1.1/6 *Lady's Pictorial*, 14.1.15; VOL1.1/29 Women's Emergency Corps. First annual report, 1914-15

[113] Cahalan. *Belgian Refugee Relief.* 334

Flushing. Her papers include a hand-made notebook containing little extracts from letters of appreciation to the Emergency Corps indicating how much their efforts helped sustain those whose lives were totally disrupted by war. One of the most significant is number 4, giving a sense of spiritual or psychological assistance having been given.

Writing about work women had done in France and Belgium, the Quaker MP Percy Alden, who was involved with refugee relief in the Netherlands, asked in November 1915: 'It is difficult to exaggerate what has been achieved by Women's Emergency Corps.[114] He asked: 'Has the war discovered any Florence Nightingale or any other women who will stand by her as typical of the spirit of the present age?' He mentioned 'that heroine Nurse Cavell', and Georgiana Fyfe who had already received the Order of Leopold for her work taking out a Glasgow convoy to Furnes and Dunkirk in 1914 and staying in Flanders to care for the refugees who 'are still in their villages behind the firing lines'. However, Grace Vulliamy was not among those listed; perhaps because her major work of rescue still lay ahead of her and some was secret, even from Alden.[115]

<u>Folder of Extracts from Letters of Appreciation to the W.E.C.</u>

Samples –

1. Letter of Sir William Ward, quoted above:

2. I hear the WEC never fails to help a difficult case.

3. Thank you personally on behalf of my sister and family for all your kindness, and to tell you that they will be most comfortable at H… They are not lacking of anything …

4. 3 February 1915 Just to thank you ever so much for the very kind way in which you have held out a helping hand to me. It is not only in a practical way you have made my burden of the moment easier to bear.

5. Dear Emergency Corps

> You have sent me a most delightful lodger, and I want to thank you a thousand times. I wonder what I can do for you now? – etc.

---

[114] IWM. SUFF 60. 117 Percy Alden. *South Wales Daily News.* 8.11.15.

[115] *South Wales Daily News.* Cardiff. 8.11.15. *Alden: 'Florence Nightingales of War.'* SUPP 60.117

6. Je viens vous remercier de toutes les bontés que toutes vous m'avez temoignée. J'éspere que Dieu vous benira toutes'

(I come to thank you for all the goodness of which you have given evidence to me. I hope that God will bless you all ').

CHAPTER 5

COMMISSION & LAST LINK IN THE CAVELL CHAIN

Refugees in Holland and Britain
Everywhere refugees were seen as a health hazard and spies were feared. In England, the Local Government Board was responsible for public health and so, with the agreement of the Belgian authorities, before being allowed to cross the Channel refugees were subjected to medical examination.[116] By 22 August, Mr Reyntiens and Mr Wintour of the Board of Trade were in Ostend arranging with the Admiralty to bring refugees over to England on the following Monday. Nicholas S Reyntiens, who had been lent to the Local Government Board, was organising refugee registration with Dr Reginald Farrar, the Board of Trade's medical inspector.[117] Examination of the refugees was undertaken through a Board of Trade Committee run by Reyntiens, who, like Grace Vulliamy was of Belgian extraction. All who were accepted were given a card showing name, birthplace, age, profession, and other personal details, but some people were prevented from departing.[118] Reyntiens was responsible for the international Double White Cross Committee, whose secretary was also secretary to the American Consulate, and whose aim was to assist non-combatants, paying fares for both Belgian and English passengers. Its clothing department, which distributed between 500 to 1,000 items daily, was superintended by an Englishwoman, Mrs Coster. Reyntiens and Farrar were helped by the Quaker Percy Alden, who was later involved with refugee relief in the Netherlands, and from early December by Grace Vulliamy.[119]

It was estimated that nearly half a million Belgians poured into towns such as Flushing (Vlissingen), Middelburg, Bergen-op-Zoom and Breda in Holland. From there most wanted to come to Britain. The suspension of the Folkestone steamer service meant a reduction in refugee numbers arriving in Britain from France and the Netherlands but still about 1,000 to 2,000 a day landed. On Sunday 11 October about 1,500 refugees arrived at Tilbury from Rotterdam, and 2,000 from Ostend.[120] The influx of refugees

---

[116] Report of the Work Undertaken by The British Government in the Reception and Care of the Belgian Refugees. 1920. HMSO.
[117] Cahalan. *Belgian Refugee Relief.* 95
[118] BEL 1/20 Cd7763. p.17 Appendix: Mr. Reyntiens' Report. Rules
[119] See K.Storr. *Excluded from the Record.* 22
[120] Nicholas S. Reyntiens. 21.10.1914. BEL 1/20 Cd7763

was reputed in September to amount to 20,000 in one week alone. There were similar numbers of refugees around 13 October during the military 'race for the sea', when Reyntiens and Dr Farrar explained that they were unable to inspect all the refugees, and this happened again in January 1915. Young men of military age were removed and not allowed to board because they were not refugees, but potential soldiers.

Women's Emergency Corps and the Local Government Board

A very short time at Flushing convinced Miss Vulliamy that she could be more useful there than in London - 'there is so much to be done and so many to be helped' - and with some reluctance, as linguists were much in demand, the Women's Emergency Corps agreed to allow her to continue there. So she returned to London in December to hand over her department at the Corps, and then went back to settle to the work in the Netherlands.[121] Now Grace's position as a British Government employee gave her certain privileges. For example, on 5 December she received a permit to proceed to Holland the next day on LGB business 'without personal search'.

Government Commission for the Transportation of Belgian Refugees to England

In Flushing Grace Vulliamy worked with Mr Massey, Mr Reyntiens, Dr Farrar, and Percy Alden who was Liberal MP for Tottenham and Warden of the Canning Town University Settlement. Together they made the arrangements for transporting 1,200 refugees to the UK each week.[122] Initially, the policy was to admit only heads of families, women and children from devastated districts and the severely wounded, but soon the crush at French and Belgian ports made it impossible to adhere to this. From the beginning of January, Dr Farrar took over the control of the service at Flushing, assisted by Mr Massey who remained in sole charge from 15 March till the end of that month when the service ceased due to submarine warfare.

> Miss G Vulliamy was for some time assisting the officers of the LGB at Flushing in bringing over Belgian Refugees to England. Miss Vulliamy is now the representative of the FWVRC at Rotterdam. I hope that it may be possible to facilitate her arrangements for obtaining a passport and permit quickly as she is returning to Holland on board the SS Copenhagen on Saturday.

[121] Vulliamy Papers. The Netherlands camps. GCV

[122] Vulliamy Papers. Summary of War Work of GCV.

Miss Vulliamy's archive contains a very large number of photographs and we have to assume that she took many of them. Photography was very popular amongst those who could afford it and many middle-class people took it up. These included prisoners-of-war on parole. Donald Harkness, an RNAS bomber pilot on parole in Holland, was one such. The entry in his diary for 11 June 1916 shows he engaged in this activity while on active service in France. He wrote to his mother:

V.P.K stood for Vest Pocket Kodak. This was a small, folding, easily portable camera, as its name implies. They were the first cameras to use the 127 roll film introduced by Kodak in 1912. One version of the VPK was called the 'soldiers' camera'. The 'autographic' camera back had an area through which notes could be written onto the paper backing of the film. The drawback to this 127 film was the small size of the prints which most people would want to enlarge. The next size of film would be a 120 film with images correspondingly larger and more easily viewable. The photographs above were taken with this size film. It seems probable that Miss Vulliamy had this kind of camera and that she was able to develop and print the snaps herself or get others to do it for her.

Plate 5.1. Grace's Colleagues on Board the SS Copenhagen

The photographs shown below are in one of Grace Vulliamy's albums dating from that period. The fact that she is sitting indicates her significance within the group.

> I am enclosing a few more of my snaps, taken, developed, and printed by myself. A rumour came round just before I left, that all cameras had to be returned to England forthwith so we set to work that afternoon to photograph every mortal thing on the station whether of interest or not. Everyone must have had his photo taken at least 30 times during the day and I enclose some of myself taken with my old V.P.K.[123]

Grace Vulliamy was right about the need for her work now being in the Netherlands. Working for the Quakers enabled her to be appointed as representative of the British Consulate General at Rotterdam for the purpose of meeting and assisting all British returned civilians and soldiers who arrived in Holland from Germany and occupied Belgium. However, this was an era of volunteerism and the first English organization to offer assistance to the Dutch Government in handling Belgian Refugees in Holland was that of the Religious Society of Friends, the Quakers, who operated through their newly re-formed Friends' War Victims' Relief Committee (FWVRC).

Military

On 9 October, the remaining garrison at Antwerp surrendered, the Germans occupied the city and some British and Belgian troops escaped to the Netherlands to the north and were interned for the duration of the war. Amongst them were 15,000 British Marines at Groningen, nick-named "Timbertown" by the British. Most of the British soldiers who came into Holland during the war were interned in the camp near Groningen. Dutch people formed a committee in Amsterdam to provide comfort, recreation and occupation.[124] After first providing books, sports requisites, gymnasium apparatus, laying out tennis courts and skittle alleys, the Committee organized scientific classes for those men who wanted to use their time in studying. Of these classes the instruction given in Deep Sea Navigation proved most popular and was of great help to many of the interned men. Later the British Board of Trade was approached with a view to sending examiners out to Groningen so that the regular examinations might be taken. The results of these examinations were 'very gratifying to the excellent instructors for different branches of the Marine Service.'[125]

---

[123] Donald Harkness. *A World War I Adventure.* Authorhouse. 1914. 251

[124] 1 Vulliamy\Box 1Vulliamy papers\Vulliamy Box 1, Notes. **WEC** Grace's account of outbreak of war.

[125] Vulliamy Papers. The Netherlands camps. GCV

Plate 5.2 Photos of the Commission at Flushing, 1916

Top left: Miss Vulliamy sitting at the front on the right, wearing a hat, a white blouse with a black bow. Adelaide Livingstone is standing next to her.

Top right: Mr Massey is the bearded man standing second from the left; Dr Farrar is sitting wearing the hat which was to be so important in helping prisoners to escape, as also bottom right.

Bottom left: Mr Massey, Miss Vulliamy and Mrs Hutchinson, who otherwise does not figure in the Vulliamy papers.

The officers had some privileges so they were able to sleep in hotels in Groningen. Later, family members were allowed to join them in the Netherlands. Some were even given permission to go to England on a four week leave, as long as they swore on oath to return and not to escape. This privilege ended on 12 November 1914, after two German officers, despite their oath, made a successful escape attempt. The official German reaction was to declare that no German officers were allowed to give their oath any longer. In December fifteen British officers escaped from Groningen after the British Government gave the same advice to their soldiers. The Dutch now needed to lock up the interned foreign troops. In Groningen this was not possible and a better place was found in an unused fortress, Wierickerschans, in Bodegraven. On 14 January 1915, thirty-eight British and one French officer were brought to Wierickerschans by train. The train stopped at Nieuwerberg and from there the men walked three kilometres to the 'Schans. They stayed there for about a year. The imprisonment ended in December 1915 when the British Government gave permission to the officers to take the oath. Most of the officers gave their word of honour and these were allowed to leave the 'Schans. By January 1916 all of those had left for hotels, pensions and the homes of nearby civilians. After a few days a group of ten to fifteen German officers were locked inside the 'Schans until April 1917. However, after their three week stay in Groningen, officers Hodgson and Morrell were transferred to Wierickerschans. Together with the other officers, Morrell left in January 1916. Hodgson, however, escaped internment and made his way back to England where he sent a postcard to the commander of the fortress. Morrell and some others also made an escape plan. This was probably not a serious attempt. They dug a six metre long tunnel from their bunkhouse underneath the fortress wall. After a few weeks the tunnel was discovered by the guards. The plan would never have worked, however, because of the large body of water surrounding Wierickerschans.[126]

Being interned in a neutral country meant that these men were prisoners to a greater or lesser extent, and under Article 10 of the 1899 Hague Convention were often put on parole not to try to escape. Francesca Wilson sometimes went with Grace to a café where she met these men, and felt that she had 'brought flirtation to a height of perfection rare with the English … an art. Wilson described Grace Vulliamy as:

> 'an attractive woman always in a whirl of activity and excitement' who 'brought stimulus into the lives of the interned officers who were often let out on parole. She had an interesting time welcoming prisoners who escaped from Germany, or were returned on an exchange basis.'[127]

Despite being born into a Quaker family, Wilson had at first been rejected as a relief worker by Ruth Fry. She described the experience:

> Ruth Fry, in charge of the Friends' London office, granted me an interview, but it was in vain that I stressed my fluent French and

[126] Morrell Life History.

[127] Francesca M. Wilson. (1944) In the Margins of Chaos, Recollections of Relief Work in and Between Three Wars, (London:John Murray) 1, 6

willingness to do any kind of work. Ruth told her she was already doing useful work giving a home to Pauline and Jenny (two Belgian girls). What was Francesca's motive for wanting to leave it? Was it a genuine concern for Friends' work and the relief of the unfortunate, or only the love of excitement? 'Baulked by the perspicacious Miss Fry' she went to Holland with Jenny to see her sister and husband interned in Urk, Zuyder Zee.[128]

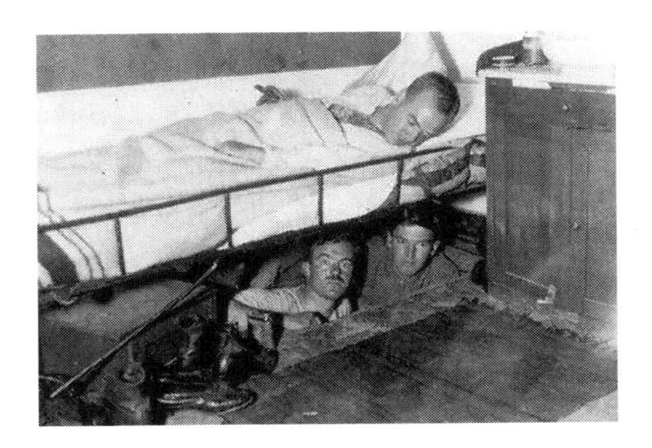

Plate 5.3 Morrell (bottom left) and two other officers with the tunnel entrance underneath the bed
Courtesy Chris Morrell and Maryrose Hughes.

However, in the summer of 1916 the Friends were willing to send her out because their work in France had expanded so much. She subsequently served in various areas of the world and wrote, among other books, *In the Margins of Chaos* about Serbian relief and *Rebel Daughter of a Country House* about the life of Eglantyne Jebb, founder of Save the Children.[129] Presumably Grace Vulliamy was thought to have a 'genuine concern for Friends' work and the relief of the unfortunate' since there is no indication she went through the normal processes before starting work with the Friends.

Once Grace was in Flushing#, she was in the perfect position to help escaped military prisoners and civilian internees to get on board ship and so across to England. The three male members of the Commission - Massey,

---

[128] Francesca M. Wilson. *In The Margins Of Chaos: Recollections of Relief Work in and between Three Wars.* Foreword by J.L.Hammond. John Murray, London. 1944. 3,9

[129] Wilson. *In the Margins of Chaos.* Wilson. *Rebel Daughter*.

Reyntiens and Farrar - were requested to sign an undertaking not to assist any POW's who were interned in Holland to escape; some of them were men who had returned from Gallipoli. There are times when being female makes women invisible and this can be useful. Grace Vulliamy used this sexist prejudice to her advantage to make arrangements to get escapees away to England. She wrote: 'Fortunately I was not requested to sign.' She explained:

Plate 5.4 The Local Government Board in Flushing

> For the Medical Exam the customs kindly lent us an office and for our convenience placed all their papers behind a curtain. Unfortunately, one night when I had three men hidden behind the curtain, one of the officials had forgotten some paper and came to see if he could get it. My heart stood still! So did three other hearts behind the curtain. Of course Dr Farrar was quite unaware of the existence of the three men. We were at the time busy examining a family of refugees and had to take a chance. 'Perhaps it would be wiser for you not to come in now; you are a married man and we think these children have measles.' He was fortunately married, so he withdrew hastily and gratefully. Dr Farrar give me a surprised look which I answered with a sigh of relief.

It is not known how Grace Vulliamy first became involved in the work of escape but it seems that it began almost immediately on her arrival at Flushing. Her comment about Dr Farrar being surprised might be to protect him from suspicion.

> Dr Farrar always wore an old fashioned half top hat. This hat was a godsend, for when some of the interned – who were not on parole – were able to escape and get as far as Flushing, the problem arose of how to get them shipped to England. It seemed to me the simplest way would be, to get them down to the docks at night when we embarked the refugees and then unbeknown to Dr Farrar borrow his hat which was so well known to the sentries. This I did on each occasion. The sentry saluted 'The Hat'. I would then, somewhat later, fetch Dr Farrar to the boat to see someone who might be ill and ask him to hurry and not worry about a hat. On leaving the boat he would return wearing it.

Dr Farrar's hat can be seen in the photos on the previous page, top and bottom right. However, Grace Vulliamy had further methods of getting men on board, without using the hat.

> We had a transport of severely wounded from Germany, on average once a month, so we were also able to use this channel to help men to England. The Dutch Red X were responsible for checking off the numbers of men, and their representative stood one side of the gangway and I the other, and if I had men in hiding – after bandaging them up to look as if wounded, I had to try and distract the Dutch representative by drawing his or her attention to some other object and then a few minutes later say definitely 'Yes, this is 118' while they had doubts as to whether it should not be 119 but thought I was correct.

Escape from occupied Belgium became extremely difficult. In the early months of the war it was comparatively easy to cross the frontier. Before long the Germans electrified the border and 'Belgian boys risked their lives, imprisonment or death trying to cross this terrible frontier with its electric wires and German guards. It was said 34,000 made the attempt in the first year of the war.' Electricity was something quite new and the results of touching the wire, carrying at least 2,000 volts, were at first totally unexpected. A special 6-sided wooden gadget was made in Rotterdam that created a space through which someone could crawl or a message passed without touching the wires.[130]

One of the newspaper cuttings Grace Vulliamy kept was of an article entitled: 'Escaped Prisoner's Story'. This was about Albert Champion, a French Private, a prisoner near Verdun in May 1916, with a terrible story of the prison camp at Cassel. He twice tried to escape, but failed and was punished by being kept underground on a diet of 100g of bread daily and

[130] David Jason, 'Secret Service.' TV programme. 6.12.17

beetroot soup every four days. After his second escape attempt he was kept this way for two months. He also received lashes from a whip. At last he got hold of a compass and map and did manage to escape. Grace wrote on the bottom of the cutting that she crossed to England with Champion in August 1917.

However, various people, especially women and civilians were trapped inside the occupied zone for the duration.[131] An Englishwoman, Miss J H Gifford, was one such. She worked at the Chateau Charles-Albert, Boitsfort, south-west of Brussels, a boarding school for English girls. Miss Gifford was appointed Sous-directrice of Ambulance H, Annexe 31 with 50 beds in one of the village schoolhouses.[132] She:

> began to prepare 20 beds there as a convalescent home for officers, the British in Brussels, under Dr Thomson, head of the British Red Cross, intending, if sufficient funds could be raised, to use it for that purpose – Miss Cavell also asking me to run it in connection with her nursing home.'[133]

She wrote:

> ... nearly every man one knew or heard of was a prisoner. Rich and poor, young and old, they were packed together like herrings in a barrel for sleeping and were provided with very meagre and very rough fare. ... Later all were sent to Ruhleben, the centre of imprisonment for civilians.

Details of the appalling treatment meted out to British prisoners of war by the Germans horrified Miss Gifford. The soldiers had been told that Britain had started the war and Britain's decision to uphold the 1839 Treaty with Belgium amazed them. 'For a scrap of paper, Great Britain is going to make war?' said the amazed Chancellor, Bethmann-Hollweg. Consequently the Germans were furious against the English and hated them much more than their other enemies. Miss Gifford made an unsuccessful attempt to visit British wounded. She recorded 'the British were always more rigorously treated than the other Allies.' The Germans allowed Belgians to feed French prisoners, but not the British. A pianist of French parentage, inscribed as British, was released on urgent French remonstrances: 'A British subject, but to be treated as a Frenchman' was written on his passport. The British were restricted as to bounds – including Miss Gifford.

---

[131] Gifford. IWM 93/22/1

[132] IWM 93/22/1, Ch. IIa, no page

[133] IWM 93/22/1, Ch. IIa, 10

She was told 'There is quite sufficient space in Brussels for an Englishwoman.' She was a guest of the Duchess du Croÿ during this time and said:

Plate 5.5 Exchanged Wounded Prisoners of War. Flushing. Holland. 1916

> really at first it was pitiable to see what skeletons so many of these ex-prisoners were. Several of them were almost like idiots, the result of the awful privations and experiences they had undergone. ... No parcels ever reached them working in Belgium; and if it had not been for food surreptitiously given by Belgian women out of their own scanty store, the greater number would never have seen Blighty again... others had gone through the terrible experience at Fort Macdonald near Lille when first made prisoners. There they were thrust into a room compared to which the Black Hole of Calcutta must have been as Paradise, and packed so tightly that even the dead remained standing. The food was flung at them, as to dogs and water was practically nil. No wonder many went raving mad. The Punishment felt most was when Huns took away their photos and keepsakes, worse than corporal punishment.[134]

[134] IWM. 93/22/1. Miss J H GIFFORD. Pages, 50, 52, 104. Chapter VIII

Nurse Cavell

The Belgians devised ways of helping escaped prisoners, but by September 1915 it had become well-nigh impossible to cross into Holland.[135] Miss Vulliamy wrote:

> We had from time to time men who had escaped from Belgium with the help of Nurse Cavell. We were prepared for these men, and had temporary passports arranged. On another occasion five men turned up and unfortunately celebrated their freedom in town, and on their way back gleefully informed the Dutch Police that they were soldiers escaped from Belgium thanks to Nurse Cavell! The Police escorted them back to the hotel where we had housed them. I had to explain that the men had had too much to drink and that they were not responsible for what they said, anyway I said I will show you their passports … a silly idea that they are heros (sic) because we had been discussing Nurse Cavell at supper – so all was well. The Police seem quite satisfied so all ended well.

Grace Vulliamy's use of the word 'we' in these paragraphs is significant. It was 'we' who were warned of the escapees' arrival, although who the others were, is never explained. Nor does she say who prepared the passports. This is exactly as it should be. Every member of an escape network had to keep quiet and most did not know who the others in the chain were. Miss Vulliamy was not the head of a network but neither was she just a nurse. Instead she was part of an active, amateur intelligence network, as was Cavell. The documents strongly indicate that Grace Vulliamy became the last link in the Edith Cavell escape chain by enabling the men to get on board ship and cross the Channel. Some photos show her with men she described as 'last lap from Cavell'.

This raises the speculation as to whether she was doing humanitarian work simultaneously with passing military intelligence from Belgium. As is often the case so much depends on definitions – here, what is meant by 'military intelligence'. She undoubtedly passed on information about the treatment of prisoners and helped with escapes. Grace Vulliamy herself gave minimal interview information about this period in her life. She was aware of the sensitivity of her work and that she could be accused of spying, as was Cavell. Further, as we saw above, escapees could give themselves away and put the lives of their helpers in danger. Some men stupidly even sent cards to Cavell from England thanking her for her help!

---

[135]*Edith Cavell.* Diana Souhami. E edition. *Edith Cavell: Nurse, Martyr, Heroine*. London: Quercus, 2010

It is unlikely that Cavell and Vulliamy ever met. But they were only at one remove away from each other. Some of their contacts can be seen in the form of a flow chart. The most likely contact to be of interest in this connection is Adelaide Livingstone

As an English person, Grace Vulliamy would not have been in a position to cross the border from Holland to Germany or occupied Belgium, but a neutral could do it. For example, Miss Stickney, an American Quaker, who later became Dame Adelaide Livingstone, a member of the Commission with whom Grace Vulliamy worked, in the early days of the war was able to cross the border without risk. Stickney, a member of the Women's International League, often travelled between the UK and Belgium, escorting German women from London and bringing out other refugees. When Miss Stickney was taking parties of girls back to Germany, she found that port officials could be intrusive, reading the girls' letters and confiscating books and newspapers. A medical student who had invested all her money in medical books but been refused her degree because of her nationality, wanted to go to Switzerland for her degree. She got through. However, in late February a party of forty was delayed in the searching rooms because a woman had been discovered the previous evening with £58 in gold concealed in the padding of her hair!

On her marriage to a British officer Adelaide Stickney-Livingstone was no longer a neutral and had to discontinue these rescue activities. Escorting women back to the Continent from Britain was undertaken only with Home Office approval, liaison with the American Embassy and arrangements with steamer and railway companies but had to be stopped when the issue of permits was stopped for a fortnight;[136] up to that point there had been weekly parties of girls returned to Germany. These refugees and their escorts used the Zeeland shipping line between Flushing or Dieppe and Folkestone.[137] This was the shipping line that Grace Vulliamy used when escorting prisoners.[138] It is impossible not to imagine the two women meeting and talking on board. On land, they were friends who met and had dinner together.

---

[136] *Jus Suffragii,* November 1, 1914. 193-4

[137] *The Friend,* No. 40, 2nd October, 1914, 730

[138] IWM. Suffrage & Politics 10.1. Report of the I.W.R.C., August 1914 to April, 1915. 12

Plate 5.6 Last lap from Nurse Cavell

Mary Sheepshanks,[139] a member of the International Women's Relief Committee, who pressed the Foreign Office to take action to help refugees in Holland by bringing them to England, wrote that 'as Dame Adelaide Livingstone she continued her trips into Holland, where she came into contact with Nurse Cavell.[140] Sheepshanks was usually very accurate, but this is unlikely. At present there is no evidence that Cavell went into Holland after war was declared – it would be most unlikely the Germans would give her permission; and as Miss Stickney, Adelaide could only get into occupied Belgium as long as her American nationality was unambiguous. Nevertheless, this shows that woman's enforced nationality and name change resulting from marriage could have far-reaching effects beyond the purely personal. However, because Stickney had reported to Lord Robert Cecil he later enlisted her aid in the Prisoners of War Department under Lord Newton, whom she accompanied to The Hague to confer with German generals on the treatment of prisoners.[141] Grace Vulliamy's photos show Adelaide Livingstoneat Flushing and on board the

---

[139] and it was from her office of the International Women's Suffrage Alliance (IWSA) that the 'unheeded, last-minute entreaty to every European Ambassador in London from the world's women's movement' went out on 31 July 1914 calling on them 'to avert the threatened unparalleled disaster' of the First World War.

[139] How farsighted that description proved to be! _Spinsters_ 213 Swanwick: Sheepshanks Secretary to Fight the Famine Council

[140] Women's Library, London. Mary Sheepshanks 7/Yyy8. It has not proved possible to confirm this.

[141] Women's Library 7/yyy8

S S Copenhagen. Livingstone was given the role of Assistant Secretary in the London end of the Commission. The two women kept in touch throughout the war. For example, Dame Adelaide invited her to lunch on Thursday 25 July 1918 when Grace Vulliamy was involved with prisoner exchange.

There were different escape routes for prisoners of war. One included Miss Cavell, Mons. Baucq who was shot on 12 October 1915 with her and Princess Marie de Croÿ who in 1932 published *War Memories*.[142] The Duchess de Croÿ hid soldiers and escaped prisoners; she helped:

> deserving cases with money or clothes' and made false passports. Naturally each member was working more or less secretly, it being a greater safeguard to know only one or two of the society.... Someone *such as a farmer or peasant burned the man's uniform and clothed him* in any rags he possessed and then forwarded him as best he could to Brussels. There the 'question of hiding was most difficult, as there were spies everywhere and the Military Police were always searching people's houses for something or another.

Miss Gifford said she offered to hide any men Miss Cavell cared to send but it was found too difficult to get them so far out of the line of route. The next step was providing the guide to take them to the frontier. Gifford said 'Many of the guides were splendid men, but unhappily on many occasions the runners, who carried contraband letters, were shot, even in the street. Once, knowing they were being followed, they simply waited for their pursuers and strangled them – 'your life or mine!' By November and December 1914 Cavell had helped about twenty men to freedom. In the months that followed she helped hundreds.[143] This implies that many other people, including Grace Vulliamy, were carrying on helping men from the border onwards and through Holland in their escape. From November 1914 until July 1915 a steady stream were sent on to Cavell and a network of clandestine help for lost soldiers grew up. Throughout the country cells of resistance interlaced, balancing caution with risk. Chateau Bellignies, the home of Prince and Princess de Croÿ, became the HQ of one cell.

> One Belgian peasant couldn't be got away because he kept failing to pick up the guide. The village curate helped pass dozens of men

[142] IWM 93/22/1. Gifford. Chapter XIV. 62

[143] *Edith Cavell.* Diana Souhami. E edition. *Edith Cavell: Nurse, Martyr, Heroine.* Diana Souhami. London: Quercus, 2010

and was initially sent away to Germany. Mdme Quiry, with a patisserie near the Porte de Namur, was very helpful. ... She was later imprisoned by the Germans and suffered both in body and mind so much that they induced her to become a 'mouton' that most treacherous of employments. This led to the imprisonment of many people with whom Mdme. Quiry worked.'

Miss Gifford wondered how she had escaped being denounced.

On 5 August 1915, Edith Cavell was arrested by the Germans and kept in solitary confinement until her 'trial' on 7 October. Others soon followed her into captivity, including Marie de Croÿ who was sentenced to 10 years imprisonment.

> After Miss Cavell's execution a long avis was posted up. I give the following translated extract ... 'Whoever knowingly aids in any manner whatsoever, an enemy of Germany in concealing his presence whether by giving him lodging, by clothing him, or by giving him food is liable to the same punishment –death or penal servitude.' It was only when public opinion had been aroused by Miss Cavell's execution that the German Government began to refer to her as 'the spy Cavell.'[144]

This somewhat naïve definition gives no clue that a spy could be other than a foreigner. However, acquiring 'information of any value' could be done very casually and even unintentionally. For example, on 16 October 1916 at The Hague, Donald Harkness, who crash-landed on 17 September 1916, met all the interned officers and had:

> lunch at Central with Captain Fryer and Jamieson. We had a talk on the way with a Belgian chauffeur to the American Consul at Ghent who told us a lot of interesting facts in regard to our bombing raids there.'

Another even more potent example was on 4 November 1916 when he 'had tea at the Royal and sat near the Turkish Minister again. We had an interesting discussion on Secret Service work here.' One of the professional spies that Miss Vulliamy knew was Paul Dukes and it is probable that she met him in Holland. She had his two English addresses: one at Furzebank, Bridgewater, Somerset and the other at 22 Ebury Street, London, SW1 in one of her little Address Books. They were in contact during her time in Poland when he gave her significant help with workers.

---

[144] Gifford, 40.

Like many prisoners of war Harkness suffered from boredom and frustration with the endless days of waiting. He was no sooner processed and given borrowed clothing when he began meeting an incredible array of people from high-ranking military types to people of very high standing in the Dutch and UK social circles. This is another clue as to how information could be passed on. He also rather enjoyed 'the clandestine, non-violent activities of the Society of Friends and often assisted Miss Vulliamy with one of her most important tasks: that of repatriating English citizens released from Germany.' He made contact with numerous members of the Allied underground and took pictures through his muffler of people and places he knew were forbidden – primarily to augment his journal but also to assist the war effort if ever called upon. Yet all the while he felt as if he was living in a surreal prison, one without walls but a prison still. Unlike real prisons, however, there were ways of leaving this one, at least temporarily, without breaking any international laws. As time went on Don Harkness and his fellow inmates discovered what those ways were and just how to use them to their advantage. One way was through a 'house used extensively by smugglers on the border between Belgium and Holland. The front door was in Holland, the back door in Belgium.'[145]

Whether he used this house in helping Arnold Jacques Chadwick to escape is unlikely. Chadwick, a Canadian airman, had escaped in October 1916 from German occupied Belgium where he force-landed. He was placed in Don Harkness's care while clandestine transfer arrangements to England were made. To keep German spies from discovering and detaining him Don Harkness hid him in plain sight while they waited for a boat to smuggle him back to London. On 8 November 1916 Harkness was 'with Chadwick all afternoon and went back to his hotel, the Victoria, where Bedwell, from the British Consulate, Rotterdam, called to tell us when the Rotterdam boat for England was to sail.'[146]

Christmas arrived while they were waiting. On Christmas Eve they met Miss Barber, Miss Vulliamy's secretary, 'with whom they are all staying.' The 'all' included Chris Morell and the Hon Major Trefusis:

> We strolled along to their house, not far from the church, and met the all-important Miss Vulliamy. She is a wonderful woman, full of inexhaustible energy and extremely clever. She speaks many languages and is the head of the "Society of Friends" a Quaker

---

[145] Harkness. 344, 354, 358, 387
[146] Harkness, 358-363

institution founded for charitable purposes though not herself a Quaker. Her duties include the looking after of Belgian refugees in this country, interned soldiers and sailors, sale of the work of Belgians, care of escaped prisoners and expelled civilians from Germany, and Secret Service work.

We all attended Miss Vulliamy's place at Daendels Street for Xmas dinner, where we had a most amusing evening. Two or three of the Quaker conscientious objectors were also present. They assist in the Society of Friends shop et cetera.[147]

Harkness's account of this escape shows how many people were involved to a greater or lesser extent in helping people get to England. This included the Consulate, as he mentioned, and, of course, Grace Vulliamy, of whom he held a very high opinion. He implies that she was acting under the direction of the Secret Service. The editors of Harkness's book wrote:

As important as Miss Vulliamy, first name unknown, may have been to the Belgian and internee relief efforts and the Society of Friends, there is little information available on her today. These entries are all we have on the remarkable Miss Vulliamy. The

Society of Friends chapter in The Hague, however, which she apparently ran, operated on many of beliefs fundamental to the parent Quaker organisation, in particular conscientious objection to the war; charity work; and an aim towards building up a new world rather than fighting to destroy the old one. It is unclear from Don's entries just how religious this particular chapter was, though they no doubt shared the same fundamental Christian teachings of the parent group which had its beginning in 17th-century England.

[147] Harkness, 371

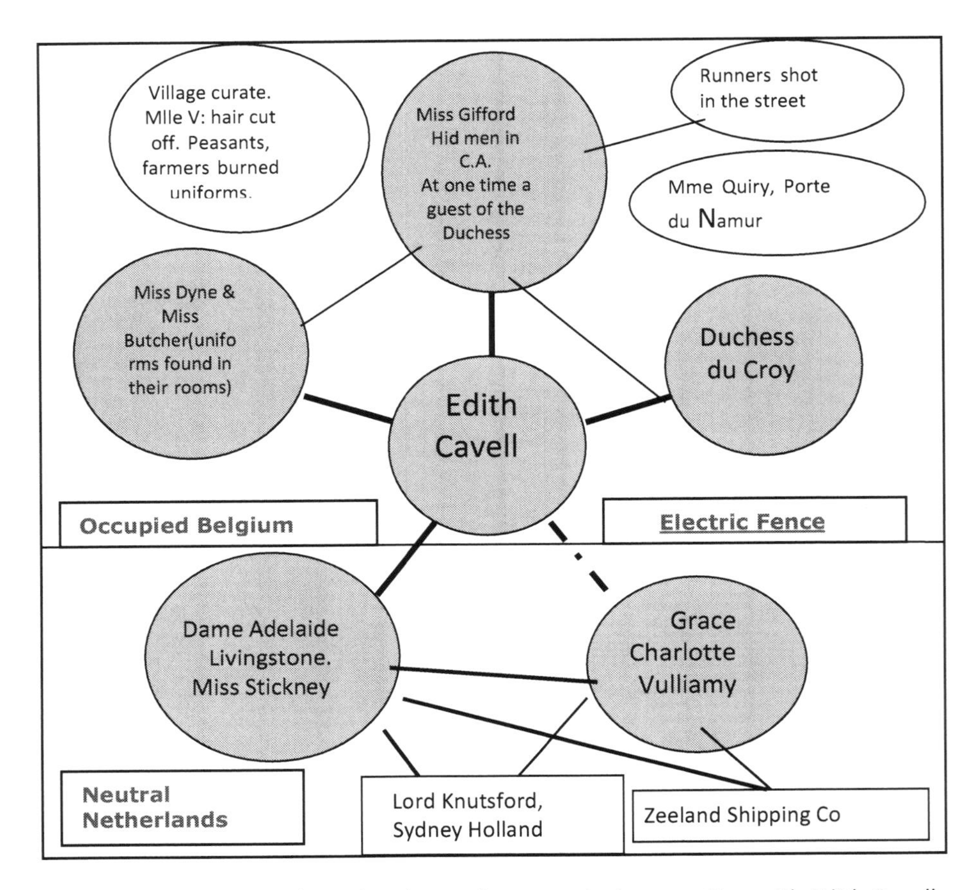

Plate 5.7 Flowchart chart showing various peoples' connection with Edith Cavell

Some of these details are inaccurate. The Society of Friends did not have 'chapters'. This was to use Masonic terminology. People who knew nothing about the Friends had difficulty explaining it to others. Nevertheless, this paragraph is useful in confirming Miss Vulliamy's position in the relief work.

In spite of all those who had paid the ultimate penalty, the work of rescuing prisoners went on without interruption till the Armistice. Grace Vulliamy's part in the work of rescue and spying also continued throughout the war. It was not until 1918 that the Germans realised that she was English, so perfectly was she able to speak Dutch!

CHAPTER 6

QUAKERS, CAMPS, CIVILIAN PRISONERS AND GRACE. 1914 – 1916

The President of the Local Government Board, Herbert Samuel, requested on 9 November 1914, that four Quakers, Arnold Rowntree, Seebohm Rowntree, E Richard Cross and Percy Alden,[148] should go to Holland to see the refugee situation there for themselves.[149] Seebohm Rowntree had investigated poverty in York, determining a poverty line in terms of a minimum weekly sum of money 'necessary to enable families... to secure the necessaries of a healthy life'.[150] After his visit to the Netherlands, Rowntree said the Dutch were absorbed with the task of looking after 'their Belgian guests'.

The Dutch, like the British, invited the homeless Belgians into their country, and Belgians in all conditions were pouring in at the rate of some tens of thousands a week. The Dutch threw up large camps of army huts to provide shelter for those who wanted to remain in their country and Belgian and other refugees were sent from Flushing in Zeeland Steamship Company boats to Tilbury, London's major port, where they were met and taken by train to metropolitan refuges where Grace Vulliamy arranged that interpreters were available. The first boat arrived on 6 December, and there was a service on four days per week, so that by Christmas, when many people were under the illusion the war would be over, the number of refugees transferred was 2,820.[151] From 8 January, further arrangements were made for transport from the Hook of Holland to Tilbury

---

[148] Arnold Rowntree was a Liberal MP for York, Seebohm Rowntree, a social reformer and industrialist, E Richard Cross, a Fabian and 'the master mind in working out … the plan for a league of nations,' and Percy Alden, a 'Radical Liberal' MP for Tottenham, London.

[149] Friends House. FWVRC. General Committee – 1.12.1914.

[150] Those in primary poverty did not have enough income to meet the expenditure necessary for their basic needs. Those classed as in secondary poverty had high enough income to meet basic needs but this money was being spent elsewhere so they were unable to then afford the necessities of life. See *Land and Labour, Lessons from Belgium* (1910) https://en.wikipedia.org/wiki/Seebohm_Rowntree 3/11/2016 4:55 PM

[151] BEL 1/20 Cd7763. LGB report on the Special Work of the LGB arising out of the war. Up to 31.12.1914

Grace now became involved with different categories of civilians who were all prisoners to a greater or lesser extent: among them were those who were housed in camps in Holland, and those who were trapped because there were no ferries, or they had other travel problems such as lack of passports, and amongst these specially selected men were hidden. These will be discussed in the next chapter. Later, there were prisoners being returned to their own countries by the authorities.

Grace Vulliamy and Quakers in Holland

Plate 6.1 Gasterland Belgian Internment Camp Brick Kilns Used as Homes

The Dutch were at their wits end to provide accommodation for the refugees and in Gasterland brick kilns were used as shelter. As shown here in Grace's photo it can be seen that they provided nothing more than very basic and very dirty shelter. While Britain had then received less than 80,000 refugees, Holland had ten as many; or considered in proportion to her resources and population, she was undertaking forty times as much. The result was that another large influx of refugees 'found its way' to England times.[152]

[152] https://en.wikipedia.org/wiki/Seebohm_Rowntree 11/03/2016 17:02

The Society of Friends expressed grave concern at the state of affairs. Percy Alden tried to arrange on behalf of the Government to bring over 20,000 refugees, but the current rate of 1,000 or 1,500 per week was far too slow. They wanted to keep in touch with other Committees already at work, including the Women's Emergency Corps, which in Holland meant Grace Vulliamy.[153] Alden was convinced that personal supervision by a representative from the initiating body in regard to any money or scheme administered in Holland was all-important and that the provision of some wholesome occupation for the Refugees was vital.[154] These views indicate one of the several reasons why the Friends asked Grace Vulliamy to supervise the work that was set in motion once they made money available. On 8 December 1914 Philip Burtt was added to the Friends Committee to deal with Belgian refugees in Holland. He and Arnold Rowntree were both members of the Friends War Victims Relief General Committee and Grace Vulliamy was to have considerable dealings with them during her time in the refugee camps in Holland.

Quakers arrive in Holland

By January 1915 the numbers of refugees entering Britain were reduced because the crisis, stimulated by the fall of Antwerp, was over, but thousands were trapped in the Netherlands. Early in 1915, Philip Burtt and Fred Rowntree approached the Dutch authorities with offers of help in the camps and suggested giving money. Upon learning that the best way they could be useful was by going into the camps and supplying the 'life' in these settlements of people who were provided with food and shelter but without any of the activities of normal human life, the Society of Friends offered themselves for this purpose. Grace Vulliamy begged them to spend the money providing employment so that the refugees could help themselves, rather than existing on handouts while remaining idle. This was a principle she applied throughout her life: if people could work towards their own support, they should. It not only provided an occupation, but it helped maintain self-respect under circumstances over which they had no control. Shortly afterwards, in May 1915 Miss Vulliamy received a cable asking if she would organize the work if Quakers put up the money. She agreed and began organising employment in the refugee camps all over Holland.[155] The

[153] Friends House Library. Belgium Sub-Committee Minutes. Box 9, parcel 3, folder 1. 15 December 1914.

[154] Friends House Library. Belgium Sub-Committee Minutes. Box 9, parcel 3, folder 1. 6 January 1915

[155] Vulliamy Papers. Summary of War Work of GCV.

authorities were favourable, in particular Baron von Tuyll, Chairman of the Dutch Government Commission for the Employment of Belgians, and the summer of 1915 saw the establishment of English workers in the four camps.

Grace Vulliamy became the Friends' representative in Holland and liaised between them and the Dutch authorities – this was of particular help to the Friends who did not speak Dutch. This was completely different from the way people usually joined up with the Quakers to help those in distress. Normally, prospective workers first had an interview where the relevant Committee decided whether the applicant was sufficiently in accord with the Society of Friends to become one of their workers. There is no hint that Grace Vulliamy went through this process. Those who were not members of the Society of Friends, discovered that working with them was a completely different experience and many people found it difficult. Group activities and decisions were organised through committees and when decisions had to be made it was necessary for everyone to accept the decision before discussion ended. If there was one dissension, discussion continued until all were in agreement. It seems that Miss Vulliamy was able to adapt to this with comparative ease. Indeed, she was consulted and gave her opinion on adding new members of different committees. Administration was based first in Rotterdam in an office lent by the American Relief Commission and then at The Hague.[156] Grace's friend Beatrice Harraden used this office when writing for the Commission; it enabled her to go into the camps where Grace was working and help there too. She is shown here on the left. Seeing the kind of organisational work that Grace did caused Harraden to refer to her as 'Dutch Boss' while signing herself simply 'Boss.'

However, there were times when Quaker methods caused problems. For example, the Meeting held at Utrecht on 1 September 1916, was told that Howard Rowntree was being sent to France by the London Committee. It was felt that this was a very bad decision. He had won the confidence of the Dutch authorities and had good knowledge of the work, having helped with the civilian prisoners passing through the Netherlands from Germany from the beginning. Rowntree himself said his present work was his right work. This was an allusion to the Quaker concept of 'Inward Light', envisaged as 'that of God' which spoke to each person individually. Nonetheless he went

[156] A Ruth Fry. *A Quaker Adventure*. Nisbet & Co., 1926. 104-5

where the London committee sent him but was back in Holland not long afterwards.

Plate 6.2 Beatrice Harraden (left) with workers at Dutch refugee camp

Camps

Dutch authorities were responsible for the establishment of camps, and each camp had a commandant appointed by the Dutch. Most of these men were understanding, but one or two seemed to think they were guarding criminals and acted accordingly. There were four large camps in existence at that time, one each at Gouda, Nunspeet, Ede and Uden. Nunspeet, with capacity 13,000, was opened at the beginning of November for the 'undeserving' or 'undesirables', that is, those who were poor or whose means of support was questionable. Nunspeet was an unhealthy place with earthy roads paved with discarded sheets of asbestos. Here, and at Roosendaal, soldiers guarded prostitutes' quarters and rooms where refugees suffering from disease were placed in quarantine.[157] It was understood that desperately poor women turned to prostitution as a survival mechanism so to prevent this women were supposed to be accompanied by a man, or their family. If they were on their own, they were regarded as prostitutes.[158] The camp commandant, Dr Muller,

---

[157] Abbenhuis 2006: 99. For a discussion on the use of the term 'prostitute' see Storr. *Excluded from the Record.*

[158] Storr. *Excluded from the Record. p.*99

was described by Burtt as 'an autocrat' when he and Miss Vulliamy visited Nunspeet. Burtt wrote to Ruth Fry:

> We knew he would be on the high horse, poor man he cannot help it at his time of life and he is getting very worried at his responsibilities, so we mounted a similar steed and duly sorted out problems. I should like Miss Vulliamy to go there alone next week. Nunspeet is going to be difficult, but of greater possibilities.[159]

The fact he wanted Miss Vulliamy to go alone indicates that she had powers of negotiation and conciliation in accord with what the Society would want. But she was also very firm and would stand her ground. Burtt and Rowntree initiated a plan for building wooden houses, the plan being adopted as one of the main activities of the Friends Committee.[160]

The camp at Gouda was long and narrow, bordered by a canal and by far the smallest, containing about 1,600 men, women and children, and instead of specially erected wooden buildings as in the other camps, the refugees were housed in empty greenhouses in which formerly grew flowers, maidenhair and asparagus ferns. Tables and forms were arranged inside and used for sleeping and eating, cooking and laundry. Miss Vulliamy wrote:

> It was sad to see there strong, young men, sleeping or lounging about with no occupation, and here it was a cheery thing to pick out the handy men, joiners, carpenters, smiths, etc and put them at work on the little wooden houses which had been approved by the Committee of the Society of Friends for erection.

At the further end of the camp was the house in which the Friends workers lived. Katharine Alexander from Worthing was in charge and the basic work of making mats and slippers was initiated by her and proved successful.[161] It was very soon apparent that there was a great need for organised employment and recreation among the hundreds of people. In January 1916 Miss Vulliamy and Charles Morrell, one of the officer prisoners, went to Gouda to find someone who could be a servant and the next day escorted him to Galvanistraat where Morrell was living. Refugees

---

[159] Friends House. FWVRC Box 9, Parcel 3, Folder 3. Correspondence With Rotterdam Office. British Government Commission for transportation of Belgians to the United Kingdom, Zeeland Hotel, Vlissingen. H.P.Enkey, signing letters therefrom. 6 July 1915. Report, Burtt to Fry from Rotterdam

[160] http://www.guise.me.uk/articles/quakeradventure/chap13.htm

[161] V.P. Ruth Fry's Report 21-28 August, 1915

often arrived with their clothes dirty and badly torn but people in England sent out parcels of clothing for refugees' use and Grace was involved in the provision of clothing for 3,000 refugees.

Workshops

Plate 6.3 Picture of crèche at Amersfoort

When the Society of Friends first started industries for the Belgians in the Netherlands they knew nothing about the Dutch Officials and asked Miss Vulliamy to liaise between them and she started workshops. These were often regarded by the refugees as sites of resistance against the German invaders, ways in which Belgian culture survived and could flourish. She organised employment for the first few months and by degrees industries were started in all the different camps without any friction with the Dutch. Miss Vulliamy, Miss Pim and Mary Rees arrived at Nunspeet on 12 October to prepare.

By August 1915 in Uden Camp alone there were some 1,800 men and women regularly working as basket makers, smiths, brush-makers, and rug-makers. Grace wrote to the Women's Emergency Corps for wool so that they could make rugs. Toys, shoes and specialised embroidery work for women, appliqué work using Egyptian designs, were also undertaken. Miss Vulliamy also started up crèches to free the mothers and give them time to work without their babies. A market was found for the goods either within the camps or elsewhere, the workers being paid sometimes in 'points' to be eventually realised in coin as this became possible, sometimes in clothes, or household requirements. Miss Vulliamy also worked at Uden with Vida Mardon and Irene Brison. Uden was one of the largest camps for Belgian refugees in Holland, opening on 20 December 1914. It catered for 5,400 refugees.[162]

Workers

Workers sent out by the Quakers arrived in Holland expecting to be sent to certain places and to have particular duties. This sometimes caused problems for Grace Vulliamy, who might have other ideas about needs on the Field and the candidates' suitability for specific places and tasks. From the Home viewpoint it was logical that workers wanted to know where they would be going and what their duties would be. Further, Ruth Fry would have in mind what requests the Field Committee had made for new workers and try to fit volunteers into the gaps. This didn't work, because Ruth did not fully know what was happening in Holland – the physical conditions, the changes that had occurred between letters (perhaps due to being delayed or going missing), and as Grace said, personality was all important, more so than the skills. In one instance a woman who was inclined to suffer from a bad throat was sent out, but the camp she had been told she would be going to was totally unsuitable because it created exactly the health problems the worker suffered from. The Home Committee were unaware of that. In addition, workers' expectations were sometimes unrealistic, perhaps too idealistic. A woman who returned to England suggested that the needlework in the different camps should be overseen by an expert. This seemed sensible, but there were excellent logistical reasons why in practice it couldn't work and Grace Vulliamy went to considerable lengths to explain these to the Home Committee via Ruth Fry. In England conscription became law in January 1916 with the Military Service Act imposing compulsory active service on single men between 18 and 41, although there were certain exemptions. The Act created problems for the Quakers. The Government agreed to allow all those on the Continent to be exempted, but then called individual men back for Tribunals. This caused anxiety for all workers, plus the time taken dealing with this meant less time given to refugees and their problems. The fact that male workers were exempted because they were conscientious objectors might have meant that any health problems they had were not mentioned. Many of them seemed to have health difficulties, but so did the women. In April 1916 Grace Vulliamy wrote to Miss Fry:

> I hope that Miss Dolling is crossing with Miss Gunter and that she will not catch cold on the way home. You will remember that in my last letter I said I would be very pleased to have her back here again if she could get a doctor to certify that she is absolutely fit.

[162] V.P. Ruth Fry's Report 21-28 August, 1915

However, I have talked to Miss Nichol and others who have worked with her and find that she is more trying to live with than I had realised. The doctor has described her as 'hysterical'. She hardly seems usable for the camp life out here and I would find it difficult to know where to place her. Her good work amongst the boys hardly seems to compensate for her other disadvantages. If she has a tendency towards pneumonia or consumption our little wooden houses do not seem to be the place for her.

Cottages

By March 1915, the 'little wooden houses' at Gouda were equipped with basic requirements including table, chairs, curtains, kitchen stove and brushes; they were being built on land rented by the Society of Friends and were their property. The ideas behind the buildings were to give work to men in the camp, and so that when the war was over, the cottages could be sent to Belgium to be used as temporary homes in the destroyed villages. They were to be occupied firstly, by the carpenters who built them, and then by other families, but to qualify, the workmen must have worked continuously for three months. The question of the rent and equipment of the houses was very fully discussed by Grace Vulliamy with Ruth Fry, Baron de Tuyll, Fred Rowntree, Mme de Schepper of Gouda and representatives of two other camps.[163] It was to be one gulden a week for a three-roomed house, and 75 cents for one with two rooms. A further small additional amount was to be paid for 26 weeks to refund the cost of equipment such as jugs, basins, doormats – these to become the property of the tenant. It was important to the Society that the tenants took pride in their cottages, keeping them clean and tidy, and undamaged. They were also expected to keep their gardens tidy and properly cultivated – this meant growing vegetables for food. Garden seeds and seedlings were supplied. If the Camp Commission or the Society were dissatisfied with these matters, the tenant could be deprived of the use of the cottage.[164] Although Holland was not one of the belligerent countries, it was one of the many neutrals that suffered as a result of the war.

It occurred to Ruth Fry that the work would be greatly helped by the establishment of a Depot in London where the goods made in the camp might be sold. She wanted to include other Belgian industries, for example the lace and crochet work done locally under the direction of different Belgian ladies. Grace Vulliamy had been helping to find a market for this work. The struggle

[163] V.P. Ruth Fry's Report 21-28 August, 1915

[164] Vulliamy Papers. Society of Friends Cottages – Vluchtelingen Kamp, Gouda.

of lace workers was considered central to the tragedy of Belgium.[165] Women tried to retain their workforce, but due to wartime restrictions, ran out of materials and a market. Foremost among the American Relief Committees was Herbert C. Hoover's Commission for Relief in Belgium. (C.R.B.)[166] They were able to work in occupied Belgium where a women's committee approached them with proposals; eventually Britain, as a belligerent, allowed imports of thread and agreed to take lace for sale. It was agreed that no lace would be sold on the open market in occupied territory so that Germany should not benefit.[167] After the war, $1,000,000 in net proceeds were divided between the individual workers according to the value of the lace made.[168]

By July 1915, several newly erected Society of Friends workshops, a foundry, two large carpenters' shops and an archway with 'SOF of England' proclaimed Quaker involvement.[169] In the camps, streets made of the wooden houses were named after those who had helped the refugees, such as Fred Rowntree Street, Avenue of Baron Von Tuyll and Grace Vulliamy Street. This was the first of two such streets that were to bear her name, the other being in South Africa. Almost the last of the huts facing a children's playground was the cottage for SOF workers displaying the SOF 'Star' insignia. There was great demand for English lessons. The longer the refugees' exile went on, the more 'normal' life became. n July two of the houses were taken for an exhibition with everything made by refugees and for sale.[170] In many instances materials were provided free of all expense to the refugees or their instructors The supervision of such work was divided by gender, men overseeing the work of male refugees employed as tailors, shoemakers, and smiths, while women directed lace-makers, knitters and embroiderers. Grace Vulliamy organized exhibitions in her home at 59 Daendelsstraat, Den Haag. Miss Vulliamy had permission from General Onnen to make anything at Amersfoort and sell anywhere.

---

[165] Kellogg, Charlotte. 'Women of Belgium'. http://raven.cc.ukans.edu/~libsite/wwi-www/Ckellogg/Wbelg.1.htm. Downloaded June 2001 (hereafter referred to as Kellogg, WB1, WB2, WB3, as appropriate). Kellogg, WB3, 5

[166] Kellogg. WB2, 2

[167] Kellogg, WB3, 6

[168] Hoover. *An American Epic.* Vol. 1. 410-411

[169] *The Friend.* 23.7.15

[170] 20.7.1915

Plate 6.4 Vulliamy Street, Gasterland Internment Camp, built where the brick kilns had formerly been placed

On 22 August 1915, Ruth Fry travelled with Fred Rowntree and Violet Vulliamy to Flushing where Grace met them. Violet, Grace's sister, helped in Holland during holidays and is mentioned below in the letter from Jessie Harry.[171] She stayed in Holland from August until 16 October 1915 working at Uden where Lillian Gunter was based. Lillian worked with Grace in Poland after the war. Grace, Fred, Ruth, de Tuyll and Dutch owners of the camps later had a discussion about the Hostel, maternity work, and the need to find sufficient sales outlets for the work that the Belgian women produced. A Field Committee, with representatives from each of the camps, and Grace Vulliamy herself, was formed in consultation with Grace. Her work was now very extensive and Ruth Fry was very much struck with the efficient and admirable way in which she managed this complicated work. She commented on Grace's wide knowledge of individual refugees and how to help them and felt that the Home Committee would warmly appreciate it. However, Fry recognised it was impossible for Vulliamy to continue all that work single-handed and it was imperative that a helper be sent out to her - not attached to any one camp but able to help her wherever required.

[171] FEWVC/M1A General Committee Reports

Coordination between the camps meant that Grace Vulliamy spent much time travelling between them, but this was unavoidable.

Grace Vulliamy's knowledge of individual refugees was undoubtedly due to the fact that she did everything possible to help them as particular human beings with personal difficulties, not just as part of the category: 'refugees'. There is much evidence of this, for example in an undated letter from a British refugee, sent from 36 Albany Street, Regents Park. Many words are underlined, sometimes twice, as though the writer wants Grace to be aware of what points she considered important. It seems she had problems finding suitable work and Grace had helped her.

> Thanks so much for card. I really cannot tell you how very grateful I am to you for all you have done for me, words cannot express my feelings, …. I will also go to Miss Fry as you told me … Thanks awfully about shoes for Mr Harry and I'm sure he will be glad to get them as [in] his letter today he says 'do send me if possible.' Babies send them their biggest kisses of thanks and our best love and a thousand of thanks for your kindness to us which I shall never forget. Not forgetting Miss Violet … also a kiss from babies for her. Always very gratefully, Jessie Harry.

'Miss Violet' was Grace's sister. An example of the small tasks that Grace undertook which meant so much to the prisoners was when the wife of a South African Infantry man who was a PoW in Germany sent her a postal order and asked her if she would make him a parcel of sweets, chocolates, and so on. Many people she had helped like this kept in touch for quite some time.

Miss Vulliamy's mother, Anna Museur Vulliamy, who regardless of what the law said about married women's nationality, clearly regarded herself as Belgian, was concerned about the amount of travelling her daughter had to do. She prepared a letter on 12 June 1915 to send to the editor of the *East Anglian Daily Times* telling him how Grace had been sent by the Local Government Board to Holland in the spring to bring over a further 20,000 people. She said after completing this work the Society of Friends asked her to stay on to organise relief for the better class Belgian refugees in Holland whose lot was 'most pitiable – so pitiable that many of them preferred to return to Belgium, under the grip though it was of the German invader.' The camp where her daughter was working was four miles from the station and the heat at that time was 'almost tropical'. She and her fellow-workers had to visit daily the various points of the camp and tramp to and from the station which made them footsore and weary and wasted much valuable time. Grace urgently needed the use of a small car. She was an experienced motorist, having had her first car, a Rover, in 1910, and would drive the car herself, take the greatest care of it and would have it attended to by a refugee chauffeur, the commander of the camp having offered the free use of a garage. Surely, said Anna Museur Vulliamy, there must be some motorists who have cars which are not just now in use. This plea resulted in a reply from N. Ruth Courtauld of Dorset Square, London, offering a 1913 two seater Ford which she had not used since November. She said it would actually hold three people as there was an emergency seat, and a tray fitted on behind for luggage when the third seat was not wanted. The engines were in good condition. However, it would probably take a fortnight at least to get it overhauled as all motor shops were very busy at that time and they had also lost a great many of their workers to the Armed Forces. Also a licence was needed from the Board of Trade so that the car could be sent to Holland. Mrs Vulliamy liaised with Fred Rowntree to get the car sent out but he had to correct one item in her appeal which 'gives more credit to our work in Holland than we deserve.' He needed to point out 'The huge camps which you speak of have been built by the Dutch Government and not by us. We are rendering what assistance we can in the employment of refugees in the camps, particularly in connection with hut building and their equipment, including rug making and so on.' He concluded: 'Miss Vulliamy's experience in Holland is of the greatest value to our work.'

Plate 6.5 Violet Norah Vulliamy with Jessie Harry's children expelled from Germany

This rather strange photograph (Plate 6.6) of four people in the car and a man wielding a starting handle is identified by Grace as 'G C Vulliamy and Ford, Vluchtoord, Uden'.

Plate 6.6 The Ford car with Grace driving

In accepting Mrs Courtauld's kind offer, Mrs Vulliamy gave her a nudge to get the work done quickly. She wrote 'if the repairers knew the purpose for which the car was required they would make a special effort to get it done as quickly as possible.' To Fred Rowntree, Mrs Vulliamy said if the Society had insufficient funds to pay the carriage she would pay for it herself. The car went over on the *SS Copenhagen* from Harwich and in September Mary Rees went out as Grace Vulliamy's assistant. Grace was most grateful for her: 'she seems excellent'. To give her still more help, a portable Blick typewriter was sent to make correspondence, reports and accounts easier.[172] Recognising that her handwriting was difficult to read, she wrote: 'Thank you very much re Blick. It will be a comfort, even more to those who read.' On 4 October, 1915, Grace wrote to Ruth: 'Hurrah for the Blick. There is so much to write about.'

Much of Miss Vulliamy's correspondence with Miss Fry was concerned with staffing problems. Miss Vulliamy was concerned about the health of some of the women sent out: Miss Mitchell was not very strong and Miss Gunter didn't seem strong either. Winter would be difficult for them. But Miss Vulliamy herself also had health problems from time to time and although Miss Fry had several things she needed to discuss on Grace's next visit to England, she wanted her to have a holiday and sleep for several days! In October, some children needed supervision on the journey across to

[172] FEWVC/M1A General Committee Reports. 1915, March – September. 27th September, 1915

England. Miss Vulliamy would normally do it but this time Miss Fry was reluctant to ask her. She suggested giving the stewardesses on the Zeeland boats a large tip to get them to do it for her because she was sure Grace ought to have a rest on the boat. Miss Fry herself was not strong and sensitive to others. There was also the matter of work to be considered. More work was needed for men and boys; and more men to be sent out to help Mr Rowntree. An undergraduate or wounded officer could be the type of person to look for.

Some temporary workers were VADs, waiting for their first posting. To replace the Whitings, who had been so 'awfully useful and done such good work', Grace intended to write to their VAD officer to ask if they could stay until the date for their being sent to France was finally fixed. Miss Gunter, who was 'very good and liked by all' suggested a Mrs Marshall who was at the Bristol settlement. Settlements were places where social and educational work were undertaken by middle-class socially aware women for poorer people living in the area. For example, *The Times* advertisement for Classes in Belgian Cookery on March 11 is an example of the work done at the Passmore Edwards Settlement where a demonstration was to be given by a refugee from Antwerp. She was a trained teacher of the *ecoles menageres*. It was pointed out that Belgian working-class cookery depended largely on the use of vegetables. They made wonderful soups and the method of preparation was different from British: onions figured largely as an ingredient, chopped fine, and browned in dripping before being mixed with other things.

Recreation

In November, Burleigh Fincken joined the Mission. He had experience with Boy Scouts and his father gave a car and a Magic lantern, which was used for the children but could also be a useful aid for fund-raising.[173] This picture shows the beginning of the Scout Troop at Nunspeet. Uniforms, like everything in the camps was either donated or made there. The boys sent a letter to Grace Vulliamy on 2 October 1916.

> We are very happy to see you back so soon and we hope you are quite well, all the scouts do their best that they can become good scouts. ... Now dear Miss Vulliamy we have bought a little present which we hope you will be very happy over. Now hope we existing for a long time the S.O.F. The dear greathing (sic) from all the Scouts.'

[173] 18.11.15

A big problem was finding suitable outlets for the camp work. However, a shop was opened in The Hague that they called La Ruche, the Beehive, where they sold lingerie and lace. Belgian lace had a very high reputation and many women had earned their living by making it. Grace recognised lace-makers were underpaid for this time-consuming, painstaking work, but did not know how to combat this. Lace patterns were ancient designs that reinforced Belgian identity or related to the current situation.[174] Women in occupied Belgium are known to have used different knitting stiches as a way of recording important information, so this might also have been done in lace since the women used designs relating to the 'current situation'. In wartime it was difficult to get the fine thread needed and Miss Vulliamy sent some completed lace across to London for Miss Fry to look at and see if it could be sold over there, probably, since Ruth Fry was sister to Roger Fry, in the Bloomsbury Group's Omega workshops, with profits being returned to the makers. During this time Grace came across a Roman Catholic convent where they were starving as they were dependent on the sale of their lace which they had not been able to sell since the outbreak of war. She took all the lace they had, went to Paris, sold it all there and brought them the money.

They were so grateful they gave her the most precious thing they had – a bunch of carrots![175]

Charles Morrell, mentioned above, worked at La Ruche. He had a temporary commission as a Lieutenant attached to the Royal Flying Corps and was an observer in a type BE2c biplane. He and his pilot, Lt Ernest Edwards Hodgson, were forced to make an emergency landing on the Dutch side of the border near Axel and so were interned in Groningen. After three weeks they were transported to the fortress of Wierickerschans near Bodegraven. Miss Vulliamy visited this fortress and on one occasion in March 1917 had her photograph taken there with five male prisoners.

On parole, Morrell was so frequently at La Ruche, shown above, that some people assumed it was his! He did in fact have an office above it. The two ladies in this photo are thought to be workers in the shop.[176] La Ruche has what looks like a ladies' blouse on a stand on the right and other lace garments displayed on the window sill; on the left the cover of the cushion was probably crocheted. The curtains also have a wide lace edging. These

[174] Kellogg, WB3, 6

[175] Eva Vulliamy's account.

[176] My thanks to Chris Morrell for this photo and information.

may have been in patriotic Belgian colours as a sign of resisting the German occupation in Belgium.

Plate 6.7 First start of Boy Scouts, Nunspeeet.

One of Grace Vulliamy's tasks was showing important visitors around the camp. For example, photographs show the Princess de Ligne arriving with her limousine and chauffeur who was often one of the prisoners. His Excellency the Hon. Prosper Poullet, Belgian Ministre des Beaux Arts, another visitor, who had a permanent office at The Hague, visited the crèche at Amersfoort. Without consultation with the Friends, the Dutch somewhat arbitrarily put him in charge of the workshops so Grace Vulliamy, Fred Rowntree and Harold Ellis organised an interview with him at his hotel at The Hague. He told them he had been given responsibility for the work in the camps' workshops as from the 1st of that month and was continuing the employment of the refugees within them. Fred Rowntree needed to explain firmly that the workshops had been built at the expense of the Society of Friends on land rented by them from Mr De Schepper and they intended to continue to rent it as long as the 64 houses which occupied a portion of the land remained on the site. But they were glad to offer him the free use of the workshops on the understanding they remained Friends' property. With regard to the cottages Rowntree enclosed a copy of the memorandum drawn up and agreed to with Mr De Schepper, and pointed out that the intention of the London Committee was always to send the cottages to Belgium when the war was over to be used as temporary housing there for the refugees. The problem was sorted out satisfactorily.

Plate 6.8 Grace with Belgian nuns

There were needs outside the camps to be met as well. At Amersfoort for instance, scattered about the town were about 4,000 women and children, the families of Belgian soldiers interned in a camp a few miles away. The district had a population of around 3,000 and the Belgians were living in distressing circumstances because they wanted to be near their men. The money granted to them was 75 centimes for each woman and 50 for each child; there was no provision for their lodging and prices in Holland were at that time very high. A large empty granary at Koppel, which held about 300 people, had been lent by a Dutch merchant, but the rest of the 4,000 women and children were housed as well as could be managed. One woman with her son lived in a cupboard of a room, just the length of the bed, with no air except through the door. When her husband returned on leave the boy slept on a mattress in a garret above.[177] Some people took refuge on boats and relief workers help supply them with food. By 1916, the Friends had erected

[177] Vulliamy Papers. Holland camps. GCV

20 wooden cottages at Amersfoort, and were completing a large one to be used as a school.[178]

Plate 6.9 La Ruche, The Hague.
Courtesy Chris Morrell

Civilians in war-time

Being a civilian in a war zone in wartime was especially difficult. The Hague Convention of 1907, meant to protect civilians, nevertheless stated that the 'Wearing of distinctive uniform or badge, including by Voluntary Corps organized under military law [are] entitled to be treated as belligerents …[and] treated as PoWs.' This was despite the fact that their insignia, the Quaker star, was recognised by both belligerent sides as being similar to the Red Cross. Indeed, for the civilian 'direct personal intervention would involve their being treated with greater severity than the soldiers themselves.' The uniform colour was similar to German uniforms and made local people uneasy. There was a strong Quaker feeling in favour of giving them up.[179]

---

[178] TNA. MH8/6

[179] 26.10.15

Plate 6.10 Miss Vulliamy escorting Mons.Poullet and others, visiting the Society of Friends crèche at Amersfoort .

Grace Vulliamy was often under severe pressure, although she was never rude or terse, but there is a difference when she had time to deal with something in greater depth. She may not have suffered fools gladly and got rather irritated with the Home Committee not seeming to understand the needs of those in Holland. She was relieved when Ruth Fry was on the verge of making a visit. Ruth was inclined to get confused and face-to-face contact could help to sort things out. Some of the pressure arose from the danger which surrounded them. Quakers held the right of free speech and in France some members doing relief wrote letters mentioning the coming and going of troops. This sort of thing risked the work the Friends were doing and here it also threatened Holland's neutrality. Ruth Fry wrote to Barry:

> We must be even more careful of expressing opinions on any controversial matters in Holland and I think perhaps it would be well if our workers had a copy each of the enclosed memorandum, as we cannot be too careful in this matter, for the whole of our work might be undone otherwise.[180]

[180] Ruth Fry to Barry. 16.11.15

Plate 6.11 People taking refuge on boats. Holland 1914

There was also censorship to deal with and other official rules concerning printed matter. Sibele Lang, who did not give her credentials or write on headed paper but was obviously known to Miss Vulliamy, sent a letter by the Legation 'bag', due to problems with the censor delaying letters. She discussed the question of propaganda in Holland, of books in particular. The whole question of literature for neutral states was in the hands of a Committee appointed by the Government. They controlled all written or printed matters leaving England and the only way of publishing pamphlets and so on for the Dutch or the Americans was via them. She wrote:

> I think it is admitted by everyone except certain official circles that the whole thing has been gross … this government Committee which really amounts to a scandal. Any evidence that is collected will help to shake them – only it must be strong and convincing and irrefutable. An official will get round almost anything!

She was also concerned with the sale of goods made by the refugees.

> Brushes cost fabulous amounts over here. I feel the unfortunate consumer would be relieved if your cheap ones could come on the market. Best wishes from …. Sibele Lang.[181]

[181] 17.12.15. 55 Seymour Street, London. Lang to Vulliamy

Meeting and transporting Refugees and released Interned through Holland

In February 1915 the British Government agreed to exchange sick and wounded PoWs between Britain and Germany across the Netherlands and the first exchanges began almost immediately. The number of prisoners to be repatriated or sent for internment either in the Netherlands or Switzerland or for exchange was agreed between the belligerent governments and then put into effect by a Commission. Selection depended on the prisoners' medical condition as determined by certain agreed principles. For example, one of the conditions for direct repatriation of sick and wounded was that they were not expected to recover within a year. Those who might be expected to recover within this time could go to Switzerland. A total of 7,800 wounded German PoWs were repatriated in this way, and 4,700 British soldiers. The Dutch Minister of Foreign Affairs also permitted civilians imprisoned as aliens in Germany and Britain to move to the Netherlands where they lived like other refugees.

Grace was continually seeking to make the transport of prisoners go more smoothly and she had the comfort of the prisoners constantly in mind.

<u>Description of Arrival and How They Were Dealt With</u>

> We had been informed that a contingent of civilian prisoners would be sent through early in each month and after our experience with the first lot I made up my mind that I would do all in my power to ensure that adequate arrangements should be made for the reception of these people. To this end I made certain suggestions to the British Consul in Rotterdam (who transmitted them to the Foreign Office in London) and in this way we were able to arrange that food tickets should be issued for supplies on the journey from the German frontier to England to be paid for when passengers could afford to do so and the cost of which would be borne by the British government, these to be filled in and endorsed by the representative of the Society of Friends while travelling with them on the train so as to avoid delay and discomfort at the port or on board. ... We were also able to arrange for the Consul to meet the train in order to check visas and passports while travelling and for money to be exchanged on the train at the ruling rate of exchange. And most important of all that the invalids should be separately and specially provided for and the Negroes accommodated apart from white people. We also had the assurance of the Central Charities Committee in London that with the assistance of the British Red Cross the sick and mental cases would receive the necessary care and attention upon arrival at Tilbury.

Transport of the civilian and wounded prisoners to or through Holland was complicated because three different railways had to be used - one for the exchange of severely wounded, another for the transport of civilian prisoners and the third for all other transport. This meant that several stations would be used and those from Aachen would go via Venlo. Grace kept a drawing of Venlo among her papers but we are left to guess who the artist was.

At the end of October 1915, after the LGB withdrew its official involvement in the transfers of civilians to Britain, the Foreign Office asked the Friends to send representatives every month to the German frontier to meet British civilians being repatriated from internment in German camps such as Ruhleben. The Under-Secretary of State for Foreign Affairs, indicating his expectation of the usual hierarchical arrangements, addressed his letter of 29 October to the 'President of the Society of Friends' (sic). He explained that:

> Sir Alan Johnstone, the Minister at The Hague, said it was impossible to detail a member of the staff of the Legation or the Consulate to meet the trains at Bentheim, where the British must leave Germany; a delegate would need to spend three days each month at the frontier station. He asked if the Society of Friends in Holland could delegate one or more representatives to undertake this work, particularly in view of the excellent work already done by them in connection with Belgian refugees in Holland. Mr Barry of the Friends ... proposed going into the matter with Miss Vulliamy and the Central Office in London

After the usual Committee deliberations, they decided to accept the Foreign Office suggestion. A letter from Grace to the Burgomaster at Roosendaal indicates the way in which the Authorities were involved, but also the amount of work connected with just one contingent, and Grace's concern for the well-being of all. Her writing is not always easy to read, as she recognised, but this is what she wrote on 5 January 1916:

> You have, I believe, been invited by the Netherlands Minister for Foreign Affairs to assist Mr Barry and myself when meeting the British refugees from Germany as delegates of the Society of Friends. We have just heard that tomorrow, Thursday, about 120 civilians are coming through, 40 of them Africans and perhaps 20 women and children. We intend to bring them down to Rotterdam and send them to England from there. ... If we might telegraph to you to have some simple accommodation provided for the party for the night at Roosendaal. We should be able to wire you from Gennep giving exact numbers as soon as the train comes in, in any case before 8 o'clock. As we hear that there are four stretcher cases I should be glad if the local Red Cross were able to meet the train

> with stretchers. I arrive at Gennep 3.51 tomorrow and I should be very grateful if you would wire me there at the station as to whether it is possible for you to arrange the accommodation if necessary. (Signed) GC Vulliamy

Grace described to her sister Eva how prisoners' exchange began and after the war Eva wrote:

> ... while she was working in the camps the exchange of sick prisoners of war was started. She found that everything was being done for our men from the moment they got on board the boats but no one was doing anything for them while they were crossing Holland. Grace went to the British Ambassador but he said he could do nothing as he had received no instructions, so she met each train and saw to the comfort of the men supplying them with tobacco and suchlike things... Among each batch of returned prisoners were some for whom the mental strain had been too great and these she looked after herself on board ship as she knew what a temptation it would be to some to throw themselves into the sea.

However, there were some events which when looked back on caused considerable amusement.

> A rather amusing incident happened with one batch of men. Amongst the first trainload there were sixteen affected mentally and she wired to her friend who was helping her at the port to keep them safe until she arrived with the next batch. Something went wrong with the wire and she arrived to find sixteen furious men locked into a room and her sixteen mental cases scattered on two ships. She had already been working 36 hours with no sleep and very little food but dare not risk letting any of the sixteen go without her so she spent the night finding out where they were on the two ships and collecting them. When she finished it was time for breakfast. One of the officers who had been helping her suggested going in to a restaurant and having some breakfast but she was so tired she kept dozing and heard a woman say to her friend 'is it not dreadful the way these drunken women get hold of the young officers!' But she was too tired to care whether or not they thought she was drunk. After she had done this for some time the Government realised what was happening and took over the responsibility of meeting the trains but asked her to be in charge of it.[182]

[182] Eva Vulliamy.

Plate 6.12 First exchange of wounded from Germany. February 1915

The Society of Friends was asked to co-operate with the Dutch Government in meeting and transporting Refugees and released Interned through Holland. The Quakers were in charge of the passenger traffic and met all British civilians arriving from Germany and Belgium and asked Grace Vulliamy to be their Representative. Mr Maxse communicated with her regarding the Red Cross's concerns. For example, he explained it was very difficult for him to obtain the necessary particulars of British subjects because they were scattered at various addresses throughout Holland.[183] She assisted in organising reception at the Belgian-German frontier, often meeting them herself on the journey to Flushing. Mrs Rozelaar and Miss Rees, Grace's assistant, went to Boxtel to arrange with the Relief Committee to provide refreshments and then to the frontier to meet the men from Ruhleben, then notifying Rotterdam and Flushing as to departure. While she was working for the Friends for the British Foreign Office she started interviewing British civilians who were allowed to leave Germany. Cables were sent from Berlin saying, for example, 50 niggers, six insane and she would meet them at the frontier and arrange for them to be put up in hotels, hospitals, etc. and brought those who could travel backwards and forwards

[183] Copy of letter from Maxse to Secretary of Dutch Red Cross. 19.5.17

to England herself. The passage was often a rough one and it was arduous work to care for the people. At Tilbury invalids were put in charge of the Red Cross and the rest were taken by the Central Charities Committee, who arranged accommodation for the homeless. This work was undertaken through liaison with Mr Monk, Prisoners of War Dept., Royal Court, House of Lords. Miss Vulliamy's description of this work reveals her attitude to the personal side of these events.

> I remember once, when owing to shortage of German doctors, women and children were allowed over the frontier to go to the Dutch doctors, a woman arrived thin and poorly clad in a large shawl and carrying a sick baby – but on her return two hours later, she certainly had put on half a stone [in weight] and the baby many lbs (pounds). I had my suspicions – but it was no business of mine, still I felt almost sorry to see the Customs Officer also had his. He gently pulled the shawl aside, and the ½ stone fell out in the shape of cheese, butter, bread etc etc.

The first train was in early November. Miss Livingstone met the train at 3 am and despite the hour gave hot drinks to everybody who wanted them. Mr Barry remained at Rotterdam and generally supervised arrangements besides picking up stragglers who came through Rotterdam instead of going direct to Flushing. The Consulate rang up that morning and congratulated all concerned.[184] There was also a letter from one of the prisoners, Norman Pogson, addressed to the Secretary of the Society of Friends, and dated 28 November:

> Belated, but sincere thanks of the British civilian prisoners released from Ruhleben Camp, Germany, to Miss Vulliamy and her lady assistants for the touching reception given at Boxtel, Holland, on their arrival on Dutch soil at 1.30 a.m. on 7th November. The German authorities hadn't provided any food all day and they were extremely hungry. But their days of captivity were over and they were no longer surrounded by enemies but were being greeted by friends. May I ask you to communicate the contents of this letter to Miss Vulliamy and everyone involved.

Changes were made as a result of this experience and on 22 November, the Friend Philip Barrett wrote from Rotterdam to Ruth:

> In future, as soon as the Consul General receives information from the American Ambassador at Berlin as to the coming

[184] V.P. Letter no 30. Headed paper. Nov 8th 1915

forward of these prisoners, he will advise Mr Barry at our office at Rotterdam and he and Miss Vulliamy will make the necessary arrangements for refugees to be met at frontier, needs administered...and welfare attended to. Enclosed is copy of letter from Sir Alan Johnstone expressing his satisfaction.[185]

On 4 December Mr Maxse, the British Consul General at Rotterdam, appointed Grace Vulliamy as representative of the Consulate for the purpose of meeting and assisting all British returned civilians and soldiers arriving in Holland from Germany and Belgium. Grace wrote:

> When escaping prisoners arrived at the frontier they were often not sure whether they were in Holland or not so they made for the nearest Post Office and bought a stamp.

Grace Vulliamy's appointment as Consulate representative was immediately put to good use. She saw Maxse the same day and told him she felt that things were not arranged for the civilians' arrival. She'd been told there were four insane and three stretcher cases and had asked Miss Livingstone to settle about the refreshments for which she'd received a quotation. However, she needed a complete list of names ready on arrival so the people could be taken for their passports. She was going over to England with them and if it were necessary on account of the insane people one of the men workers would accompany her. Those identified as insane were what today would be called 'shell-shocked'.

This time, as on the previous occasion, a list of those who were to go had been prepared but they were told on the last morning that five would be kept back, though which five was not announced until the final list was read. One man was turned back at the frontier for no apparent reason and his wife and three children were sent on without him.

Such action, which would appear to be entirely arbitrary, would subject not only the prisoner but the wife and family to a great deal of unhappiness and stress; this could have a negative impact on the British Home Front, which would potentially be what the enemy wanted.

Miss Vulliamy arranged for medical assistance and provision of food in advance of the arrival of such trains. Her Report indicates the complex

---

Friends House. Box 9, Parcel 3, Folder 3. Correspondence with Rotterdam Office. British Government Commission for transportation of Belgians to the United Kingdom, Zeeland Hotel, Vlissingen. H.P.Enkey

nature of caring for the people on their journey to freedom and the amount of preparation needed.

Plate 6.13
Society of Friends working in Holland, pictured outside The Friends hut showing the Quaker star

. At Boxtel, *en route* for Flushing, we were met by Dr Merkens of Flushing, who attended to the sick as we travelled.

> We reached Flushing at 1 a.m. and there found another member of the Society of Friends who had hot soup and other refreshments prepared. While the food was being served, passports were being visa-ed, but this formality was not over until 6 a.m. and the boat taking the travellers over to England sailed at 7.30 a.m. Upon our arrival at Flushing, the cases of sick were dealt with immediately by the Consul and Dr Merkens, assisted by two Red Cross nurses sent from England for the purpose and then removed by them directly to the boat. Special attention was needed for the mental cases so two members of Friends accompanied the party to England. The negroes needed a good deal of supervision. On the same boat were 81 wounded who had travelled via Roosendaal and there was also a small party of destitute English from Brussels. The boat reached

Tilbury at 4 o'clock and cards of instruction were given to destitute people by the Central Charities Commission.[186]

The port of embarkation needed to be changed and on 13 December Miss Vulliamy suggested parties should go by Great Eastern or Batavia Lines from Rotterdam instead of Flushing. This change necessitated attention to all the details of the journey. Prisoners would need probably three meals on board and a card or ticket system would be wanted for food on the journey from the frontier to England, to be paid for by those able, and free to the destitute. Tickets should be sent from England, filled in by the Society of Friends on the train and to be handed on arrival to the person in charge. The Consul should meet the train at Boxtel and visé passports on the train so avoiding delay at Flushing in early hours of the morning. The Society of Friends would undertake to change money on the train at the rate of exchange of the day. On 7 December they only received 15 shillings for 20 marks. Negroes and invalids should travel in special compartments from Germany. On arrival at Tilbury, the Red Cross should have immediate accommodation for all mental, nervous and sick cases and proper waiting rooms provided. This was to be a regular event and parties were always to leave Germany on 6th of the month.

It was necessary that people such as Burgomasters with whom Miss Vulliamy had dealings recognised her authority so Mr Maxse wrote to Mayors at Rotterdam, Roosendaal, Zevenaar and Oldenzaal asking them to help her in every way possible when she was acting as Delegate of the Society of Friends. On 16 December Maxse wrote to tell Grace that this had been done. It gave her greater authority on her journeys to and from the frontier with prisoners.[187]

Grace also became concerned about the German prisoners returning to their own country. Knowing that the Friends Emergency Committee would be in a position to help these men, she wrote to them at Friends House, London, to ask if there was anything they could do. They began investigating whether their organization in Holland was able to undertake this.[188] This virtually put it back into Grace's hands.

As we saw above, soldiers were mentioned as arriving in Holland from Germany and Belgium. The Quakers refused to have anything to do with the

---

[186] V. P. Report on the journey of British Civilians from Germany to England, 6 December 1915. Friends House, Box 9:4:5

[187] 16 December 1915

[188] Box 9:4:5 Exchange of Civilian Prisoners. Emergency Committee Minutes, Book 1. 12 December 1915

military as a protest against war, so the work of helping the military prisoners was very time-consuming, involving travelling, waiting at various train stations, getting the prisoners on board ship and ensuring their welfare. Grace decided to leave work in the refugee camps because Quakers and the Belgians could work there, but the:

> difficulty of handing over the work here makes me wonder if it's right to leave. It is complicated by constant change of workers, difficulties of travelling, also the civilian prisoners.[189]

Sooner or later things would come to a head and Miss Vulliamy was forced to choose. In the meantime, her work remained voluntary and some kind of remuneration and reimbursement of expenses was necessary to enable her to continue.

PAY

On 19 March, 1915, Mrs Falk, now Secretary of the Women's Emergency Corps, wrote to Mr Burtt, telling him that Miss Vulliamy had left for Holland the previous night and saying: 'I do not know what arrangements you have made with Miss Vulliamy about payment etc. but I conclude that she will be on the same terms with you as when she was working for the LGB.' Nonetheless, during April and May she received no remuneration. This was gender discrimination – it being assumed that a woman was always financially supported by a man, usually husband, or father. In May she wrote to Mr Burtt

> I hear that the Corps is leaving Bedford College at the end of this month, I don't quite know what to do as I have all my furniture and if I am over here I cannot see to a flat, can you tell me at all how long you would like me to remain here. I am afraid I cannot afford to go on. I thought Mrs Falk had arranged but she writes to make arrangements direct with you. I wish I could afford to do all voluntary work but I can't. The LGB paid me £9 a week, that naturally included all Hotel Expense.... perhaps I could have £5 per week to include everything, but I must go to England for a day or two to see to all my belongings.

It seems that she was able to return to sort out her affairs because by 1 June Miss Vulliamy had not only returned to England with Philip Burtt but then also gone back to Holland, two of her many trips across the dangerous English Channel.

[189] Vulliamy Papers. 9.8.16

She was clearly skating on thin financial ice. Grace's frequent changes from working with one organization to another may look like career moves for more experience or more money. This is not so. In every case her work came to an end because war conditions changed or she moved to where her particular skills could best be put to good use and need was greater. The Women's Emergency Corps offered her something, but she did not accept as she was then able to give her services without remuneration and WEC was supported by voluntary efforts, in contrast to the Local Government Board, funded by taxpayers. When that work ended, she began work for the Friends and asked them for £5 per week. In September 1915 they offered her £4 a week, to include expenses such as travelling. This meant she was partly using her own funds for support. In February 1916 she mentioned to Consul General Maxse, she might have to give up because of lack of funds, but the Foreign Office offered to pay her a fee for the civilian work to enable her to continue.[190] The Commission was brought to a close in November 1916, but the work continued through the auspices of the British Consul-General in Rotterdam and in that year 2,224 refugees were brought over.[191] By March 1917 it was recorded that the Red Cross owed her 'quite a lot.' By then she had been appointed their Representative.[192] It seems likely that her 'own money' came from a bequest from her father after he died. Although in his Will he left everything to his son, Lionel, it was administered by Grace's brother and from this she possibly had some kind of income. It was typical of Grace that she was also concerned about pay for others and amongst her papers is a 'pretend' official note about payment for the 'typing men' at Rotterdam.

In July, 1915 John W Barry, a Quaker, who attended Quaker Committee meetings with Grace at Rotterdam and knew her sister Violet, told Ruth Fry:

> Last Monday I paid a visit to the boat which conveyed the British Prisoners to England. They were grateful to us for our visit. Many officers and soldiers told me I was the first Englishman to talk with them since their imprisonment ten months ago. They told me many of the British prisoners are employed making munitions. Seems a terrible policy for the German government to adopt towards their prisoners.[193]

They were to learn of even worse treatment as more prisoners came through.

---

[190] Grace Vulliamy to Ruth Fry. 27.2.16.

[191] IWM BEL 1/15. 46th Annual Report of LGB, 1916 –17 Cd 8697, 1917. 17

[192] Friends House. Box 9:3:2. Box 9:3:3 13.3.17.

[193] J Vulliamy Papers July 5, 1915

Meeting Prisoners

This work continued until September 1917 when she left the Friends to work under the British War Office arranging for British PoW's who were to be interned in Holland. At this point her work was no longer for civilian refugees, but for the military and remained so until after the Armistice. She was a woman who responded to difficult situations and her work in refugee camps had become routine. She now acted as British Red Cross and YWCA representative in Holland and felt that the need for help was greater among the military. Miss Vulliamy was Major General Sir John Hanbury Williams's representative, making all arrangements and meeting all prisoners at the frontier, the first batch arriving on 29 December 1917, taking particulars during the journey, very often of over 300 men, and telegraphing them to England to warn of their arrival the same day. General Hanbury Williams was appointed by the British government to represent the interests of the British prisoners in Holland; Major General Onnen, Dutch Military Officer in charge of prisoners interned in Holland, was doing the same job on behalf of the Dutch. At the request of General Onnen, she became attached to the Dutch Medical Service as liaison officer until the Armistice and she remained in Holland at the Armistice to assist repatriation.

CHAPTER 7

WORKING WITH THE INVISIBLE ARMY, CIVILIAN REFUGEES, PRISONERS AND QUAKERS.

Invisible Army

The undercover import of Belgian armament workers had begun by 11 March, 1915. These men became known as the 'Invisible Army.' They were coal and iron, railway and other skilled workers the Belgian and English governments were anxious to get out of Holland and Belgium - men who were spirited out of Holland and occupied Belgium to serve in France or clandestinely recruited to do industrial work in Britain or France. The 'Invisible Army' were trans-shipped to France on Zeeland boats.
Miss Vulliamy learned that the LGB had consented to send all relatives of workmen wishing to go to England to the Uranium Hotel at Rotterdam. Six to seven hundred working-class people were kept there until they were able to leave. Many were part of the 'Invisible Army'. Their removal was always conducted furtively because of the discrepancy between stated and real aims in order to safeguard Holland's neutrality and so that it could continue. It may be this to which Grace Vulliamy was referring when she wrote to Agnes Conway at the Imperial War Museum saying she did not want her name known because of the 'secret' work she undertook for the British Government, which she would write about at the end of the War.[194] She fulfilled this obligation in January 1920 and Agnes Conway wrote thanking her 'for the account of your work which is exactly what I wanted.' She added 'You must be proud of having accomplished so much and I hope you will be equally successful in Poland.'

On 15 March, 113 specially chosen workmen arranged for by the Local Government Board (LGB) from Holland arrived at Folkestone on the Flushing boat and were sent to West Brompton by special train. Folkestone became responsible for accommodating the 'Invisible Army' for different lengths of time. When Leonard B Franklin, the LGB's Representative on War Refugee work at Folkestone, wrote his final report which ended 1 May 1915, he said that the amount of money spent at the port had doubled due to the fact they were now responsible for the 'Invisible Army.' Nonetheless, they needed to be careful. A suspension of the shipping service due to submarines caused delays. Delays led to leakage in numbers – men would

[194] Storr. *Excluded* p.109

'vanish.'[195] However, to help control this, at a conference in Tilbury it was decided that in future, the Invisible Army was to be landed in Gravesend and would be entrained for Folkestone.

Strand Hotel, Flushing – civilian refugees

On 11 April 1915, Violette Goffart, the wife of the Belgian Consul General for Holland, wrote to Grace asking for help for the refugees. People had to wait 18 – 21 days before being able to embark. She spoke of 'Congestion in a little town of 20,000, where Hotels are rare, living dear, and the commercial spirit of the inhabitants strongly developed,' a euphemism for exploitation of the refugees by the inhabitants. She continued 'The situation has become more aggravated since 18 February when the submarine blockade commenced.' This intervention might have taken place partly as a result of a letter written by a Mme Leclercq-Demeur who applied first to M. Paul Hymans, Belgian Minister in London, exposing her own 'unhappy situation', the manner in which she had been 'exploited by certain hotel keepers and the manoeuvres of doubtful characters who swarm about these unfortunates, particularly the women'. She asked that 'a sort of Home' could be created where families could have board and lodging, and where they would only be associated with people of their own social condition. This request had been passed to M. Julien Davignon, Minister of Foreign Affairs who passed the appeal to Mme Goffart's husband, but at a time when the 'very existence of Belgium is at stake,' it was doubtful if official action could intervene in time to do any good. Mme Goffart did all in her power to assist 'interesting' cases that were brought to her notice, but alone her actions were limited. She wished specially to draw attention to the 'moral benefit that work brings to our exiled women'. She asked that 'such families be given some useful work to do to occupy their time such as the making up of linen, clothing and so on for the unfortunate soldiers and refugees. The women would make up the materials put at their disposal by the Committee … I am confident that nothing but good will be attained.' On 25 March, M. Goffart, the Consul General, wrote to Miss Vulliamy saying he had learned that thanks to her initiative an English Society had taken the Strand Hotel at Flushing with the intention of making it available for bourgeois families with very limited resources wanting to go to England. He concluded: 'Que grace a votre initiative.'[196]

Miss Vulliamy and The Society of Friends

---

[195] HO 144/1358/261916. IWM BEL 1.5/3

[196] 25 March, 1915 from Consulat General de Belgique, to Mme Vulliamy at Flushing. 'Thanks to your initiative.'

The English Society mentioned by M. Goffart was the Society of Friends. During the early months of 1915 Miss Vulliamy's activities and journeys across the Channel started to be recorded by the Friends War Victims Relief Committee in London, indicating she was cooperating with them by then. At their April meeting the Society of Friends reported that they had asked Miss Vulliamy to start a Hostel at Flushing for better class Belgians and of course, by the time this record was made she had already taken steps to do so. It was on their behalf that Grace arranged the rental of the Strand Hotel in Flushing and fitted it up for reception of 70 stranded Belgians 'of the better class', who were given hospitality by the Dutch. Provision was made to shelter people prior to embarkation while they waited for their passports to be processed and until England was able to arrange for escorted transport for them.[197] This was at the lowest cost to themselves. Some of these people were relatives of the 'Invisible Army' workmen. Miss Vulliamy was therefore undertaking for the Quakers tasks which were of a type to overlap with the work of the Commission. The people were recorded as being 'mostly of a different type from those inhabiting the refugee camps', and as the majority knew little or no English or Dutch, she also saw them as 'being very much exploited by the Hotels.'[198]

Mr Goffart sent her two copies of the *Flushing Courant* in which was an article praising in glowing terms the work that she had carried out with such 'remarkable self-abnegation and devotion'.[199] First of all it praised the Society of Friends and then moved on to show how Miss Vulliamy had changed circumstances as far as possible but also helped the refugees on a personal level .

There exists in England a great charitable Association of which the usefulness in these times of distress is not sufficiently known. We speak of the Society of Friends which has done such an enormous amount of good to Belgian refugees. This Society has taken here the Strand Hotel with a view of offering hospitality to Belgian families of the better class, during the time they are compelled to wait for their passports before going to England. These poor people are often in very straightened circumstances. The work that is being carried out and accomplished under the able direction of Miss Vulliamy is incredible. This lady by her great experience in charitable work, is truly admirable.

---

[197] Vulliamy Papers. Holland camps. GCV. Ruth Fry's Report 21-28 August

[198] Vulliamy Papers. Holland camps. GCV

[199] 17 May, Goffart. Extract from the *Flushing Courant,* 15.5.1915

Sorrow and suffering, she knows well how to soothe and to help, and no one goes away without assistance and consolation. We have seen six orphan girls who arrived at Flushing, goodness knows from where, and who by her goodness will find later a home in England. Miss Vulliamy has found in Mr and Mrs Enkey the well-known merchants of Venlo, two excellent assistants. Mr Enkey is specially engaged in superintending the construction of some portable wooden houses and the Belgian workmen engaged to build them may later on transport them to Belgium for their own use.

Plate 7.1 Strand Hotel

On 25 May the London Friends War Victims Relief Committee discussed the Women's work amongst refugees at the Strand Hotel. They noted that work done there by Miss Vulliamy and Mrs Enkey so impressed Madame Violette Goffart that she was anxious to continue it. Expenditure of £15 was authorised by the Friends for the provision of materials for women's classes.[200]

It was necessary to keep the hostel open until the boat service restarted but finances were a cause for concern. Who would pay? There were 70 people in the Strand Hotel, with an extra 13 for meals. The cost of this was £3 per day, plus £2 for rent per day. This was the cheapest available since boarding in town would cost more. The LGB at Rotterdam was in same situation, keeping 600-700 people in the Uranium Hotel. The issue of social class was important in this context. Enkey said 'All our people are of superior class' and mentioned their Library at Ede.[201] This was a matter of finance because the LGB were only responsible for poorer and therefore

[200] Friends House, FWVRC. Box 9.3.1. Belgium Sub-Committee Minutes. 25th May 1915. Secretary's Agenda. Women's Work amongst refugees at Flushing.
[201] Friends House. FWVRC. Box 9:3:3. 24.4.15. From Enkey to Burtt.

working-class people. Also because of the secret nature of the procedure working-class people needed to be kept separate as far as possible. There was always a tendency to boast about escape or let things slip inadvertently. The fewer people who were aware of what was going on, the better. The Uranium Hotel was where refugees awaited passage to England. Most had escaped the live electric wire and double barricade of barbed wire at the frontier, constructed from April 1915.

Grace Vulliamy stayed in Flushing until April 1915 when owing to the submarine warfare transportation of civilians had largely diminished. On 24 April 1915 Mr Enkey of the Commission wrote to the Quaker Mr Burtt explaining that the:

> 'Regular Mail and Passenger service of Zeeland Co from Flushing to Tilbury and the LGB Refugee service from Rotterdam to Tilbury have been suspended by order of British Government since 20th inst. But it is necessary to keep the hostel open. Miss Vulliamy sees that they are kept occupied in evenings and given English lessons, then games. During the day they do housework, knitting, sewing. All aprons worn by our 'staff' [are] made by the refugees in the house.'[202]

The Hague Women's Congress

Most people would take it for granted that the reason for this suspension of services across the Channel was due to submarine activity. However, international women's organisations had planned to open the First International Women's Congress at The Hague to discuss possible peace terms which they intended to present to the belligerent governments in the hopes they would start talking about peace and so bring the war to an end. Special arrangements were made with the Zeeland SS Co for the party to travel in two contingents on 24 and 25 April. The British Government regarded the event with shock and horror and on 16 April the British committee of the Congress had a letter from the Home Office saying it was refusing permits to 180 delegates and cancelling those already given. Regular commercial ferries from Folkestone to Flushing were suspended and women's organisations believed this was to prevent the 180-member British delegation from attending. It is impossible to be sure.

[202] Friends House Library. Box 9, Parcel 3, Folder 3. Correspondence with Rotterdam Office

Even though she was no longer a member of the Emergency Corps, friends there remained in touch. She received a letter from Beatrice Harraden dated 8 February 1915.[203]

> My dear Lady
>
> So very sorry not to have answered your interesting letter before, nor acknowledged your kind card. I've been so busy doing some article on the Commission for an American magazine and … and other odd jobs this war brings and doing a little of my book and then recovery from my various efforts. But Nessie and I so often talk of you and I wish always I were there doing (or trying to do) that interesting work. But now I am anxious about your safety. I know we all have to take our chance over the Channel.
>
> I have missed you very much at the Corps – it feels altogether different now. I believe we are to have a public meeting for the Hospitality Department but the difficulty is to get new (and good) speakers.
>
> I am so interested to hear of this new carry on at Flushing. …
>
> Affectionate greeting and my love.
>
> Yours always
>
> Boss

'This carry on' possibly referred to the Women's International Congress.

Quakers and Refugees

The original aim of the Quakers was to help the refugees who were in camps, but they were also beginning to help released civilian prisoners and on 8 October John Barry wrote from Rotterdam:

> Today I have been assisting the British invalids from Germany and although one is busy – yet I feel that this work should not be neglected. There is no association in Holland doing this kind of work and as we are in close touch with the British Consulate we can do this work without any friction. What is the feeling of the Committee on the matter? The 'prisoners' come through once a month.

[203] Addressed 3 Fitzjohn Mansions, Netherhall Gardens, Hampstead, N.W. Date is unclear but looks like 1915.

Indicating its financial commitment, the Committee gave its permission for Barry to continue. Several of the members of the Friends Committee were very influential men, such as MPs or having access to MPs. These matters were reported to Government as a result of which the Foreign Office suggested the Quakers becoming involved in Holland with the refugees, if the Dutch and the Belgians agreed. Grace recorded:

> 'In regard to English, Belgians and others who were passing through *en route* to England, towards the end of 1915 the British Government officially asked for assistance from the Dutch Government, with whom the Society of Friends were requested to co-operate, in meeting and transporting Refugees and released Interned through Holland, and from November onwards we met the regular monthly contingents which Germany sent through.'

The Quakers at Rotterdam decided to accept the Foreign Office suggestion that they should become involved with the refugees in Holland. They had consulted the Consulate and understood that the authorities would be pleased if Quakers supervised all the arrangements. Barry wrote; 'In the meanwhile so far as this Party is concerned Miss Rees, (Miss Vulliamy's assistant) and Mrs Rozelaar will go to the Frontier to meet the men from Ruhleben and will notify us at Rotterdam and Flushing as to departure.' He concluded: 'I had some talk with Miss Vulliamy yesterday and she assisted in the making of these arrangements.'

As we saw in the last chapter, by 4 December 1915 Grace had decided to leave work in the refugee camps because Quakers and the Belgians could work there, but there was no-one helping the military or civilian prisoners from Germany in the way she was able to do. However, she was unable to put her decision into effect until early 1917. In the interim Grace also heard the men's reports of how the British were treated worse than other nationalities by the Germans. The lack of food was in part due to the British blockade, but it was also due to a particular animosity. Such information was to be constantly repeated, not only by prisoners, but by civilians such as Miss Gifford trapped in the occupied area of Belgium.[204] Grace Vulliamy wrote:

> We were generally advised of the number of people coming through by the special train set aside for the purpose, and among these were many sick and stretcher cases, cases of insanity, women and

[204] *The Times*. 17.2.15

children, and also negroes.[205] No arrangements for distinction as regards colour, race or sex were made on the train: some had a little money, some had none, and any money they had was German and therefore useless until exchanged. The border station was Gennep, those bound for England travelling on from there to Flushing, and so – on. I therefore arranged with a good doctor to join the train on the frontier and to see that stretchers and other medical necessaries would be in readiness at Flushing, and on the 6th December I went up to Gennep to meet the first party coming through in this connection, taking two workers with me.

The sick people were dealt with immediately by the Consul and Dr Merkens, assisted by two Red Cross nurses sent from England for the purpose and then removed by them directly to the boat. While the food was being served, passports were being visa-ed, but this formality was not over until 6 a.m. and the boat taking the travellers over to England sailed at 7.30 a.m. As there were a number of negroes in the party, two members of the Society of Friends were detailed to accompany the prisoners to England, in order to give their attention to these and, if necessary, to the insane.[206] They arrived at Tilbury at 4 p.m. where the sick were taken over by the British Red Cross and the destitute by the Central Charity Committee.

Some of the cases of civilians were very hard: there was, for example, a little woman who had taught English in Germany for 18 years, and who had all her friends there as well as her connection, and no-one and nothing to go to in England. She had been expelled with so little notice that she had only been able to bring £6 with her in money, and her references had been retained by the police in Germany.

Had these unfortunate people known that the War would last for years to come, their despair would probably have weighted them down to a state of inertia, but then there was always the hope that it would soon be over, that this upset and uprooting and exile was for a short time only, and, unhappy though it was, all would soon revert to its former normal state. But the sick, homeless and destitute were to continue pouring into and through Holland for many a long weary month before return to former interests could be contemplated.

---

[205] Negro. This term, now considered offensive was the usual term applied to people with dark skins. They were thought to be less self-controlled and therefore more inclined to cause trouble than white-skinned people.

[206] These were likely to be men suffering from what came to be called 'shell-shock.'

A description of the transport of the wounded soldiers was published in the Rotterdam newspaper by a sister of the Red Cross. She said nurses were chosen on account of their knowledge of the two languages to take and fetch the English and German prisoners. This gives important reasons for Grace Vulliamy's involvement and responsible position – ability with languages and the fact that she was a nurse. The nurse continued:

> the men I can give a true picture of the feeling on either side. The gratitude of the English over their reception in Holland and on board ship was much greater than that of the Germans ... their first meal was given to the English on board and from groups of the wounded as well as from members of the ambulance came expression of amazement and rapture at 'having such a nice meal. White bread! Meat!' Their gratitude was touching and from the reserved English was most expressive. The Germans on the contrary had hardly a word of thanks to say a fact which struck us very much. Their meals consisting of ham & eggs, strawberries for breakfast, beef-tea in between meals and meat, potatoes and strawberries again seemed a usual occurrence and no occasion for astonishment which proves that they had equally good food in England. They merely remarked on the strawberries as being a treat. Over all of the Germans said they had nothing to complain of their treatment in England. The English in a composed and serious manner told us 'we will try to forgive we can never forget.' The hospital trains we were told are even better in England than in Germany. At the last exchange a German was heard to say, 'oh but the English Hospital trains are wonderful.'

The Red Cross Sister finished by saying that she was not in any way prejudiced and hers was entirely neutral report.

In fact, there were 85 men from Ruhleben in this first contingent; the oldest was sixty-four years old. There were also at least seven sixteen-year olds, mostly fishing apprentices like Charlie Smith. On arrival at Folkestone women members of a local relief committee gave the prisoners coffee, cigarettes, buns and newspapers.

Children

Children were of special concern to all caught up in the war. Refugees who escaped from occupied Belgium included children. They arrived at Rotterdam needing everything and were fist sent to the Uranium Hotel at Rotterdam and also to Flushing. It was thought that Mrs Fisher at Aldeburgh might be able to help.[207]

---

[207] Box 9.3.3. Burtt to Fry from Rotterdam. July 8th 1915.

Mr and Mrs Fisher of Aldeburgh, Suffolk, went to Flushing some time in February under the auspices of the British Commission for the Transfer of Belgian Refugees to England, the Government organization for which Grace Vulliamy worked. In September 1914 Mrs Fisher, whose father was Sir Henry Trueman Wood, Secretary of the Royal Society of Arts, had opened a Belgian Children's Home in two houses facing the sea intending to provide boarding for 50 girls aged 6 – 16 from professional and commercial classes but due to the chaos in Belgium the home was not full. Now, twenty-three children were specially selected to go back to England with the Fishers and were given free passage by the Commission. Girls stayed at the Home for different lengths of time, sometimes quite brief periods, moving away because parents moved to obtain work, or even to return to Belgium, while some removed their children because they were worried by the Zeppelin raids on other nearby coastal towns such as Yarmouth.

Plate 7.2 Aldeburgh Belgian Children's Home

Grace's photo of the children in neat uniforms and hats, posed in a group outside the home, implies that she knew this home and the Fishers personally.

The steamer which brought these children to England was the last refugee boat to leave Flushing before 17 February, the date announced by the Germans for the commencement of unrestricted submarine warfare. They refused to guarantee that neutral boats would be exempt from torpedo attack[208] so the Dutch Government therefore stopped the service of their boats which they had made available to the British to transfer refugees to England. This resulted in the holding up of many hundreds of people who, in the hope of the boat service being resumed, preferred rather to remain at Flushing and starve than go into one of the camps. Grace Vulliamy worked in these camps until September 1917.[209] The reference to starvation was not pure rhetoric. Early in 1915 the lamentable state of the children in Belgium led the German Government to consent to a proposal that a number of failing children should be sent each month into Holland to be fed, clothed and cared for, for a period of four weeks. The sufferings of Belgium's children at that time may be judged by the fact that 200 came each month from then until the end of the war, each one of whom held a doctor's certificate of ill-health. Tuberculosis was the great scourge, the result of bad and insufficient food over a long period. The worst of those cases were allowed to remain indefinitely in sanatoriums in Holland.[210] After responding to the German declaration of war by issuing its own, Britain initiated a blockade of German ports, cutting off access to resources such as food, textiles, coal, and iron, a tactic intended to starve the Germans into surrendering. The Commission for Relief in Belgium (CRB), run by the American Quaker Herbert Hoover with the agreement of Germany and Britain, brought in otherwise prohibited goods, especially food; money raised in Britain was channelled through it.[211] As a result of the blockade and other wartime methods such as the burning of crops by retreating invading troops, by 1916 famines began spreading throughout Germany, Austria and Hungary. These famines continued throughout the war, reaching a climax in 1917-1918. After Germany's surrender in 1918, the blockade remained in effect until the signing of the Treaty of Versailles on 28 June 1919. Grace Vulliamy was to see the results of the blockade, the famines and the Russian Revolution for herself and try to alleviate them when she worked in Poland and Russia after the war.

The records that Miss Vulliamy left about her work in February 1915 indicate that this was a key month when she began to enlist the help of individuals, asking their help in escorting refugees to the UK and obtaining 'hospitality' for them there. On 4 March 1915, when the boat service had been suspended, she wrote to Jervist H Coats, of Ellangowan, Paisley, thanking him for being ready to take her two families, including the Van de

[208] IWM. BEL 6.4/1

[209] Vulliamy Papers. The Netherlands camps. GCV

[210] Vulliamy Papers. Holland camps. GCV

[211] *Excluded.* P.57

Poels who had 'suffered so much' and who she was hoping to bring to England in the middle of the following week. She wrote: 'I will put them up in London for one night and send them on to Barshaw House the next day, wiring in advance.' She continued: 'The distress here in Flushing is 'simply appaling. (sic) All refugees are being sent to three military camps. There are so many cases where the husband or the wife have already gone to England and now, except by the paying boat, there is no means of sending them over to England'. She wrote: 'I am sorry to be returning to England myself, but if one stayed here much longer, one would be absolutely stonybroke.'

The Vandepoels wrote to Grace from their accommodation in Upperthorpe, Sheffield in January 1916 asking if they could use her names for their expected baby. Evidently, they had been shy of asking her, and Grace responded that if they didn't ask she would not feel that they were treating her as a friend. She had seen them off at one of the London stations and they were sad to say goodbye, feeling how dear she had become to them as she had also taken care of their parents. Mr Vandepoel wrote: 'You see, I have done what a foreigner ought to do, when he comes in a strange country, that is to learn, as soon as possible the language, styles and manners of the people he is going to live amongst, and it has given me an advantage … to write to you in your native tongue.' They ask if Miss Vulliamy had made any advance in learning Flemish, not that they wanted her to write in Flemish, because it would take a lot of time, and Grace was extremely busy helping so very many people. Then Vandepoel wrote again about using her names for their baby who would get the name 'Grace' whether a boy or a girl. 'Now excuse me, dear Miss, but your writing about your names is altogether unpardonable, for my wife and I we agree to find your names lovely … it is not for a name but a remembrance.' They hoped Grace Vulliamy might be able to visit them, knowing she had no acquaintance in Sheffield with whom she could stay. Then they gave a piece of their family news. They had heard that a younger brother, who by Belgian law was a soldier, had been transferred from Antwerp to Germany as a prisoner and asked her, if she saw their mother, to tell her not to worry. They sent 'all a ship of kisses' from their small son Henri and added thanks for the Christmas presents they had just received. 'I remember your hearty, good and generous character, and your kindly face.'

On 26 July 1916 Grace Vulliamy wrote to the Prince de Ligne at the Belgian Legation, The Hague, asking him to 'facilitate the departure of Maria Vanderpoel for England. 'Her father is seriously ill, and they have sent for her. She has been my personal maid for some months and I can vouch for her in every way. I very much wish to take her with me to-morrow, July 27th, to Flushing.' Presumably this was another member of the family who were living in Sheffield. Grace knew the Prince de Ligne personally and on one occasion at least went to a dinner that he and his wife attended. See Chapter 9, Plate 9.8 for a menu card with his name on it.

Grace's travels across the Channel
On many occasions Grace Vulliamy herself accompanied the prisoners to England often sailing on Captain Fryatt's boat.[212] She crossed the North Sea 46 times, and ten of the boats by which she frequently travelled were mined, captured, or torpedoed but she was always fortunate enough not to be on the boat on those occasions. Several times the crossing took four or five days owing to fog or to other effects of war. In 1914 and early 1915 they darted through the night in a ship painted black, and had to sleep in life belts and, to her disgust were 'not even allowed to make a cigarette!' They were always thankful to arrive in England. The mention of a cigarette further identifies Miss Vulliamy as a 'New Woman', those who at the end of the 19th and early 20th centuries pushed the limits allotted to them by male-dominated society. They were pilloried and satirized by Horatio Bottomley of *John Bull* and Henry Mayhew's journal *Punch,* because the New Woman was affluent and sensitive, who exhibited an independent spirit and was accustomed to acting on her own. In Grace's case, it does not seem to be entirely because of affluence, since she needed a salary, but rather the position she held in society and the fact that the term New Woman always referred to women who exercised control over their own lives be it personal, social, or economic.

Captain Charles Algernon Fryatt (2 December 1872 – 27 July 1916), to whom Grace Vulliamy referred, was a British mariner who was executed by the Germans for attempting to ram a U-boat in 1915. On 28 March 1915, as captain of the *SS Brussels*, he was ordered to stop by the *U-33* when his ship was near the Maas lightvessel.[8] Seeing the U-boat had surfaced to torpedo his ship, Fryatt ordered full steam ahead and proceeded to try to ram the *U-33*, which was forced to crash dive. This action was in compliance with orders issued by Winston Churchill to captains of merchant ships. For this action, Fryatt was awarded a gold watch by the Admiralty. The watch was inscribed *Presented by the Lords Commissioners of the Admiralty to Chas. Algernon Fryatt Master of the*

[212] See Chapter 4

S.S. 'Brussels' in recognition of the example set by that vessel when attacked by a German submarine on March 28th, 1915.

When his ship, the *SS Brussels* was captured off the Netherlands in 1916. It is recorded that Fryatt and his crew were sent to the civilian internment camp at Ruhleben, near Berlin, but this probably only applied to male members of his crew. This image from Grace Vulliamy's collection, dated 1916, shows stewardesses from the SS Brussels at Holtzminden, near Hanover.

The Mayor of Harwich opened a fund to erect a permanent memorial to Fryatt. A similar fund was opened in the Netherlands. In 1919, Fryatt's body was exhumed and returned to the United Kingdom where it was reburied with full honours. His coffin was landed at Dover and transported to London. On 8 July his funeral was held at St Paul's Cathedral. Hundreds of merchant seamen and widows of merchant seamen and fishermen attended. Representing the Government were many members of the Admiralty, the Board of Trade, the Cabinet and War Office. A public house in nearby Parkeston is also named in Captain Fryatt's honour.

There are distinct similarities between what happened to Fryatt and what happened to Edith Cavell, executed by firing squad by the Germans on 12 October 1915, an event that horrified the world. A memorial service was held for her in St Paul's Cathedral on 29 October.

There were other problems in travelling by boat partly due to tides, but also to the fact that this was war. Grace Vulliamy wrote:

> Once I crossed in an Admiralty boat to see a seriously ill relation and asked if I could be away two days and be able to catch the boat to return. The Admiralty said 'yes', but when I returned to London they informed me it had left, and had been torpedoed. My friends in Holland telephoned the Consul to ask about me and were told that I was on board and the boat was sinking, so when I turned up two days later 'they seemed almost to regret to see me alive and well.'[213]

Evidently Grace's wry sense of humour remained intact regardless of personal and political conditions; it is more than likely that her father was the sick relative she went back to England to see.[214] He died on 29 March 1915.

[213] Vulliamy Papers. Grace's Account of Prisoner Exchange.
[214] Vulliamy Papers. Grace's Account of Prisoner Exchange.

Plate 7.3 Stewardesses from SS Brussels

Grace's Colleagues and Friends

Visiting cards show how people she met in one place might continue the relationship in another. These cards were used by people who, on going to visit someone who they found was not at home, left the card to show they had called. For example, Mrs Francis Acland of the Belgian Repatriation Committee, Lady Townley and Sir Walter Townley, Lord Apsley of the British Legation,[215] Fred Rowntree, V F W Cavendish Bentink, Secretary to the British Legation, and Mr Walter Long, President of the Local Government Board all called on Miss Vulliamy in London.[216] There are also three of Miss Vulliamy's own cards prepared post-war ready for her to leave for other people when necessary. One gave her address at Littleholme

---

[215] Eldest son of the 7th Earl of Bathurst.

[216] including one from Alice Masaryk,

[216] who was then a member of the National Assembly, daughter of the first President of Czechoslovakia; the Princess de Ligne, who thanked her for some photos, Major General Carton de Wiart of the British Military Mission in Warsaw, (a much wounded soldier who was born in Brussels).

in Hertfordshire, but on the same card was printed the 'Grand Hotel, Krakow', another in her role as Organiser of the British Committee for Relief in Warsaw and yet another as representative of The Save The Children Fund also in Warsaw, together with Mrs W.G.Max Muller, wife of the British Consul-General in Budapest.[217] W. Haldane Porter, a civil servant who presided over the Aliens Branch (later Immigration Branch) and its staff of Aliens' Officers (later Immigration Officers), used his card as a means of introducing Miss Vulliamy to an unnamed third-part

But in addition to such people, Miss Vulliamy was in touch with old friends such as Lena Ashwell until the end of her life and they spent time together whenever possible. There is a hint in one of Grace's letters that their relationship was physical as well as emotional and practical. If this is the case it perhaps helps to explain the enduring nature of their friendship. There was an official link between Grace Vulliamy's work for the YMCA and her actress friend, Lena Ashwell. The YMCA was responsible to military authority for the 'lodgement, general care and good behavior of the Lena Ashwell parties' in Holland. At the end of January 1917 Grace wrote to Lena to let her know that 'some time soon' she would be in England. Lena hoped it might be possible for them to go back together on 2 March and then she would be able to stay in Holland for two weeks. She wondered what kind of ship she would go over on. Sail ships were giving place to steam, paddle steamers were still in use in some places, including cross-Channel, but there were also occasions when Miss Vulliamy and Lena Ashwell travelled on Admiralty boats. Such visits gave the two women an opportunity to spend time together. Grace was not particularly interested in Lena's acting or work on the stage but she undoubtedly spoke to Lena about her own work, and engaged her sympathy for the prisoners. This carried over into her work after the war for those who suffered as a result of the Russian Revolution.

[217] The main players in the 1914 Crisis: Sir Edward Grey; Sir Arthur Nicolson, Permanent Under-Secretary at the Foreign Office; Sir Eyre Crowe, Assistant Under Secretary of State at the Foreign Office; Sir Francis Bertie, British Ambassador in Paris; Sir George Buchanan, British Ambassador in St. Petersburg; Sir Maurice de Bunsen, British Ambassador in Vienna; Sir Edward Goschen, British Ambassador in Berlin; Sir Francis Villiers, British Minister in Brussels; Dayrell Crackanthorpe, British Chargé d'Affaires in Belgrade; W.G. Max Müller; British Consul-General in Budapest and J.F. Jones, British Vice-Consul in Sarajevo

CHAPTER 8

RUHLEBEN

From October 1915 the Society of Friends were made responsible for meeting British civilians and transporting them first to Flushing and then across the Channel to England. Many of these people were men who had been imprisoned in the civilian internment camp at Ruhleben, some since the very beginning of the war. These Ruhleben prisoners were sent among other civilians through to Flushing. Their release started 15 November.

When war was declared fishing ports like Grimsby and Boston immediately felt the impact. On Tuesday, 4 August 1914, several vessels, including some owned by the Great Central Railway, were in German ports unloading their catch and the men were interned, many leaving wives and families to fend for themselves.[218] This contravened the rules of war, which had not yet been declared between Britain and Germany. The captured fishermen, who included young apprentices, were transferred to Spandau, a Berlin suburb, and housed on the Ruhleben racecourse.[219] The Boston Fishing Company, like Grimsby, employed apprentices, mostly from orphanages. The Apprentices Home was run by Mr Brightey and his wife, who was known as 'mother' to the boys. Among those taken prisoner were Albert Stearns, John Wilmot, Robert Foster, Thomas Cornford, Charlie Smith, John Graham and William Henry 'Lizzie' Harris, most of whom are on Grace Vulliamy's lists of escorted prisoners. 'Lizzie' wrote most of the letters home for the other boys, including one to Mr Brightey.

> 'I suppose you missed us when we did not come home. I am pleased to say that both the crews and the apprentices are all safe and well in Germany as prisoners. We are being treated with every respect, and with the greatest of civility. We have plenty to eat and tobacco is allowed us. ... We have the crews of the *Lindsey, Kesteven, Porpoise* and a Grimsby trawler here in Cuxhaven. ... Tell 'mother' not to trouble about us as we are faring well... With very best regards, from your boys ... We are seven jolly fishing apprentices just captured at sea.'

---

[218] *W.H. Jackson.* Grimsby's War Work : an account of the Borough's effort during the Great War, 1914-1919, together with the Roll of Honour. *W.H. Jackson, 1919. www.Lincolnshire Genweb Project. Downloaded 7.2.2008*

[219] Stopper & Maltby. *Boston Deep Sea Fisheries. p.17. Lincolnshire Standard,* 22.11.1914. Some items they brought back with them are in the Grimsby Fishing Museum.

It is risky to take this letter at face value although they were still in Cuxhaven and possibly among friendly German fishermen, but they might have been aware that criticism of their captors could result in reprisals. In addition, the apprentices would want to appear as positive as possible to their readers at home and possibly expected to be released very quickly. When they got to Ruhleben conditions there 'for the first 12 months were horrible' but improved when 'parcels began to arrive from England'. Local English newspapers began appealing to people to 'Send food parcels to prisoners, including those at Ruhleben'. Parcels from home soon became vital to their survival.

Miss Vulliamy's lists of British civilians from Germany dated from this period show that many of them were from Dr Weiler's sanatorium at Ruhleben and from quarantine in the Lazarette. Those repatriated on 6 October 1917 had illnesses including neuritis in the leg, consumption, heart and liver problems and gallstones. These were serious illnesses, particularly for mature men living under prison conditions, the youngest aged 34, the oldest 54. Several of them were destitute and most had been interned in the first months of the war. There was even a little boy who had been born in Berlin in September 1911. Many were very bitter about their treatment in the camps. Yet despite such difficulties, most had somewhere to go. All were escorted by Miss Vulliamy on their journey from the German frontier through Holland. She learnt much about Ruhleben conditions on these journeys although of course she did not visit the camp herself. Nevertheless, the information she garnered contributed to her document entitled *A Few Points to Dispel False Impressions*, (see Appendix).

Of course, it was not only fishermen who were sent to Ruhleben. All British males within Germany became subject to internment on 5 November 1914, the day war was declared. They came from all aspects of society and included individuals from the professional classes and business community, as well as academics, students, sportsmen and even travellers and holidaymakers. One page of one of the lists made by Grace Vulliamy includes a Draughtsman-Lace Designer, a seaman and a cook. Two politicians were interned. In the camps, civilian internees were treated differently from military prisoners of war - they were allowed privileges; for example, playing sports and putting on theatrical productions.[220] This happened only after they had asked for and been given permission. Despite this apparent leniency, prisoners were liable to be constantly insulted by their captors because Britain was held responsible for the war. Using the

[220] 421 Foreign Office: Prisoners of War and Aliens Department: General Correspondence from 106. FO 383

words of one of the prisoners, whose name she put in brackets at the end of the extract, Grace recorded:

> The case of the civilian who finds himself in an enemy country at the outbreak of war is peculiar. He has no status and is immediately deprived of all rights – civic, domestic and economic. The soldier reckons upon imprisonment as a possible factor in his career, while the Officers and NCO may look forward to release after 18 months of imprisonment. Military prisoners received treatment according to rank in ways agreed upon by an international convention. Officers and men do not cease to draw their pay. To the civilian prisoner, deprived of earning his living and thus his claim to that independence which is the right of every... and becoming therefore a burden to his family and friends, is added yet another humiliation and cause for depression. Is it because a civilian is supposed to feel his position less acutely that no provision for his release after 18 months is made? (Digby R Lawson)[221]

The Ruhleben racecourse became the principal internment camp for male civilians. Men were then interned *en masse*; it had over 4,000 internees, all men.[222] But originally there were no specially built huts for them to live in. They were given the stables, complete with the dirty straw which had been horses' bedding, and the loft above provided additional space to lie down at night. Six men were allocated to each stable and in the lofts as many men as could lie down – about a hundred. It was miserable and overcrowded; unheated, even in winter, although in hot weather it could become very warm. There were no special rooms in which to eat their food or spend their time in the hours of darkness and bad weather. Want of occupation, worry about and lack of news from the outside world made for depression. They also had to take a long walk to wash themselves or their clothes in an open shed but there was nowhere to dry their washing except their living quarters - the stables, which consequently became permanently damp. It was always muddy. Charles Winger, one of the men interned here gave further information:

> The barracks were flanked by dustbins and refuse boxes and the smell as well as the flies and mosquitoes issuing from these and the neighbouring marshlands, in summer made sleep impossible.

---

221 GCV. Chapter II

222 Douglas Sladen (Ed.) *In Ruhleben. Letters from a prisoner to his mother.* London. Hurst and Blackett. 1917. 10

> There was no drainage or flow of water; the sanitary arrangements were entirely primitive and spitting to a degree unknown and unsuspected in the freedom of ordinary life constituted an ever – increasing menace. (Charles Winger)[223]

This drawing of men queueing and two others knee high in mud holding cans for their food beautifully illustrates the comment that 'The prisoners had to walk with their food bowls to distant kitchens and queue for their insufficient food regardless of the weather.'

Plate 8.1. Mealtime at Ruhleben

The following one, undoubtedly drawn by the same unknown hand, possibly depicts two German guards and the Camp Commandant. Another prisoner, J W Hughes, describes their frustration at the captivity:

> As time went on and these prisoners saw little or no prospect of release urgent enquiries began to be made by them as to the reason of their indefinitely prolonged captivity and the reply from our Government was that 'military reason' made it necessary for them to remain there as "the handful of captives at Ruhleben are the means of preventing two fresh enemy divisions from entering the field." The vast majority of the prisoners were always ready to offer their lives for their country, but in view of the "military" nature of the reason of their detention, one cannot help feeling that they would have been more justly treated had this been made clear to them from the start and put upon a military basis. The impulse which sustained them to a point of protracted and courageous endurance [would be]

[223] GCV. Chapter II

much strengthened. A definition of their task and status in an authoritative message from England would have given a new direction to their lives and a fresh inspiration to their thoughts and their efforts, which were bound to grow bitter and resentful when faced for years with a ... seemingly unnecessary sentence of imprisonment. (JW Hughes)

Plate 8.2. Germans at Ruhleben

The first party of released prisoners from Ruhleben came into neutral Holland on 7 November 1915 when a few at a time were included among the prisoners sent through to Holland. From then onwards the Friends met the regular monthly contingents which Germany sent through. Consequently, Miss Vulliamy spent many hours at the various frontiers. In February 1916, it was reported in the *Lincolnshire Standard* that a ship was arriving at Tilbury the next Monday with 600 British prisoners from Germany. There were eighteen from Ruhleben; John Graves was one, with '104 wrecks of soldiers, he the only Bostonian.'[224]

Two members of the Society of Friends were detailed to accompany the prisoners to England, especially as 'there were a number of negroes in the party' in order to give their attention to them. Comments about 'negroes' occur frequently and it is taken for granted that the reader will understand why they needed a great 'deal of supervision.' In many cases, prisoners escorted by Grace included 'the sick, insane, niggers and thieves!'

[224] *Lincolnshire Standard.* 12 February 1916

Evidently, her primary concern was with alleviating distress, but it is also clear that she was something of a social snob and accepted current prejudices without question.

When six members of Society of Friends met the first prisoners at Gennep there were 96 men, 13 women, nine children and 47 negroes. The train arrived two hours late. Miss Vulliamy arranged for medical assistance and provision of food in advance of the arrival of such trains.

> The majority of those who came looked ill and bore evident signs of their experiences in camp. All returning civilians complained of their treatment at Ruhleben. One and all showed great appreciation of the reception prepared for them, and evinced unbounded delight at meeting English people again. We heard from them that one of their company had died on the journey and there were among them two stretcher cases and four cases of insanity. Boxtel was the station nearest the German frontier and there we were met by Dr Merkens of Flushing, who attended to the sick as we travelled. We reached Flushing at 1 a.m. and there found another member of the Society of Friends who had hot soup and other refreshments prepared. Upon our arrival at Flushing, the cases of sick were dealt with immediately by the Consul and Dr Merkens, assisted by two Red Cross nurses sent from England for the purpose and then removed by them directly to the boat. Special attention was needed for the mental cases so two members of Friends accompanied the party to England. The negroes needed a good deal of supervision. On the same boat were 81 wounded who had travelled via Roosendaal and there was also a small party of destitute English from Brussels. The boat reached Tilbury at 4 o'clock and cards of instruction were given to destitute people by the Central Charities Commission.[225]

Whenever Dutch people are mentioned Grace referred to them as 'good' or 'kindly'; this was general practice. The British and their Allies tried to prevent food supplies reaching Germany by means of a naval blockade, food being a weapon of war. Germany retaliated with submarines sinking Allied merchant, food-carrying ships. Nevertheless, the Dutch made it possible for food shipments, largely from America, to get to occupied Belgium through the auspices of the Commission for Relief in Belgium (CRB), run by the American Quaker Herbert Hoover, with the agreement of Germany and Britain. This brought in otherwise prohibited goods, especially food; money raised in Britain was channelled through it. The Dutch placed strong emphasis on humanitarian activities as a method of staying out of the war,

---

[225] Vulliamy Papers. Report on the journey of British Civilians from Germany to England, 6 December 1915. Friends House, Box 9:4:5

increasing the value other nations placed on its neutral status. The description of the Dutch as 'hospitable', 'good' and 'kindly' adopted on both sides of the belligerent lines assisted in this. One worry was that if America entered the war, which it did on the 6 April 1917, such humanitarian activities would have to stop.

Two members of the Society of Friends meeting this train were already in the area at one of the refugee internment camps and so did not travel to Gennep with Grace Vulliamy. They all had a long wait because the train:

> arrived two hours late, but the railway authorities kindly allowed it to wait there another hour in order that refreshments might be given out to the travellers. They were helped by the Protestant clergyman and his wife and by the wife of the local doctor.

The Friends, with Grace Vulliamy's expertise to assist them, also attended to the 'insane,' people who were suffering with stress-related mental disturbances. Douglas Sladen, who is quoted later in this chapter and was a friend of Lena Ashwell,[226] describes the effect of the years of restraint and strain on 'the strongest of the prisoners,' as nerve-pressure 'all due to the soul-wrecking regime of the Camp.'[227] Mental illness was here being recognised as due to life in the prison camp, not to any individual psychological weakness. It took a very long time before the Military and society in general was able to recognise that lifestyle contributed to psychiatric disorder.

One severe irritant in Ruhleben was the requirement that they adhere to German patriotism. An unidentified newspaper cutting included in Miss Vulliamy's papers entitled 'Memories of Ruhleben - Flagstaff story' tells that in the middle of the camp and on every possible occasion - the Kaiser's birthday, a victory - the flag was run up.

> One day the cord was found to be cut through. Own up! Or the whole camp is to be punished. Ordered three days' CB [confined to barracks]. So there was no exercise except the walk to the kitchen for the dole of food. We were civilian prisoners, whose only crime was being the wrong side of the boundary when war was declared. Many were relying on English supplies of food so each man took his tin pannikin and marched to the kitchen singing 'Tipperary'. The Authorities hadn't

---

[226] Ashwell. *Myself a Player*. Michael Joseph. 1936. 185

[227] Sladen (Ed.) *In Ruhleben*.

got enough food until they used the supplies for the whole week. Men were actually starving in the first winter of the war.[228]

Despite being prisoners in Germany, by arrangement between the German and British Governments men received their money from England. They had to pay, for example, if they were in the lazarette. On the train out of Germany, some had a little money, some had none, and any money they had was German and therefore useless until exchanged. On board ship they were expected to pay for their own food. However, food had to be provided for a certain number of the party who were found to be absolutely penniless. One such was William Rudd who had been interned on 25 August 1914 having been taken off the *SS Kesteven,* one of the boats from Boston. On repatriation, on 28 January 1917, in a group supervised by Grace Vulliamy, he gave his address as 49 Duke Street, Boston and needed his fare, food and tickets because he had no money, but said he would be all right once he got home. On the same boat were 81 wounded who had travelled via Roosendaal and a small party of destitute English from Brussels.

The boat arrived at Tilbury at 4 p.m. where the sick were taken over by the British Red Cross and the destitute by the Central Charities Committee. The term 'civilian' hides the fact that there were women and even children included amongst these prisoners. Miss Vulliamy's concern for individuals is evident in the report about the little woman who taught English given in the last chapter. This ended with information about:

> A Mr Hunter, who was missed on the boat, had not been reported when the Tender left.[229]

The first civilian exchange was of 79 people, including five women and one child. There were three stretcher cases and one nervous case. This was not unusual. In fact, in the exchange that took place on 7 May 1916, there were nine men who were 'completely insane,' and one woman who was 'nervous bordering on insane' who needed constant attention, with ten being destitute. Grace Vulliamy noted that German born women married to Englishmen now found themselves in an invidious situation. A letter published in the suffragist magazine *Jus Suffragii,* on 1 September 1916, explained the problem married women now faced:[230]

> Whoever comes into frequent contact with German wives of aliens interned at Ruhleben will have been able to judge of the tragedy of their

[228] Vulliamy Papers. Newspaper cuttings.doc

[229] Vulliamy Papers. Holland camps. GCV

[230] *Jus Suffragii.* 1 September 1916

fates. Many had never been out of Germany, had lived there with husband and children, never dreaming until the outbreak of war but that they were Germans. Suddenly their eyes were opened and they were stamped as aliens, enemies. The physical, but still more the mental suffering of such women, not only here but in every belligerent country, is beyond description.

(signed) Thea Mertelmeyer, *Die Frauenbewegung*

'Aliens' in this context refers to British or other Allied men and was the legal term widely used rather than 'foreigner.' Women had no choice but to take the nationality of their husbands on marriage; therefore if British women married German men they became enemy aliens in their birth country. This did not change until 1949 in Britain.

This group of prisoners reported that there had been food riots in Germany and said the food in Ruhleben was worse every week. Milk and butter were almost unobtainable and soap tickets were being issued. The Germans had arranged with the *Wagons Lits Co* for a restaurant but finding there were two Germans sent with it the British told people not to go into it – the food was expensive, and they thought the Germans were there to listen to conversations. Grace told *Wagons Lits* they would always have sufficient food and the restaurant was not necessary. This helps explain why the Germans refused Grace Vulliamy permission to be on the trains in 1918 when they discovered she was British, not German: perhaps she was also put there to listen to conversations? Dr Hobhouse, who had been sent over by the Red Cross from England, took charge of the prisoners on the boat. On this transport there was no doctor on the train and although the German doctor offered his services they were refused, highlighting the lack of trust between the two nationalities. Grace asked that subsequently the medicine chest should always include hypodermic syringes with heart tonic and an opiate. The City of London Red Cross Hospital were consulted and decided their orderlies could not be trusted with such dangerous drugs because they had no medical training, but that if Miss Vulliamy was going to be there, there would be no problem. Miss Vulliamy's reputation and training were sufficient.

Family relationships could become especially stressful due to the war. Amongst one party transferred in July 1916 was a boy of 16 whose stepbrother was in the German army and who had another brother in the British Army. Such torn loyalties must have been very difficult to deal with. There was also one lame prisoner and one suffering from internal problems, thought to be caused by mistreatment when a prisoner, and another in a highly nervous condition. On another occasion that month[231] when five highly educated prisoners crossed at Gennep, they said that if 'measures were not taken to obtain the release of men still interned in Ruhleben, the camp would soon be little better than a mad house.'[232] After British and German governments agreed to exchange civilian prisoners over the age of 45, the others at Ruhleben realized they would remain captive a very long time.

As mentioned above, prisoners in civilian camps like Ruhleben were able to entertain themselves by various means including putting on plays. One, ironically entitled 'The Prisoners' Friend' written by O P McDonald and others, initialed by ELH and JHBS, was produced on 15 August 1918. However, one scene, though fully rehearsed, was banned shortly before production by the camp's British Amateur Dramatic Society Committee and was therefore never played in public, probably because they did not want to incur repercussions. Nevertheless, the duet 'Newton the Teuton' was sung at a smoking concert with great success. Lord Newton was the Minister in Charge of Prisoners of War and therefore supposed to be sympathetic to their difficulties. The well-known tune for this ironic song was 'Gilbert the Filbert' with music by Herman Finck, a very popular British composer. It had been performed in *The Passing Show* of 1914 by the popular Basil Hallam, who as Captain B. H. Radford was killed in 1916 when he fell to his death because his parachute failed to open. The song begins with one of the 'female singers' singing 'you are known to all as a fearful dud, there are thousands thirsting for your blood' and Newton replying:

> 'But as they are in Germany
> That really doesn't worry me.'

In the play, in addition to Lord Newton, the cast included Mr Hope, his Confederate, five girls (who of course were played by men) and Reggie an Escaped Prisoner of War. The scene was set in Lord Newton's room at the Foreign Office in London in August 1919, indicating that the prisoners expected the war to last at least this long. In the banned scene Newton and Hope gloat over the fact that they have managed to delay repatriating the prisoners by various subterfuges such as moving them from place to place while giving the impression they were going to Holland. In other words, they are acting like the German captors. Newton says 'I ought not to praise myself but I don't mind saying that they ought to adore me, though I'm very much afraid they don't.' A song entitled 'The Prisoners' Friend' was sung to the tune of 'The Disagreeable Man' from Gilbert and Sullivan's 'Princess

---

[231] 7.7.1916

[232] V Papers. Report 11.7.16

Ida' with music by Arthur Sullivan and words broadly the same as Gilbert's. The final two lines of this are:

> '... but though I check their vices by all the means I can
> The prisoners all say I'm such a disagreeable man
> And I can't think why.'

At the close of the scene the 'girls' make it clear that he is a traitor to his trust, he does not love the prisoners as he claims, and then they carry out the first part of his punishment which is to de-bag him - that is, remove his trousers! The final pages of the copy of this play given to Miss Vulliamy carry notes explaining the actual events to which the play refers at any given point. For example, during the year beginning about 1 August 1917 prisoners in the 10th Army Corps command were forbidden to have the envelopes of their letters. Another example is that the official explanation of the several large moves to different camps in Germany in December 1917 was that the officers so removed were going to a concentration camp for Holland. Thus the big moves from Swärmstedt, Ströhen, and (?) Augsburg to Holzminden.[233]

One of the first English women to be concerned about Ruhleben was the internationalist Emily Hobhouse who had scathingly attacked conditions in the Boer camps established by the British during the Boer war of 1899-1902; more adult Boers had died in camps than in battle and over four times as many children.[234] Hobhouse, who was supported by the Quaker Sir Edward Fry and knew his children Roger and Ruth, was eventually vindicated and her ashes are buried at the foot of the National Memorial at Bloemfontein. She is valued in South Africa, but comparatively unknown in Britain, being deemed 'unpatriotic'. In the First World War Emily Hobhouse found a way of moving across the German and Allied lines in and out of occupied Belgium and Flanders (movements that were not approved of by the Authorities), attempting to rouse women to act to stop the war. In the summer of 1915, she went to Switzerland and Italy to incite women to act against the war.[235]

Hobhouse visited Ruhleben Camp for Interned Civilians, some of the British inmates assuming her presence was due to being the mistress of one of the German officers, which she was not. She also visited Dr Weiler's sanatorium where she considered the food was very insufficient.[236] While in Germany,

---

[233] See Appendix Prisoner Exchange 4.9. = the play

[234] Storr. *Excluded from the Record.* Hobhouse, Emily, 5, 11, 14, 48-51, 61, 131, 133-4, 163, 190, 236, 260

[235] Fsher, John. 1971. *That Miss Hobhouse.* Secker & Warburg.

[236] Sladen. *In Ruhleben.* 34

Hobhouse was able to contact Dr Elisabeth Rotten who had been expelled from England because the Government was obsessed with spying and thought she was German. Rotten was not British born, but neither was she an enemy alien, being Swiss. Some sources state that she was educated at , others that she lectured there.[237] She was closely connected with the Friends War Victims Relief Committee (FWVRC) and in contact with the suffrage movement. She undertook work on the Continent on behalf of suffragist and Quaker Committees. However, such movement across enemy lines did not meet with the British Government's approval. Elisabeth was also a German scholar gaining a doctorate for a study of Goethe while studying at Marburg, Hesse, in Germany.[238] That was enough to cause her expulsion. Another Friends' Minute dated 28th July, 1915, stated that 'Dr Rotten left England last night, by order of the Government.'[239]

A Minute from the Detention Camps Subcommittee of the Friends Emergency Committee shows that on 13 April 1915 the Friends had received a letter from Dr Rotten advising them that the Berlin Emergency Committee had been established independently, 'before they knew about us' and that 'our existence was an encouragement to them.'[240]

> Elisabeth Rotten – her name disappears without any kind of public tribute in minutes or reports. In 1952 she was nominated by the Society for the Nobel Peace Prize, but she didn't get it. She died on a visit to London in 1964. Elisabeth Rotten was Jewish.[241]

Despite censorship and other laws which sought to prevent people from communicating across national boundaries, Elisabeth Rotten was able to maintain communication with the Quakers throughout the war and her reports were printed in *The Friend,* as were those of Emily Hobhouse. Rotten became Secretary of the Berlin Committee for the Relief of Foreigners,[242]

---

[237] Switzerland Yearly Meeting. History and Biography Project. 'Let Their Lives Speak' A Resource Book. Michael and Erica Royston. http://www.swiss-quakers.ch/francais/Let%20their%20lives%20speak.pdf Accessed 11.10.2006

[238] http://de.wikipedia.org/wiki/Elisabeth_Rotten. Accessed 11.10.2006

[239] Friends. FWVRC. Emergency Committee Minutes, Book 1.

[240] Friends House Library, London. (hereinafter Friends) FWVRC. Emergency Committee Minutes, Book 1.

[241] John O Greenwood, *Quaker Encounters Vol 3 Whispers of Truth,* William Sessions Ltd. York, England, 1978, 268-9

[242] Fisher. *That Miss Hobhouse.* 251

caring for British prisoners and enemy aliens[243] in the same way that the Friends Emergency Committee helped German and Austrian people who had become enemy aliens in Britain. She was a very useful contact for internationalists, such as Grace Vulliamy, who sought to alleviate suffering caused by the war regardless of nationality. For example, the Friends Emergency Committee Minutes of 21 December 1915, records they had received a letter from Miss G Vulliamy asking whether 'we can do anything to help German prisoners returning to Germany. We decided to write to the War Victims Committee asking whether they could undertake this by means of their organization in Holland.' Elisabeth Rotten's care of civilian prisoners and interned PoWs at Ruhleben and other camps[244] earned her the title of the 'Florence Nightingale' of the Internment Camps for Allied Nationals in Germany.[245] Grace Vulliamy deserves a similar title.

Hobhouse suffered the whistle-blowers' usual fate of being treated as the perpetrator of the crime when she inadvertently left on the Consul's desk a letter to Dr Aletta Jacobs who had arranged the International Congress of Women in April 1915; revelations about her contact with the 'enemy' from this letter raised the question of whether she should be interned, and she was watched by the police. Also, she was a woman – so inevitably questions were raised about her morality and unreliability. Nevertheless, in such ways, the truth about Ruhleben conditions became known in Britain largely because men, who were more likely to be taken notice of by the Authorities, also reported the poor Ruhleben conditions. For example, on 16 February 1915 the Friends' Emergency Committee reported that Dr Cimino, an Englishman, who had just been released from Ruhleben, visited the Friends in London and told them of the camp. He said conditions were very similar to the English Concentration camps in the Boer war, exactly as Emily Hobhouse had said but which the authorities would not want to know about. There were 4,500 English prisoners, with some French and Russians; food was poor and inadequate, but most prisoners had money and could buy. The sleeping accommodation was poor, but it got warm in the evenings.

Did Grace Vulliamy know Emily Hobhouse? There were Quaker links between them, although neither one was a Quaker, and it seems unlikely, although Grace may have known about Hobhouse and her work. However, both knew Ruth Fry and possibly Roger Fry also. But that seems the extent of

---

[243] Greenwood. *Whispers of Truth*. 195

[244] Friends FWVRC. Box 10, parcel 2, folder 3. German Babies' Teats Fund. To Secretary, Ministry of Blockade. 4.1.1919

[245] Michael and Erica Royston. 'Let Their Lives Speak'. 36 After the war Rotten was cofounder of the Pestalozzi villages.

their contact. Elisabeth Rotten was another matter, corresponding with Grace Vulliamy about the prisoners during the last two years of the war, although whether they had previously met is not known. Newnham, the Cambridge College that had an important influence on many women, was nevertheless, a significant link between them. Elizabeth Rotten was at Newnham, and, as we have seen, a member of Grace's family was also there. in view of the fact that Vulliamy had been working with Rotten for some considerable time it is rather surprising to come across a letter dated 6 March 1918 apparently seeking permission for this connection from the military. Perhaps as the military situation changed Vulliamy felt it wise to bring it to their notice.

> Dear General Graham Thomson
>
> I have received the enclosed letter from Dr Rotten of Berlin and I am sending it to you to ask you to advise me how I should reply.
>
> I have been working with Dr Rotten for two years in connection with the repatriation of civilians who come through on the 6th of every month and it is, no doubt, for this reason that she has addressed the letter to me.
>
> The matter would appear to be urgent as the letter came through as an express letter and so I should be most grateful if you would return the letter to me with your advice as soon as possible.
>
> Yours sincerely,

On 26 July 1916 Grace Vulliamy wrote to the Prince de Ligne at the Belgian Legation, The Hague, Further links were made with Ruhleben on 2 March 1915 when the American-born Quaker Dr Henrietta Thomas visited the camp and spoke to an Englishman acting as Captain to one of the barracks there. She found that weekly concerts, etc, rounders and cricket were 'still allowed'. Food however, was scanty and sometimes inedible, and the heating poor and most prisoners still bought their own food. Whether this 'Captain' was 'the Mayor of Ruhleben' or not is uncertain, but his Badge, bearing his name 'Walter Butterworth', is in Grace Vulliamy's collection. He was Liberal Candidate MP for Rushworth, Manchester in the 'Coupon Election' in September 1918.[246]

[246] Vulliamy Papers. Holland camps. Ruhleben. Exchange and Prisoners. *Daily Graphic.*

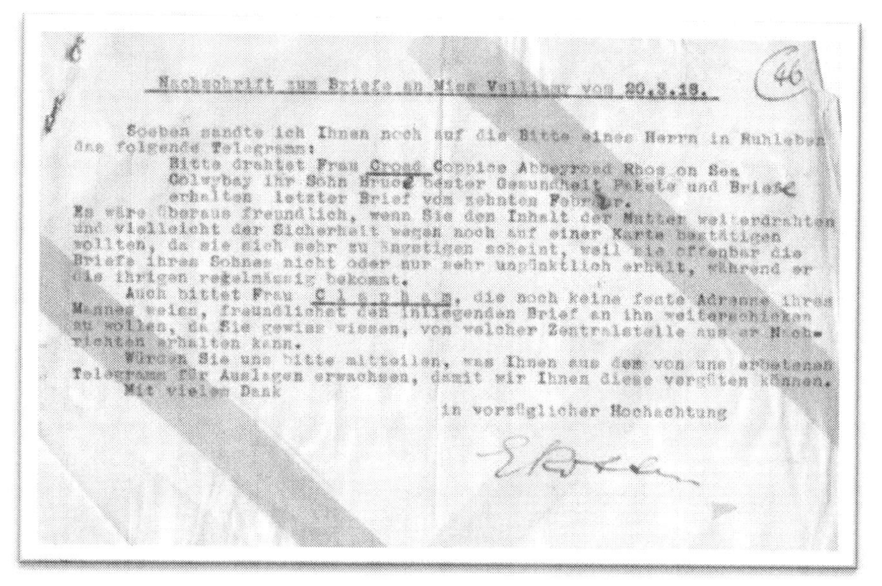

Nachschrift zum Briefe an Miss Vulliamy vom 20.3.18.

Soeben sandte ich Ihnen noch auf die Bitte eines Herrn in Ruhleben das folgende Telegramm:

Bitte drahtet Frau Croad Coppice Abbeyroad Rhos on Sea Colwynbay ihr Sohn Bruce bester Gesundheit Pakete und Briefe erhalten letzter Brief vom zehnten Februar.

Es wäre überaus freundlich, wenn Sie den Inhalt der Mutter weiterdrahten und vielleicht der Sicherheit wegen noch auf einer Karte bestätigen wollten, da sie sich sehr zu ängstigen scheint, weil sie offenbar die Briefe ihres Sohnes nicht oder nur sehr unpünktlich erhält, während er die ihrigen regelmässig bekommt.

Auch bittet Frau C l a p h a m, die noch keine feste Adresse ihres Mannes weiss, freundlichst den inliegenden Brief an ihn weiterschicken zu wollen, da Sie gewiss wissen, von welcher Zentralstelle aus er Nachrichten erhalten kann.

Würden Sie uns bitte mitteilen, was Ihnen aus dem von uns erbetenen Telegramm für Auslagen erwachsen, damit wir Ihnen diese vergüten können.

Mit vielem Dank

in vorzüglicher Hochachtung

Plate 8.3. Letter from Elizabeth Rotten to Miss Vulliamy dated 20 March 1918

On 20 April 1915, the Women's International League decided to ask Dr Thomas to speak on their behalf to Dr E Rotten at The Hague Women's Conference. Evidently there were many contacts with Elisabeth Rotten but there is no indication as to how Dr Rotten and Grace Vulliamy initially made contact with each other. Dr Rotten was a Theosophist and later became a Quaker by convincement. Both women's work was concerned with the problems of individual soldiers as indicated in this letter from Dr Rotten about a married couple who found it difficult to correspond with each other:

Dear Miss Vulliamy

I have just discovered that my comments of yesterday about Mr Lockwood were erroneously founded, insomuch that his wife, apart from the first words sent via the Red Cross, had received no news from him. However, he had at the time sent her his new address: Albert Lockwood, Ratcliff House, Barnes Street, Stepney, London. She is sending us a letter to forward on to him via Switzerland, as this route may be better at the moment than via Holland. If you would be so kind as to drop him a couple of lines to cheer him up however, that his wife has been advised of his current situation, then I would be extremely grateful. It would be a great relief for Mrs. L if she could soon follow her husband.

With many thanks and best regards

(Signed) E Rotten

Another letter from this period is again quoted in full. It is an example of the nerve-pressure caused to civilians by wartime restraint in a camp.

25 Wetherby Gardens, London SW5

November 25, 1917

Dear Miss Vulliamy

Several of the returned Ruhleben prisoners have told me of your extraordinary kindness in meeting them on their arrival in Holland. The great pleasure you gave to the men given me the courage to ask you to ?? of your great kindness also on my boy he will be among these Ruhleben prisoners who will be transferred to Holland to be interned here.

He is just 23 three years old but photos received some months ago poor boy he looks more like 32 years old. Being a very studious boy, (a student of New College, Oxford) with many interests he took a very active part in the so-called Ruhleben University and to get his mind and idealistic temperament away from subjects that worried him he has overdone study and work and I am afraid has suffered a bit from overconcentration of the mind. He was in the hospital for some time.

I would be so very grateful and thankful to you if you would give him a few words of welcome and if possible to induce the camp Dr (sic) and officials to take a kind interest in him. I don't think that I shall be able to come to Holland but could you perhaps advise me how I could go about get a fortnight leave for my boy I'm sure it would do his mind a world of good.

I am sending a book to your address which I would like my son to have on his arrival. They are his letters which were published last year by Douglas Sladen. I could not send the book very well to him before.

Please forgive me giving you all this trouble but you can imagine how anxious I feel.

Yours very truly, Mary Andrews. My son's name is Henry M Andrews.

The book is published with the title *In Ruhleben, letters from a prisoner to his mother.* It is edited by Douglas Brooke Wheelton Sladen and reveals that the author was an Oxford scholar who had been in the Officers' Training Corps before the war. While in the prison camp he lectured on modern philosophy. His name, which was not given at the time of publication, is revealed here as Henry M Andrews.

In January 1917 Grace Vulliamy told Ruth Fry that civilian prisoners from Ruhleben had been coming through almost continuously but at uncertain times. Most parties contained children who were a cause of great concern. For example, on 6 February 1916 there were younger women and children, from 'all over the world', but mostly Berlin, Hamburg or Dresden. Some were born in Germany, others elsewhere in the world. This party included Fred Erett age 15 whose home was in Ashby, Lincolnshire. Annie Stevens, age 10, was with her mother and Charles R Davis aged 8½ was taken by his grandfather to Flushing. Surprisingly, especially considering this was wartime, some children travelled alone, such as Louis Cross age 14, travelling alone to Battersea. In July 1916, three women, four children and

Plate 8.4 a page from Grace Vulliamy's scrapbook

one man were released, and Vulliamy telegraphed urgently for clothes. In July 1916 a party of five men all from Ruhleben camp came through. As they were all well educated men their remarks were considered to be of special interest. They stated, in connection with the feeding of the prisoners, that in consequence of the British Government considering measures of reprisal in England with potato allowance to prisoners withdrawn some time previously had been restored, but then German guards always went round to the dustbins each night to see if they could collect anything which might be of use to feed themselves and their families. With regard to the condition of the prisoners still at Ruhleben they said that if measures to effect their release were not soon put into effect there would be many more cases of madness.[247] As the parties came through, Grace Vulliamy and her colleagues were able to obtain impressions of the conditions prevalent in Germany at the time, though the accounts varied, of course, according to the different localities from which the prisoners came. As time went on and food, clothing and other essentials of life became more and more difficult to obtain, conditions became more distressing:[248]

Plate 8.5 Nurse with two prisoners from Ruhleben who had been repatriated They are apparently wearing the uniforms of wounded soldiers.

> The accounts of the camps however vary considerably and in April 1916 a party of somewhat stolid looking men from Ruhleben told us they had nothing to complain of with regard to the camp except that had it not been for the food sent from home they would certainly have starved.

[247] GCV Chapter II

[248] Vulliamy Papers. Holland camps. GCV

Nevertheless, Miss Vulliamy became increasingly concerned about conditions in the military PoW camps when she saw the men's mental and physical state, heard their stories, and recognised the underlying consistency in all. The descriptions of Ruhleben were similarly reliable. However, the released men had been given 'exaggerated reports of the internment of Germans in Britain, and their treatment in the camps' which she was at pains to dispel. She was not in a position to do anything directly to alleviate the suffering of prisoners as a whole – that would require talks at the highest level between Britain and Germany. She was not one to waste her time in useless sentimentality, so immediately started gathering information from individual prisoners about their treatment which in due course she forwarded to the relevant Authority. For example:

> In June of the same year [1916] a man who had been captured early in the war and imprisoned at Wittenburg reported that prisoners there were suffering badly. There has been an epidemic of typhus which had killed in large numbers and he himself for trivial offences had been flogged and then tied to a tree with his hands above his head for two hours at a stretch.

Adelaide Livingstone as Secretary of the Committee on the Treatment by the Enemy of British PoWs, sent out the report prepared by Mr Justice Younger on the typhus epidemic at Wittenburg. Conditions were indescribable. British men were sometimes wearing French, Belgian or Russian uniforms and lying about on straw on the floor sometimes dying, sometimes delirious. In at least one compound there were no beds, and bedpans were unobtainable. From this kind of personal knowledge she could certainly share in Grace's concern for prisoners of war.

With Grace's training she would have known that trying to discuss things that are private, upsetting, unformed, can feel difficult and risky, but the men managed to talk to Grace Vulliamy. She wrote:

> It is characteristic of the British soldier that once freed from conditions of discomfort, pain and suffering, he becomes mute upon the subject of his former misery and touching the prisoner much persistent and tactful enquiry was soon needed in order to extract from his unwilling lips any kind of detailed or comprehensive account of conditions in the prison camp from which he had been released. Owing to that innate reticence it was difficult for many to realise anything of the discomfort, wretchedness, misery pain and suffering which thousands of our prisoners endure for many weeks, months and even years, but when they reached Holland their minds [were] innocent of the seal of forgetfulness with which they so splendidly and so pathetically close

> to as soon as they realised their freedom and knew that those long days of unhappiness were done with for ever.

She also made *Suggestions* which she hoped could be incorporated into international agreements to prevent abuse of prisoners in the future. These can be found in the British Cabinet Papers and in the National Archive at Kew, London.

Some people's family allegiances had become especially stressful due to the war. Amongst one party transferred in July 1916 was a boy of 16 whose stepbrother was in the German army and who had another brother in the British Army. Such torn loyalties must have been very difficult to deal with, especially for one so young. In the same party being returned to Britain there was also one lame prisoner and one suffering from internal problems, thought to be caused by mistreatment when a prisoner, and another in a highly nervous condition. On another occasion that month[249] when five highly educated prisoners crossed at Gennep, they said that if 'measures were not taken to obtain the release of men still interned in Ruhleben, the camp would soon be little better than a mad house.'[250] After British and German governments agreed to exchange civilian prisoners over the age of 45, the others at Ruhleben realized they would remain captive a very long time.

In her *Memorandum* Miss Vulliamy's concern for mental welfare is clearly evident. She wrote:

> Since the transfer of 400 civilian prisoners from Ruhleben to Holland, the rest of the camp who have no hope of exchange under the agreement of 1917, seem to have sunk into despair and mental inertia, due partly to the fact that practically all the leaders of the camp have been repatriated or interned in Holland. The most serious result of this has been the rapid increase of nervous diseases and insanity, especially among the younger men. Their whole moral future is being endangered by this prolonged activity.[251]

Few at that time would have understood the 'despair and mental inertia' she mentions, putting it down to innate lack of 'moral fibre' to which the solution offered would have been 'pull yourself together'. Vulliamy clearly shows it as being the effect of 'no hope', the lack of leadership that might have helped

---

[249] Vulliamy Papers 7.7.1916

[250] V Papers. Report 11.7.16

[251] Memorandum on Conditions Amongst Prisoners of War and Civilians in Germany and Holland By GCV

the men and the impossibility of the normal activity of life, 'moral future' carrying implications of homosexuality.

She prepared several copies of a document entitled *A Few Points to Dispel False Impressions of The Camp* for distribution to those who might have had a false impression of Ruhleben's facilities and the care given, and which in her opinion needed correcting. It is reproduced in full in the Appendix. It shows that being imprisoned in Ruhleben resulted for some men in physical weakness, blindness and lunacy while some of the 'better class' who could afford it, took to drink to 'drown their sorrows' and help them get through it. Dr Wiener's Sanatorium was not excluded from her incisive criticism. Patients received indifferent attention. They were exploited and affected by doses of sleeping draughts. The food was insufficient. There was overcrowding and interference with patients' parcels. But the sanatorium is elsewhere described as more bearable than the main camp!

Ruhleben and Miss Vulliamy's activities for the prisoners were later described in a Johannesburg newspaper. When Miss Vulliamy arrived there in 1924 one of the prisoners she had helped sent a letter to *The Star*.[252] He described a raw January morning in 1917 when he brought a small party of nine ex-Ruhleben prisoners to a small station on the Dutch border. A lady approached the railway carriage and remarked:

> Well Mr Cohn where have you been? Mr Rowntree and I have been waiting for you for the last two days!'

This of course, was not meant to be taken seriously and was perhaps an example of what Wilson described as flirting. He explained that there had been a blunder with the paperwork at the German Ministry of War and that the German railways were dislocated.

> Miss Vulliamy, for of course it was she, then stopped teasing and asked if they would like some breakfast and would bacon and eggs, fresh rolls and butter do? Mr Cohn wrote 'oh would it not! Imagine after 2½ years of Ruhleben camp food and its other horrors! And I shall never forget the faces of my – so to speak – children (the eldest 78, and I, the leader, was the youngest) when hot fresh rolls were put on the table by the caterer of the Dutch station.

This letter then explains other ways Miss Vulliamy helped passengers she was escorting.

---

[252] 14.3.24

After breakfast Miss Vulliamy attended to our telegrams to friends and then took us personally down to Flushing where three of us, who could afford it, put up at an hotel; the other six she took to her home for refugees; my charges told me afterwards that they were very happy there and right royally treated. The next day this untiring lady took us to the British Consul to arrange for passports and passages to England.

Mr Cohn described Miss Vulliamy as a member of the Society of Friends, which strictly speaking she was not, but most people were unaware of this. He said that later on when in England, as intelligence officer to prisoners of war camps, he met in the course of his duties other members of the Society, he was greatly impressed by the large-heartedness of its members. He asked for his thanks to be expressed once more to Miss Vulliamy. Miss Vulliamy was helped by Howard Rowntree in the work of transferring civilian prisoners passing through Holland from German camps such as Ruhleben. She was, during this summer, thinking of leaving, but because of the difficulty of handing over the work, the complications caused by constant change of workers, the difficulties of travelling and the civilian prisoners, was wondering whether it was right to do so. However, she was able, through Francis Aveling of the British Legation at The Hague, to put the names of certain prisoners onto the list for internment and repatriation. It was evidently not entirely the choice of the Germans, therefore, as to who was to be repatriated. Her report on Allen Gordon Strawbridge who was interned at Ruhleben, was annotated with the words 'Above report handed to Mr Aveling for name to be put on list for internment and repatriation'.

Strawbridge was an Australian, born in Adelaide. About 26 years of age. He is the son of the late Surveyor-General of Adelaide. He first studied architecture then devoted himself to art. He studied in Paris some time before the war. He was very delicate from birth suffering greatly with his digestive organs which often incapacitated him for weeks at a time from work of any sort. In 1913 he had a very severe attack of typhoid which further seriously affected his health. He is a thorough artist completely absorbed in his work and of a sensitive and reserved nature. He was naturally very cheerful and optimistic but now his last letters show that he is in despair and quite hopeless with a tendency to black melancholy. There are signs that his mind is becoming unbalanced. He has not the physical strength to resist the privations of captivity which tell harder upon a sensitive nature.

When war broke out he was painting in the neutral Grand Duchy of Luxembourg. He was first detained and then arrested and though a civilian, sent to the military camp of Grissen [Gruissan]? where he was forced to consort with French black troops and Russians amongst black troops.

The racism current at the time in the mention of French and Russian men amongst these black troops and the phrase 'forced to consort with' are inescapable. There is a subtle difference in the attitude towards German prisoners – they were after all white, even though they were the enemy. Another newspaper article describes the arrival of some older prisoners at Gravesend on 13 January:

> Wearing the white cross, superimposed on the red disc – the distinctive badge of all civilians returned from Germany – nine more repatriated prisoners arrived here by the Flushing boat this evening. All are over 45, and few are under 55. All men of 55, except a ship's captain, are discharged: the Mistress of the Seas must not have the benefit of the services of a man who understands the navigation of ship.
>
> I talked with half a dozen of the men, all of whom decided that their names should not be mentioned, as the Germans read the statements in the English papers and retaliate on those known to be their friends. One told me something of the conditions of Ruhleben camp during the two years he was a prisoner there. He was first sent to Gissen, where he came into contact with some of our own soldiers all of whom were treated with scant consideration. Afterwards he was removed to Ruhleben where the conditions for the first 12 months were horrible. They improved about 18 months ago about which time parcels began to arrive from England. 'People wonder why we look so well, when the German folk are thin, pinched, and starved' said one of the returned men 'but it is not a matter for surprise when it is remembered that we have been kept by our own folks at home.'
>
> ... The arrogance of the early days of the war has entirely disappeared. No longer do the guards hustle the captives, no longer do they threaten them, or boast of what they are going to do to the hated English.... But there is one thing at Ruhleben which is almost unendurable, and that is the mud.

The article continued with information about the sanatorium and the fact that there were 'No medical comforts'. However, it also gives insights into the effect of the Allied blockade of Germany.

> All the half-dozen who told me their stories have been for various periods in the sanatorium at_Ruhleben, a place more tolerable. The Ruhleben sanatorium is in a residential quarter in which well-to-do people live. At first these people were very arrogant towards the prisoners, and the children especially, taught by the elders, were most insolent. They are now glad to linger around the compounds and eagerly snatch the bits of the food sent out from home, which the

> English toss over the 8 foot wire fence to them. That incident was even more eloquent of Germany's real economic condition than the long queues of people standing outside shops waiting for food – a sight which they saw as soon as they came along in the trains from Ruhleben to the railway station.[253]

In fact, Hindenburg's memoirs blamed 'disruptions and revolutions on the homefront' for Germany's collapse and the total German civilian deaths were 762,106, about the same as from Allied bombing in WW2.[254]

---

[253] Wiener – *Hungry Germans At Ruhleben*. Newspaper article unidentified. Grace's note 'arrived in Holland 12 Jan 1917'. 'First batch of civilian exchange men over 45'.

[254] Martin Gilbert. *First World War*. 1995. 256, 515

CHAPTER 9

GRACE'S CHANGE OF WORK. PREPARING FOR PRISONERS' INTERNMENT IN HOLLAND

Prisoners in Holland. Grace's uncertainty

Early in 1917 when Grace Vulliamy found that her help was most needed amongst the military Prisoners of War, as the Quakers repudiated connection with the military, she proposed leaving her work with them so that she could do this with impunity. The Quakers were very concerned when it looked as if Grace was leaving them. Her ability to empathize with and put herself in other people's shoes and to negotiate with authorities was noted at the time as being remarkable. Having heard from Harold Ellis of her decision to leave the Holland work, Howard Rowntree wrote to her from Uden saying that she had been much in the thoughts of the Uden workers since they heard. He wrote:

> Such a step must mean a big break for you and it must hurt tremendously to leave the direction of work affecting so many people's lives which you have seen growing up under your hand. One sometimes wonders what the Belgian refugees will feel after the war, but I am sure it will be their recollection of you and the enormous variety of ways in which you helped that will last in their minds. I do hope you feel that sense of work well done above the pain of leaving it all.
>
> May I say one thing which has always surprised me in talking to you and that is your extraordinary loyalty to the Society of Friends. I feel it just that in other circumstances you might have felt we were a body of curious cranks but during the nearly two years that I have been here it has always been a wonder to me to see you looking at problems as you conceived the Society of Friends would look at them.
>
> I am sorry to hear that you have been a-bed and hope you will soon be able to come up here. We can really offer you warmth. With the best of wishes for you in your future work.

Grace's uncertainty over the best work for her to do communicated itself to her family and on 12 February 1917, her aunt Rose of Riversdale, Ware, Hertfordshire sent a letter to Ruth Fry asking for help in contacting her. She wrote back that it was 'difficult to communicate with Holland where your niece now is' but said she was 'Posting your letter on to her. I've been expecting her to come over with prisoners, but this month's exchange is postponed.' On another occasion Miss Gunter tried to contact Grace by approaching her parents. Grace seemed wryly amused and wrote 'my parents don't know anything about me!' It is unlikely therefore that they knew anything about her connection with the Prisoner of War exchange.

HET LEVEN

De Lusitania-relletjes te Londen.

Het Lusitania-incident heeft te Londen, evenals overal elders in Engeland, veel kwaad bloed gezet. Menige winkel, waarvan de naam van den eigenaar tot het vermoeden aanleiding gaf, dat hij Duitscher of van Duitsche afkomst was, moest er aan gelooven. Op de bovenste foto zien wij het sigarenmagazijn van een zekeren Schoenfeld door een opgewonden volksmenigte vernield en geplunderd, waarom, zooals op onze tweede foto zichtbaar is, het restant van den inboedel onder toezicht der politie in veiligheid werd gebracht.

Plate 9.1 Pages from *Het Leven*
showing riots in London as a result of the Lusitania sinking

Prisoner of War Department

In October 1916 Lord Newton was appointed Controller of the newly established Prisoner of War Department and is thereby credited with negotiating the release of thousands of British prisoners of war. On 4 February 1917, Grace Vulliamy called at the British Legation at The Hague to seek a letter for Lord Newton from Walter Townley, the British Minister, because she was returning to England and was anxious to find out exactly how matters stood with regard to the exchange of wounded and civilian prisoners of war. Lord Newton should be able to give her the necessary information. On his behalf Owen Monk told Grace on 17 April that there was 'no prospect of exchanges of prisoners pending the resumption of the Dutch service between Holland and the UK.' This had been stopped due to the German announcement of unrestricted submarine warfare on 1 February 1917. On 5 February Germany declared that all waters surrounding Britain were a war zone. Now military wounded were to be sent by hospital ship flying a British flag or not at all, and this was 'made inevitable due to the German "naval" policy'. In May 1917 Grace was again thinking of leaving Holland. The exchange of wounded had been stopped again because of the torpedoing of hospital ships, and of trawlers and ships belonging to neutral countries such as Norway, Holland and America. It had shocked Britain when in November that year the hospital ship *Anglia* had struck a mine and sunk with the loss of 85 lives. The torpedoing of the liner *Lusitania*, on 8 May 1915 off Ireland, carrying 1313 passengers and a crew of 665, horrified the world. Grace was evidently stirred by these events and kept newspaper cuttings - one showing anti-German rioters in London protesting at the loss of the *Lusitania.*

Walter Townley eventually wrote to Lord Newton on 23 May:

> I have heard nothing but praise for the admirable work done by Miss Vulliamy in connection with wounded and civilians on their way to England. She has asked me for a letter to you as she wants to find out exactly how matters stand with regard to the exchange of wounded and civilian PoWs. She has seen the director of the Flushing Line who says he is willing to keep in commission for the purpose of repatriation the *SS Zeeland* which is now used to bring back Dutch subjects from England.
>
> The only information I was able to give Miss Vulliamy was that contained in the Foreign Office dispatch No. 670 of May 10 in which it is stated that the Government had every intention of resuming repatriation of civilians as soon as circumstances permit, but that at present the great difficulty is to ship from England the relatively large number of Germans entitled to repatriations in exchange.'

In further confirmation of the importance of Grace's work, Maurice de Bunsen at the Foreign Office told Townley that as the government had every intention of resuming repatriation as soon as possible, 'it would seem desirable therefore that Miss Vulliamy should remain in Holland'. This is another unusual reaction for such high-ranking government office to have towards a woman – women were held to be not only insufficiently intelligent to vote but also generally unreliable and troublesome

Grace could be under no illusion about the dangers of crossing the Channel but she did so over forty times. Grace's collection of photographs includes one of the Dutch tank steamer *Artemis* which is captioned 'German Ruthlessness at Sea' and was torpedoed on 7 February 1916, a year almost to the day after Germany's announcement. Some of these attacks indicated that German torpedo boats were becoming heavier and faster. Dutch boats were used to transport prisoners across the Channel and understandably the Dutch decided from time to time that they would no longer be used for this purpose, for example on 1 August 1916. This meant that people had no choice but to wait until the service was restored.

Plate 9. 2 'German Ruthlessness at Sea'
Artemis, Torpedoed 7 February 1916

Grace befriended a survivor from the Dutch motor schooner *Timor* which was sunk off the North Hinder[255] on 19 July 1917 at about 6.00 a.m. while on her way from London to Rotterdam with a cargo of pitch. The lugger *Eendracht III* KW102 landed the seven survivors and among them was a British girl from Gravesend who had stowed away on board so as to be able to cross to Holland and see her lover at Vlaardingen. One newspaper version of events says she was discovered when the vessel was torpedoed by a German submarine. Aged 21, she had no father or mother and became engaged to marry a Dutch sailor whose ship had been detained in London.

Plate 9.3 The Stowaway from the *Timor*

They concocted a plan to get her to the Netherlands without paying and were to be married as soon as possible. A Dutch sailor took her aboard and hid her among the sails and nets. The vessel left either on Sunday or Monday a.m. – the accounts differ. A shell from a German submarine went through the ship nearly killing the girl. She 'emerged and discovered herself to the crew as they were entering their lifeboat.' She was taken into it and they were picked up by a fishing smack and taken to Ymulden, the outer port of Amsterdam. She related her story to the British Vice Consul and was sent back to England. This photograph of the stowaway shows her on the balcony of Grace's home at The Hague.

Prisoner Exchange

---

[255] A dangerous area of the North Sea off Flushing with sandbanks creating tidal currents.

Prisoners of war are a burden to their captors. They require more than the basics of life to be provided – as well as food, shelter and clothing, guards are needed. It is to the advantage of belligerent countries therefore to organise it so that at least some prisoners can be returned to their home countries or otherwise removed. The Germans were in favour of exchange but opposed to interning able bodied prisoners in a neutral country. The British Government, especially the War Office, the Cabinet and the Admiralty considered that exchange would prolong the war. Despite this, in February 1915 the British Government agreed to exchange sick and wounded PoWs between Britain and Germany across the Netherlands and the first exchanges began almost immediately.

When the LGB withdrew its official involvement in the transfers, Friends' participation was even more necessary. In October, the Foreign Office asked the Quakers to send representatives every month to the German frontier to meet British civilians being repatriated from internment in Belgium and from German camps such as Ruhleben and they asked Grace to be their Representative. She organised their reception at the Belgian-German frontier on their journey to Flushing, housing and then transporting them to England, sometimes escorting them herself. Here, her mental nursing training and experience were vital. Also that month the Aliens Committee asked for three Belgian children aged four, six and eight to be brought to England, suggesting that Grace Vulliamy might look after them on the boat. However, the 6th and 7th of each month had to be avoided, as she took part in regular exchanges of severely wounded men from Germany on those dates. There were also additional emergency exchanges. These all involved train journeys of eight to ten hours, two or three times a week. Consequently, she spent many hours at the various frontiers.

Not all prisoners were adults. Children were especially vulnerable. Grace wrote:

> Amongst the civilian prisoners was a small child of 7 or 8, Adele Phillips, whose parents had brought her early in 1914 to Germany from S. Africa (Cape Town I think) for medical .... treatment, as it was a long [?] case the parents left her in Germany at the outbreak of war. The hospital where the child was, was turned into a Military Hospital and the child was placed in a family where she was most unhappy.

In July, Francis Aveling of the British Legation at The Hague instructed that Grace should discover where the child was and whether she could return to South Africa. She would need to be accompanied because, understandably, the child's mother did not want her to travel alone. Grace was asked if she would do it. She wrote:

> Thanks to the kindness of a German nurse we heard of the position and finally the Germans agreed to send her into Holland where I took charge of her and brought her to England.

Years later Grace 'had the pleasure of meeting her again.'

Arrangements for the exchange of prisoners from Germany into neutral Holland were made at the highest levels and necessitated a simultaneous exchange of German prisoners from Britain. The difficulty was not so much to transport from Holland the limited number of British as to transport to Holland the relatively large number of German prisoners of war entitled to repatriations in exchange. The German Hospital train was always met by the Dutch at Roosendaal and escorted by them to Flushing, where they superintended removal of the wounded from train to boat and thence to Tilbury. Grace's task was to arrange to meet the British prisoners at the border, provide food and drink when needed, and with the help of the Dutch to arrange for a doctor to take over from the American doctor, who being neutral, might accompany the men from Germany into Holland. She also needed to arrange for another doctor to meet the train at Flushing. Then the party was transferred on board ship.[256] The greatest difficulty was caused by alcohol on the train and boat which rendered the men difficult to control and Grace made arrangements to change its availability. Her role also involved liaising between different authorities, passing on relevant information such as about the condition of prisoners, making reports on each exchange and suggesting ways of smoothing relationships; one of her suggestions was that the British Red Cross should send a letter of appreciation to the Dutch Red Cross.

Only a few voluntary organisations were available to help military personnel. The Red Cross, founded by Henri Dunant on 4 August 1870, aimed to help military sick and wounded. There was no similar organization aimed at civilians, who were presumed not to need such care. However, in war civilians held society together and formed the grounding for the armed services; this was tacitly acknowledged by use of the blockade as a weapon of war and its continuation after the Armistice. The Young Men's Christian Association was founded in 1844 in London to deal with social and welfare issues of non-combatant men. In wartime this service extended to combatants. Both these organisations were dependent

[256] V Papers. 15.5.16 GCV to Sir Louis Mallet, British Red Cross

on funds raised voluntarily and although the government used them it did not support them financially. They were therefore important but limited in scope. In Holland, Grace Vulliamy acted as temporary representative of both organizations and her concern for prisoners, the conditions in which they were held, and ultimately their release and return home, was in the tradition of Elizabeth Fry. Grace organized the arrival of the prisoners at their destination, but difficulties arose through lack of on-going communication, military arrogance or disregard for suffering. For example, Mr Carbutt of the Red Cross arranged with Grace that his men would meet the prisoners at Victoria Station, but afterwards she wrote to him that 'the military authorities wouldn't allow your men to help.' One of the [German] prisoners was returned to Germany in a very dirty condition and insufficiently clad. This seems to indicate lack of concern for the Germans by the British, but is the only example found in these papers.

Grace travelled across the Channel several times in 1917 including in March when she returned to the Netherlands after taking prisoners over. During that visit to England, Lord Newton asked to see Grace and in order to save her time he suggested that perhaps she would like to see him after she had visited Lord Drogheda on the 24th. It has not been possible to discover anything more about her visit to Lord Drogheda or how Lord Newton knew about it. Nonetheless, it indicates that Grace's movements were important enough to be followed by those with interest in the same line of work. It also shows that Newton, however unpopular with prisoners, could be considerate of others on occasion.[257] 'Mrs' Livingstone was also mentioned as being very anxious to see Grace and would postpone her call until her return from France. Adelaide Livingstone was the first woman to be included in a deputation that negotiated for prisoner of war exchange, a colleague who became a close friend to Grace Vulliamy. Grace also spent some time in England in August and while there, visited General Belfield. In retirement from the Army this officer became Director of Prisoner of War work, negotiating prisoner exchanges and improvements in the treatment of prisoners.

Dame Adelaide Livingstone, also known as 'Colonel' Livingstone, was the Honorary Secretary of the Government Committee on the Treatment by the Enemy of British Prisoners of War. Dame Adelaide, formerly Miss Stickney, was an American Quaker who in the early days of the War made trips to Holland to escort parties of children, young servants, old and

[257] Letter from Owen Monk prisoners of War Department, Downing Street. 13 August 1917

helpless women and mothers with children back behind German lines[258] bringing out Allied women and girls. She was reputed to come into contact with Edith Cavell but this is unverified. She and Ellen Walshe of the International Women's Relief Committee encountered the vast chaotic influx into Flushing of 80,000 refugees in 1914 while escorting parties of German girls through Holland. On her marriage to a British officer Miss Stickney was no longer a neutral and had to discontinue these rescue activities. However, because she had reported to Lord Robert Cecil he later enlisted her aid in the Prisoners of War Department under Lord Newton, whose reputation among the prisoners was of an unhelpful obstructionist. He limited the number of parcels prisoners were able to receive, meaning many prisoners went hungry and were clothed in rags. Newton was reported in English newspapers as having made a statement in the House regarding prisoners' disgraceful treatment at an officer's camp merely because they were British. But in explanation and mitigation of the captors' behaviour, Newton said it was because the British prisoners did not behave. This caused huge resentment among prisoners and indicates how strong were attitudes towards social class. Newton was a Lord, some of the officers were not even Gentleman but members of the middle-class. In fact, most prisoners were of the middle or working classes and were an unknown form of the social order as far as those above them were concerned. However, Grace's photos include several of Adelaide in Holland. Adelaide accompanied Newton several times to The Hague to confer with German Generals on the treatment of prisoners and was able to meet with her friend Grace. Livingstone now wrote saying she hoped Grace's conversation with Belfield would have made him realise the necessity of speed and hoping Grace would be able to visit her on the Tuesday. Adelaide wrote: 'I am glad you expect the exchange to take place soon. With me it is becoming a case of hope deferred.'

YMCA and Red Cross

Around this time, when officer prisoners began to be exchanged, Grace Vulliamy was asked by the YMCA to work with them so before agreeing she needed to know what the responsibilities would entail. Baroness de Brienen cabled her saying that she would be wanted to organise clubs, workshops, and entertainments for released prisoners with the YMCA's representative and to cooperate with the executive committee. The

[258] K. Storr. *Excluded from the Record.* Peter Lang, 2010. 16, 92.

Baroness was English born, Dutch by marriage, with homes in both Holland and England.[259]

In July, Mr Carbutt also contacted her to find out if she was officially asked, would she act as British Red Cross representative in Holland. Grace said she would be glad to do it. She must have known she was taking on a lot so during September 1917 Grace finally left the Quakers and working under the War Office concentrated on the wounded and special exchange prisoners from Germany who were to be interned in Holland. In addition, the Dutch Government asked her to take over the Medical Administration and she arranged for convalescent homes where necessary, saw to the building arrangements, and other matters. In fact, she discovered her decision meant she was tied to the office desk too much. However, she was still able to meet all the exchanged prisoners at the frontier, and her presence there was no surprise to the Dutch who had refused permission to the Red Cross and YMCA personnel to meet the prisoners. In each case she took the prisoners' names and cabled them home, thus avoiding considerable delay and difficulties. From the beginning when making her lists of prisoners' names, and before they were allowed into England she was able to identify those who were really German spies who had either been at an English public school or were using the papers of English prisoners who had died. Her niece Poppy asked her after the war how she knew when such men were imposters and she replied that she 'just had a feeling'.[260]

How much her prisoner lists were appreciated is shown by a letter from Carbutt dated 9 November. He wrote:

> 're the lists which you so kindly provided of the civilian prisoners that were repatriated. These you always used to let us have when the Prisoners came to Gravesend or Tilbury and were of immense use and there was great competition to get a copy of them. Do you think you would be able to manage these lists again when the exchange is made at Boston? I know that it will be very difficult for you if they send as many men as they suggest but if you could possibly help us in this way it would be of great use.'

[259] Baroness De Brienen. Married 14 APR 1904 to Ward, Cyril Augustus, Capt., Hon.

[260] Letter from Poppy Vulliamy to Daniel Vullliamy, 27.10.1989

Preparing for prisoners' internment: premises

At this stage the British workers did not have suitable premises for offices. On 25 August, Arthur Stanley of the Joint War Committee asked her if she would 'look out for any buildings, workshops and so on, near the camps' in Holland but not to commit herself to them at this stage. He also asked her to consult with Sir Walter Townley about the Red Cross having a working committee in Holland and to suggest a few names of appropriate people. This latter request was perhaps the more difficult to fulfil: conscription meant most younger men were now serving in the armed forces or were in reserved occupations and the remaining men often filled two roles. Perhaps as a result of these 'behind the scenes' activities, on 31 August 1917 Grace proposed that Major General Sir John Hanbury Williams[261] should be in 'complete charge,' 'that the YMCA and British Red Cross would have their offices in the same building and refer to [him] on all important matters.'[262] As she was now the temporary representative of both organisations, this made work considerably more convenient for her and everyone else.

Consequently, in mid-September she went with the General to find somewhere for their offices, but it was extremely difficult to find anywhere suitable. At last he decided on a place over a theatre, with a rent of about £300 a year, which Grace considered rather high. The General was willing to pay £150, but the YMCA only wanted one room which left three for the Red Cross. Additional expenses such as for light, telephone, and taxes would come to another £50 a year for each body, but a decision needed to be made quickly or they would lose the place. In England Sir Arthur Yapp had been appointed Director of Food Economy under the Food Controller, now Lord Rhondda, and this placed a burden on him which was more than one man could carry, so he decided to give four days to his new work and keep three for the YMCA. Hanbury Williams now acted as head of the Red Cross and a working committee of about 20 people was wanted. Grace was asked for suggestions and agreed she would let Stanley know.

Whereas organising transport for comparatively few prisoners did not need a large amount of administration, the numbers now to come through were a different matter. A Red Cross representative was urgently needed to sign a contract for land seen by Lord Sandwich, (representing the British Red

[261] British POW Dept. Jan 1918. Hanbury Williams Director.

[262] Letter from 59 Daendelsstraat, Den Haag, from GCV as from Red Cross. Sindoro can't get into Boston, so Zeeland boats should be used instead. Making of artificial limbs by the prisoners proposed

Cross and the Order of St John) and offered by the town with rent one florin per year, and drainage, fencing etc at the expense of the tenant. The YMCA agreed to share land that was suitable for workshops etc. But office furniture must be paid per month and was needed immediately.[263]

GOVERNMENT COMMITTEE ON THE TREATMENT BY THE ENEMY OF BRITISH PRISONERS OF WAR.

18, Carlton House Terrace, S.W.,
6th April, 1916.

Sir,

I have the honour to state that the Chairman of this Committee, Mr. Justice Younger, has prepared the enclosed Report on the conditions obtaining at Wittenberg Camp during the typhus epidemic of last year.

The information upon which this Report is based has been collected from prisoners of war repatriated from Wittenberg, and especially from Major Priestley, R.A.M.C., Captain Vidal, R.A.M.C., and Captain Lauder, R.A.M.C., who were sent to the camp soon after the outbreak of the epidemic and who were only recently released from Germany. The Committee considered it advisable to hold back the Report until the evidence of these officers was available.

I am, Sir,
Your obedient Servant,
(Signed) Adelaide Livingstone,
Hon. Secretary.

The Under-Secretary of State for Foreign Affairs.

Plate 9.4 Letter signed by Adelaide Livingstone

So Grace now acted as Red Cross and YMCA representative in Holland.[264] These organisations both wanted her to work exclusively with each of them but she preferred to be independent and to help wherever most needed. But these arrangements were temporary. The YMCA also needed male organizers. Mr H A Dennis, a 'rattling good chap,' went out on 27 October 1917 to work in Holland accompanied by Mr Clapperton whose experience and knowledge of YMCA work would make him invaluable as Mr Dennis's colleague. On 24 August, Arthur Yapp wrote saying he was happy to agree to Grace's suggestion about the payment of expenses but

263 7.11.1917. Cable from Grace to Sir Arthur Stanley, British Red Cross, London.
264 IWM. Prisoners 17/1

Faulkner was having difficulty getting his passport, so the temporary arrangement might last longer than originally planned. Both van Tuyll and Mr Yapp thanked her for her 'splendid service' and 'all that she had pledged to do' during Mr Faulkner's visit in October 1917. She had suggested that Mr Faulkner could use her house as a temporary office. Dennis and Clapperton were to cross by the first Admiralty boat and Yapp hoped Baroness Brienen would soon be over to act with and for them. Yapp further said it was a great satisfaction to the National Council that Grace was there to co-operate with them in regard to the ladies' work.[265] This is an interesting comment in view of the fact that most of Grace's work was with men but it was usual for women to deal with women's issues and there were women and children among the prisoners, so it was necessary to have a woman helper. He added that Mrs Picton Warlow, having left for England in late October, was already there so work could start quickly.

On 30 August Lieutenant M Dillon of the RNVR at the British Consulate in Amsterdam wrote to Grace introducing Mrs Picton Warlow who had been running a Bread Fund for Prisoners of War and had also got the question of the British men's Separation Allowances settled when they were first interned. He said that an agreement about the prisoners had been ratified now and wondered whether Picton Warlow would be one of the lucky ones under this agreement. He sent to Grace copies of letters Mrs Picton Warlow had received from her Petty Officer husband who was now a Prisoner of War in Vergeltungs Lager. He wrote about the continual overworking and under feeding of the prisoners which resulted in two men dropping unconscious at work on Easter Saturday and five men being unable to continue the previous day. The work itself was not hard but the hours were far too long and food insufficient. He had written a report and sent it to the British Secretary of War and asked Grace to confirm whether this was now Lloyd George[266] which Grace was able to do. The substance of Picton Warlow's letter was confirmed by many other male prisoners who had written to their local members of Parliament about the prisoners' treatment.

Although the Picton Warlow letter was censored what remains is surprisingly explicit but the writer said he thought the Germans would allow

---

[265] Sir A K Yapp, National Council, YMCA, London. 5.12.1917

[266] In June 1916 Lloyd George succeeded Lord Kitchener (whose ship was sunk by a mine while on his way to Russia) as Secretary of State for War. Asquith resigned in December 1916 and Lloyd George became Prime Minister, with the nation demanding he take vigorous charge of the war. Many other male prisoners had also written to their local members of Parliament about the prisoners' treatment.

it to get through because they wanted the withdrawal of their own prisoners, who were rumoured to be being treated worse than the British were by their captors in Germany. On 17 August, Adelaide Livingstone wrote to Grace asking 'I wonder how Mrs Picton Warlow struck you when you saw her the other day' and hoping that Grace would have time to visit her before they went back to Holland. By 3 December 1917 Mrs PIcton Warlow's health had deteriorated. Adelaide wrote: 'Fortunately she seems to be enormously impressed with your great ability.'[267]

In fact, Capt. Picton Warlow, in a party of 40 officers and 252 NCOs, arrived at Scheveningen on the night of 23 January 1918. Another member of the party was Captain Maclean who had been a prisoner of war since 1914 Theoretically, then, both these men are somewhere in this picture. Grace got to know them both and on 8 September 1918, she was present at the wedding of Captain Alexander Maclean and Hon. Muriel Burns. The Bride was given away by Sir Walter Townley; other people known to Grace such as the Prince de Ligne, Captain and Mrs Craig, were also among the guests.

The Reception was at the British Legation. British social life somehow continued in wartime Holland.

Red Cross - Housing

Nevertheless, things were moving very slowly partly because the Dutch had made no preparation for the prisoners although they had invited them to come to Holland. Complications cropped up daily and the Dutch Red Cross was finding it very difficult even to get the boats settled chiefly on account of cost. The housing problem was also very hard; buildings for workshops and other uses seemed impossible to find and Grace thought temporary buildings would have to be erected. She asked Sir Arthur if he considered it a good plan to ask the Belgian government to guarantee to buy any such buildings after the war for transportation into Belgium.

This is where the Belgian Repatriation Fund might be useful and Grace Vulliamy wrote to Eleanor Acland asking whether the Repatriation Committee could do anything to help.[268] Eleanor Acland, (Mrs Francis Acland) the Liberal democratic suffragist, was Honorary Secretary of the Belgian Repatriation Fund which was established in September 1914 by Madame Vandervelde, the English wife of the pacifist Emile Vandervelde a member of the Belgian Cabinet and Belgian Socialist leader, whose

---

[267] Adelaide Livingstone to Grace at 'British Prisoners of War Department, The Hague.'

[268] 21 December 1915

influence, according to the *Englishwoman* (July-September 1915: 124), 'was one of the great factors inspiring Belgium's resistance'. Eleanor Acland organised fund- and goods-raising and visited Holland to see schemes for housing refugees in Dutch internment camps.[269] There are indications that she met Grace Vulliamy while there. The Fund was putting up buildings in camps to be used as houses by refugees

Baroness de Brienen was worried that the men might be sent to Gouda or Rotterdam which were completely unsuitable because they were low lying and damp. The men were coming to Holland with undermined constitutions owing to privations and neglect during their long captivity and were consequently more sensitive to cold and damp. She was convinced that the men would get illnesses such as colds, malaria and rheumatism. If camps were to be built, they must be on sand. She wanted the hotels in Scheveningen given over to the officers of whom there would be about 700. She added that the only thing being talked about in London was peace, which they thought would be before the New Year.[270] It was not to be.

There were also to be restricted districts where hospitals could not be placed but until the Dutch said which these districts were, it was impossible to start anything. The number of prisoners was also uncertain. At first it was thought there would be 8,000 but by 18 September this was thought to be more than would actually arrive. Some were going to be placed at Scheveningen and some at Sandvoort. There were also difficulties in relation to their own staff coming and going. Mr Faulkner proved to be very able but Grace found he was 'not a gentleman' so although he arranged the business side excellently his arrangements on the social side did not reach the standards required.

In order to care for the wounded it was necessary to find buildings that could be used as hospitals and medical staff were needed to look after the patients. It was also desirable that they should be kept together as far as possible and within easy reach of wherever the offices were to be. The YMCA and Red Cross were to carry out the greater part of work amongst the prisoners, so it was essential that the work of those two bodies should be centralised as far as possible. It was very likely that invaluable assistance would be given by Dutch and Anglo Dutch families especially from the neighbourhood of The Hague and Haarlem so these areas were preferable.

---

[269] Storr. *Excluded.* 51

[270] 19 September 1917. This reflected current events on the military front but of course the Armistice did not take place until November 1918.

Plate 9.5 First group of British prisoners arriving at Scheveningen for internment January 1918

Red Cross – Prisoners' Occupation

Once the male prisoners were in Holland they would need some kind of occupation and in order to provide this the men needed classifying according to their fitness for any kind of work as far as their health was concerned. Then their various qualifications needed to be taken into account and once these things were organised, the way that accommodation had been allotted might also have to be changed. Grace had seen General Onnen who said he had not yet been officially informed that the British Red Cross was taking up the question of employment and education. She asked Sir John to tell him so officially and feared that Onnen had made some plans of his own, thinking that the British government would pay.

At the back of everybody's minds while all this was happening was the hope that maybe peace would be declared before it was all put into place. During August, Britain and the Americans had captured 150,000 German soldiers, and there was a spirit of optimism in the air.

Return to England

Grace Vulliamy was also involved with arrangements for the care of prisoners when they arrived back in England, and on at least one occasion she joined parties on a boat trip on one of the rivers near Boston. Another organisation very much involved with the return of prisoners was the Central Charities Committee in London; a key figure within it was Annie

E Barnes, the acting secretary. Replying to a query from Mrs Barnes, Grace said she would be very willing to help in any way possible in connection with the civilian prisoners from Germany. In one letter to Grace Vulliamy, dated 27 October 1917 Mrs Barnes expressed amazement that after three years the Foreign Office was still unable to get speedy and reliable information about civilian prisoners from its own officials. She continued 'the muddle regarding the last party surpassed anything even I have ever experienced.' She had spent six hours on the telephone making, cancelling and remaking arrangements according to the various messages received from different Government Departments. She asked Grace to impress on whoever brought the parties across that it would save delay and suffering to the men as well as worries to the workers if all the sick cases were kept together and taken off first from the boat to the tender and from the tender to the land. When this was not done looking for the sick men was, she said, like 'looking for needles in haystacks'. They were hoping that at last the exchange was really going to begin.

By 16 November 1917 Grace had arranged to let Mr Aveling of the British Legation in The Hague know immediately she had any information about the people and was hoping to get the usual permission to go to the frontier and join the German Red Cross train. They were expecting 550 civilians in the first batch so it would be rather hectic. She had seen the Dutch Red Cross and they had promised to try and do what was wanted regarding the order for the people to be taken off the train. Dr Hymans, the medical officer in charge, was said to be an exceptionally nice man. She asked: 'Do you want civilians to have any distinctive mark? I doubt if we shall have time to get enough badges made but as the others will be in uniform I don't expect it's necessary.' The badges were in the form of a white cross, superimposed on a red disc – the distinctive badge of all civilians returned from Germany.

There needed to be constant liaison between the two Generals, Hanbury Williams and Onnen. Grace was kept fully informed, sometimes by carbon copies of correspondence between them, and was frequently asked for her remarks. It was unprecedented that a woman would be asked for her opinion let alone her advice at this period and shows the high opinion in which she was held. The Generals needed to know the numbers of prisoners coming through, the proportion of these who required medical attention, also the numbers who could go to the officers' hospital that was to be at Clingendaal, the Baroness's home, or to other hospitals and how many should be sent straight to England. Hospitals needed equipment including beds, blankets, foodstuffs and other necessaries. Grace organised all these.

Some items, such as soap, matches and bandages, were very expensive and difficult to obtain; some medicaments, cigarettes, tea, coffee, paraffin and anything in tins were completely impossible to get. There were also such mundane matters as tyres wearing out which she had to be made aware of as they needed to be bought in London and shipped across to Holland. It was officially 'at Hanbury Williams' request' therefore that Grace Vulliamy organised the first temporary Hospital for sick or wounded PoW.'s. However, Grace corresponded with Francis Aveling[271] about this because 'the Dutch were taking all the arrangements into their own hands without even consulting us.' Consequently, Sir Walter Townley, as Ambassador, contacted London to tell them this could not be allowed, especially as the British were to pay the bill, supply all materials, food, medical stores and so on. He pointed out that there were plenty of people in the Netherlands who could do it themselves, including Grace and her organisation, by which he meant the Society of Friends. Nevertheless he wanted someone senior to be sent out to select camp sites and make general arrangements. It was also necessary for someone to organise a camp for civilians.

Red Cross

The Red Cross was at last able to make more permanent changes to their representatives in Holland. On 9 November, Lord Sandwich, of the Joint War Committee wrote to Grace saying that:

> Sir Arthur Stanley obtained services of Mr Voules to take charge of the Red Cross work at The Hague, but due to the absence of his Chief Managing Clerk through illness it is unlikely he will be able to catch the next boat, so I am afraid we must ask you to be so good as to carry on for another ten days.
>
> I feel sure you will like Mr Voules. He is an old friend of Sir Arthur's, is a solicitor and has a great deal to do with Brazil. He speaks French but not Dutch. I have had two long talks with him and have put him *au fait* with everything I can think of.... I have seen Baroness van Brienen and I understand that the question of coal and fuel is being arranged at the Foreign Office.... I told Baroness van Brienen that I did not think it was any good her going out until Repatriation actually begins ... and I don't think it expedient to begin our hut building until that moment arrives.

---

271 Aveling to GCV. 27.7.1917

Plate 9.6 Waiting at hub for 3rd internment

. Finally, he wrote a few sentences about Grace's expenses being paid into her account at The Hague. In view of the fact that she frequently had to use her own money for her work, this was undoubtedly a relief to her. The relevance of Brazil to Mr Voules' appointment is perhaps that many people there spoke German or it may be simply that Lord Sandwich was affirming that Mr Voules had experience of working abroad.

Mr Carbutt of the Red Cross wrote on 9 November 'Now that we are sending out Mr Voules as Commissioner I hope things will move a little more quickly… especially as we are going to start an office in the building specially to look after anything to do with the people in Holland. I understand I am going to be in charge of it so that if you want anything done over here please write to me.

Lady Susan Townley had a collection of hospital appliances being stored by theFan Red Cross at the Legation that could be used and would save buying things in England, but it looked as if there was going to be a longer delay. It was depressing. An article in *The Times* on 19 November explained that delay in the arrival of British prisoners from Germany through Holland was Germany's insistence on an unacceptable sea route. It had been agreed that the Dutch hospital boat would use Rotterdam and

Boston, but the route between those ports was unacceptable to the British authorities and the Dutch captains. However, Cabinet Papers reveal another reason: that the German government had decided not to ratify the Anglo German agreement for the exchange of prisoners unless Germany was satisfied on the position of their prisoners in China. Prisoners in Turkey were also involved[272] and from August 1917 there are documents in connection with Turkey amongst Grace Vulliamy's papers showing her interest in these men. She corresponded with Mr E H Keeling of the Prisoners in Turkey Committee, Leicester Square, London, who told her that the Berne Agreement that was signed last December included inspection of camps. They were trying to get assurance from the Turks that the hospital ship would not be attacked but no reply had been received. Grace thanked him for his letter which had 'given me a far better grasp of the situation of the British Prisoners of War in Turkey.' She was trying to get a Dutch doctor she knew to go out there.

Plate 9.7. This picture of a Ward car of an Ambulance train is in Grace's collection

Corridor of one of the Ward Cars of the Ambulance Train, constructed by the Caledonian Railway Company, on the instructions of the War Office, for conveyance of Wounded British Soldiers in France from the Front to the Sea-board

[272] CAB/24/66

Plate 9.8 Commissioner for the British Red Cross Society in Holland
Mr Francis M Voules

In December 1917 an Exchange Agreement was signed between Britain and Turkey regarding prisoners and the inspection of camps. On 29 December 1917 it was announced there was to be an immediate exchange of 1000 invalid British and Indian combatants for 1500 invalids and that the prolonged negotiations had been a tax on the patience of Lord Newton and Sir Herbert Belfield, the British representatives. Grace tried to get a doctor out to help the prisoners.[273]

Nonetheless, despite difficulties, a party of 500 returning prisoners of war reached Dover on 18 November and 250 landed at Hull. The returning men were taken to specially prepared camps at Dover and Ripon and the wounded were sent promptly to hospital. A further 50,000 prisoners were due to sail on 20 November on Danish ships from the Forenede Company and they would sail between Danzig and Manchester. Some would go via Copenhagen where they would board liners that would take them home. Representatives of the Danish Red Cross were on their way to Germany to help with the departure of the prisoners despite the fact that a serious epidemic of Spanish influenza was prevailing. A good number of Danish surgeons and nurses had offered to care for the British on their way home and the Red Cross had arranged to provide all vessels with English books and the latest newspapers and magazines.

From time to time newspaper reports appeared which expressed dissatisfaction with the work that people like Grace were trying to do; it was thought that these were written by pro-Germans. But now, reports were written and published about the alleged bad treatment by the Germans of

[273] Letter to E H Keeling dated 18 September 1918

British prisoners of war. On 9 October 1917 May Gelderen wrote to Grace with disturbing information about the way Allied prisoners had been treated and explaining that she was unable to tell anything about a particular newspaper account or who had put it in the paper. Apparently, three Canadians who ran away were punished by being put under a boiler put for four hours with no food, and water placed just out of reach. Russians had been punished in a similar way and one had died. This sort of report became too frequent to be dismissed as propaganda and copies of the reports sent by Grace can be seen in the National Archive at Kew, London.

However, the process of being confined for a length of time with boredom and lack of contact with loved ones also created suffering and Grace heard from the severely wounded who were allowed to return to England how much the men were suffering mentally who had been prisoners since 1914 and had nothing to do while in captivity. They did not qualify to return to England because they were not physically ill. So through the influence of a friend, Grace obtained an interview with Princess Helena Victoria. The friend might have been Netterville Barron, mentioned earlier, or, more likely Lena Ashwell who was married to Dr Henry Simson, the royal gynecologist. Grace explained that through further channels she obtained an audience with King George V and Queen Mary to ask their help in getting 'our prisoners brought out to some neutral country, naturally in exchange for the same number of Germans from England.'

The Royals referred her to the Prime Minister, Lloyd George, who began to listen to her proposals when she told him that the enfranchised prisoners-of-war hated him and would never again vote for him!'[274] Grace's sister Eva recorded what Grace had told her about these events.

The men she met told Grace of the desperate condition of those prisoners who were not ill but had been captured at the beginning of the War and had been in captivity for two years with nothing to do so she went to London and asked to see the King. She saw him and he called in Lloyd George with the result that Lloyd George called a Cabinet Meeting and it was decided to get the Germans to agree to having two camps in Holland for all who had been prisoners since the early part of war. The two camps were at Rotterdam and at The Hague. The former was a very poor one and the latter a good one so Grace, having been at both, came back to London and went to the War Office to get them to send the officer who was going to be in charge of the camp over at once which they did with the result that our men got the camp at The Hague and the Germans said it was the first time

[274] Vulliamy papers. Woman of Action, 3

England had got in before them. After the war was over, Grace and an officer who had been a prisoner drew up suggestions for the occupation of prisoners of war and sent them to the War Office. These were largely carried out in World War II and young soldiers were able to study for and write the exams to qualify for their professions and with musical and dramatic entertainments there was nothing like the same mental strain.[275]

Plate 9.9

[275] Eva Vulliamy

Right and below Two pictures of the *SS Sindoro*, the ship on which many of the prisoners travelled between Britain and Holland and which is frequently mentioned in the Vulliamy Papers.

Left: The signatures on the back of this menu card show that two members of the Oppenheimer family and two of the de Lignes were present at the event, giving an idea of the social circle in which Grace Vulliamy mixed.

CHAPTER 10

PRISONERS IN HOLLAND AND GRACE'S FAMILY

Under the agreement for exchange of British and German prisoners entered into the previous summer at The Hague, regular exchanges took place between Rotterdam and Boston (Lincolnshire). At Rotterdam the train was taken directly to the quayside where General Sir John Hanbury Williams and other British representatives awaited the wounded. Reception at Rotterdam was reported as 'excellent'. A temporary hospital, which included an operating theatre, was fitted up on the quay at Rotterdam. The three hospital ships - the *Sindoro,* the *Mecklenburg*, and the *Zeeland* – had 'every comfort' for the wounded who were 'met on their arrival in Dutch territory by Miss Vulliamy representing the British Prisoners of War Department at The Hague, and Lady Susan Townley'. Nonetheless, comfort in the ship was dependent on where the invalid was placed. Despite this glowing newspaper report, there were in fact 'inadequate arrangements for the loading of prisoners on the *Sindoro* the first time' and the executive of the Rotterdam Red Cross was summoned to The Hague to explain what took place in connection with the transport of the invalid prisoners. Some of the wounded were placed so deep down in the ship that in the event of it being torpedoed or striking a mine it would be impossible to rescue them. In this second batch the men were placed nearer to the deck. Now Grace heard from the severely wounded how much the men who had been prisoners since 1914 were suffering, which as a mental nurse concerned her greatly and she began to take steps to set them free.

The number of prisoners inevitably depended on military events. The Battle of the Somme, for example, which began on 1 July 1916, had seen the worst slaughter imaginable and commemorations inevitably focus on the numbers killed. But for Grace Vulliamy it was the number taken prisoner that was especially significant. Recent on-line records give 80,000 as possible. The first day of the renewed Somme offensive in November resulted in 5,000 German prisoners being taken.[276] The number of prisoners held by both sides was an unwanted pressure on resources and an agreement was at last made with Germany in getting the men brought out to some neutral Country, in exchange for the same number of Germans from England. Grace, as an

[276] Gilbert. 1994. 297

expert linguist and organiser, was afterwards appointed by the Admiralty and War Office to take charge of the PoWs exchange.

The Dutch Minister of Foreign Affairs also permitted civilians imprisoned as aliens in Germany and Britain to move to the Netherlands where they lived like other refugees. However, when there was no boat immediately sailing for England they needed accommodation for unknown periods and some kind of entertainment, but also strict disciplinary measures to prevent drunkenness.[277] This was wartime and unguarded remarks could give away vital information to the enemy. Drunken men are not careful what they say. An agreement was at last made with Germany and The Exchange of Prisoners of War (for Holland only) Agreement signed. It was not necessarily for seriously sick or wounded. Indeed, once they had crossed the Channel, one man was so delighted to see England that he tried to swim ashore.

Arrangements for the exchange of prisoners from Germany into neutral Holland were made at the highest levels and necessitated a simultaneous exchange of German prisoners from Britain. The difficulty in regard to this was not so much to transport from Holland the limited number of British as to transport to Holland the relatively large number of German prisoners of war entitled to repatriations in exchange. The German Hospital train was always met by the Dutch at Roosendaal and escorted by them to Flushing, where they superintended removal of the wounded from train to boat and thence to Tilbury. Grace's task was to arrange to meet the British prisoners at the border, provide food and drink when needed, and with the help of the Dutch to arrange for a doctor to take over from the American doctor, who being neutral, might accompany the men from Germany into Holland. She also needed to arrange for another doctor to meet the train at Flushing. Then the party was transferred on board ship.[278] The greatest difficulty was caused by alcohol on the train and boat which rendered the men difficult to control and Grace made arrangements to change its availability. Her role also involved liaising between different authorities, passing on relevant information such as about the condition of prisoners, making reports on each exchange and suggesting ways of smoothing relationships; one of her tactful suggestions was that the British Red Cross should send a letter of appreciation to the Dutch Red Cross. Her compassion for the hungry men when it was not possible to provide other food is shown in a photograph dated 29 December 1917, handing up apples through train windows to the

---

[277] Extract from *Excluded from the Record*. p.106

[278] V Papers. 15.5.16 GCV to Sir Louis Mallet, British Red Cross

delighted men inside. Such acts of kindness would not be soon forgotten after the experiences of the prison camps.
The first contingent of British prisoners from Germany was composed exclusively of the original Expeditionary Force who were captured on 24 August 1914 in the battle of Mons. In fact, approximately 200 Mons men arrived – 37 officers and 184 NCOs. They arrived on Friday, 29 December 1917, the train having reached Venlo at 11.00. The men were drawn up on the platform by a German lieutenant and after a few formalities were handed over to the Dutch officers. The German guard then disappeared and round after round of cheers were raised. Grace Vulliamy met the first trainload of wounded Britishers at the frontier; Lady Susan Townley joined them at Dordrecht. The men were the less seriously wounded and showed great pleasure at able to chat with English ladies. In another batch there were 12 officers and 317 men in two parties and they were expected to leave for Britain on Wednesday. An even bigger contingent arrived with 871 military and civilian prisoners, including 23 mental patients and 24 invalids. They were looked after in Red Cross sheds. Much of the organisation for the care of all these people fell to Grace. Naturally members of the Press wanted to interview the men but became such a nuisance that Grace needed to take steps to limit the number of these journalists and to control their behaviour.

Another contingent arrived on 22 January 1918. In one group were four wounded soldiers to be repatriated, having lost their sight. Ruhleben prisoners arrived on the quay at 9.a.m. having been delayed for three hours at Hassum by Gennep shortly after midnight. This meant an equivalent wait for those who were meeting *en route* the 370 passengers of whom 22 were invalids, and some who had lost their reason. The Dutch gave them a warm welcome from the border and Grace Vulliamy accompanied them from Venlo where, as usual, she started to organise a list of their names, and other details such as home town and ages. A further party of 40 officers and 252 NCOs, arrived at Scheveningen at 10.00 p.m. on the night of 23 January 1918. That they were cheered while still in the train may have surprised the officers who 'had been given somewhat erroneous impressions in advance,' in other words that they were unpopular because they allowed themselves to be captured. They were expected to leave for Britain on Wednesday.

Grace was Sir John's representative, making all arrangements and meeting all PoWs at the frontier, taking particulars during the journey, very often of over 300 men, and telegraphing them to England to warn of their arrival the same day. *The Times* named her on 21 December 1917, as one who since the beginning of the war had 'done excellent work in connection with the transfer of the sick and wounded'. At some point she seems to have wanted to write a book about her experiences and her Chapter II is about this period. She wrote:

> As the parties of refugees came through we were able to obtain impressions of the conditions prevalent in Germany at the time, though the accounts varied, of course, according to the different regions from which the prisoners came and naturally, as time went on and food and clothing and other essentials of a normal life became increasingly difficult to obtain, conditions became more distressing. ...

Plate 10.1 Grace Vulliamy handing apples up to the First party of British Prisoner soldiers in a train at Helmund, Holland. 29 December 1917

Some prisoners arrived at Oldenzaal and Gennep but Sir Walter Townley at The Hague Legation was not always advised about the condition and numbers of civilians, so this caused problems. For example on 14 September Mr and Mrs Cohen left Germany with their children, accompanied by the German nurse, but the Note advising the Legation was not received until after the family had actually arrived in Holland. The man and woman were both desperately ill with what was then called consumption and is now known as TB. They also had heart trouble. No arrangements had been made to meet them and so new arrangements were put in place to try to ensure such unfortunate things did not recur.

> Still difficulties were not at an end. It was, of course, necessary for us to receive particulars regarding the number of prisoners coming through and the general condition et cetera in time to allow of our getting up to the station on the frontier, and there making the necessary arrangements for their reception. The delay in sending us this information, perhaps almost inevitable when it could not be sent direct but had to go through the medium of a third party, sometimes made things somewhat difficult for us. For instance on one occasion (vide letter to Maxse 9.11.16) we received information regarding a party to be met at Gennep only half an hour before the train went by which it was necessary for us to travel in order to be at the frontier in time. Picture us flying around and rushing off to the station et cetera et cetera. And upon arrival at Gennep we found that although we had been informed that all the prisoners were sane we had to deal with two insane men.

One of these 'arrangements' survives in the form of a letter dated 6 December to Dr Merkens. Grace had heard that 150 interned civilians were expected on 7 December and asked for his help. She told him 'some of the men are very seriously ill, please bring the necessary things with you, arrange for stretchers at Flushing and perhaps one or two of the Dutch Red Cross would help.' probably'(Belgian query)' in her report implies that Grace thought the girl was Belgian:

> On another occasion (vide letter to Max 9.8.16) we were advised first that nine women and children would be coming ... What actually happened was that... 13 women and children via Oldenzaal, many of these last without means of any sort. As we had been advised that they would come via Gennep we did not meet these poor people at Oldenzaal, who being set down there in the middle of the night, stranded. One girl of 17 (Belgian query) for instance knowing no English or Dutch and without either money or friends was escorted to Rotterdam by a Customs Official which cost us a good deal of money – as she had then to be retrieved from there and sent on to Flushing.

Plate 10.2 Grace Vulliamy meeting men of the first military exchange, December 1917

Grace organized the arrival of the prisoners at their destination, but sometimes difficulties arose through lack of on-going communication, military arrogance or disregard for suffering. For example, Mr Carbutt of the Red Cross arranged with Grace that his men would meet the prisoners at Victoria Station, but afterwards she wrote to him that 'the military authorities wouldn't allow your men to help.' One of the [German] prisoners was returned to Germany in a very dirty condition and insufficiently clad. This seems to indicate lack of concern for the Germans by the British, but is the only example found in these papers.

Grace's Social Life

It is amazing that with so much work to do Grace could still find the time and energy for a work-related social life. This is often more visible in photographs, where she is shown with other people, for example with the stowaway girl, than in the documents where her focus is on her work. However, the diary of Charles Morrell[279] gives a very different picture. For example, on 1 January 1916 she had tea with him at Gouda in the Station Hotel. The next day they had lunch together, and he saw her off to Rotterdam. On 14 January she was at The Hague and he called on her there. They worked together nearly every day for the rest of the month.

[279] See Chapter 6

The routine was similar in February. On 16 February Grace went to dinner with Charles Morrell and they spent time together on fifteen of the twenty-eight days of February. This gives a completely different idea of Grace's life in Holland, showing it as much more social than is evident from her documents. They used the shop (see chapter 6) as a place to discuss business, worked in Mrs Chilton's room, Charles 'stained Miss V's desk (and his hands)'; they went house hunting for prisoners' accommodation and offices, prepared exhibitions and went to the cinema. Mrs Chilton was the wife of a British Commercial Attaché and a representative of Queen Mary's Needlework Guild and was a very useful and helpful contact.

There was an Ice Club where they went skating and they also skated on canals and lakes when they were frozen. Friesland was an area where there were many lakes and so Grace arranged weekend skating parties to the area starting on Saturday 17 February. Harkness 'met the party (Morrell, REG, Misses Barber, Vulliamy, Nicoll, etc')' planning to go to Leeuwarden, the capital town of Friesland, picking up Mr Paley and Miss Nicholl of the Society of Friends on the way. The next day the weather was foggy and a thaw had set in. The train timetables had been altered and this delayed them, so they went about 3 kilometres out of the town towards Groningen, where they eventually found plenty of ice, but water too. Harkness wrote: 'We all succeeded in getting pretty wet, but we got some good skating.... We lunched on some of Miss Vulliamy's sandwiches.' They arrived back at The Hague at 1 am and walked out to Scheveningen

Plate 10.3 Station Hotel, Gouda, Holland

.It was a friendly, working association and in March when they drove to Amersfoort in the car with Princess Isabelle de Ligne; they had two punctures on the way and had lunch at the camp. The Princess was aged about 27 and unmarried. She supported the British Legation and the wartime charitable work of the Society of Friends. In 1920 she married Prince Von Croÿ.[280] People had dinner with each other regularly and afterwards they had 'cheery evenings' playing cards; they had drinks at the American bar and on 3 December 1916 Morrell called at Grace's house to see 'Mrs Hessin and her flapper daughters'. The word 'flapper' became common in the 1920s to indicate a fashionable young woman who had a good time and flouted convention. This is a very early use of the term. Mrs Hessin was an American lady who arrived in Holland from Germany in late 1916 after having been interned since the beginning of the war. Her husband, a Canadian, was still interned at Ruhleben. She and her two daughters were staying with Miss Barber, Grace's secretary, who lived not far from the church where Harkness met Morrell and Trefusis on Christmas Eve 1916. It was here that Harkness met Grace on Christmas Eve 1916. He wrote that they all went to Grace's place at Daendelstraat for Christmas dinner and that two or three Quaker conscientious objectors were there, men who also assisted in the Society of Friends' shop. As a military man it is almost inevitable that he would share the usual contempt for pacifists, regarding them as cowards. This is a comparatively mild mention of them, but he did not have to mention this at all. By 2 January 1917, Grace was 'as usual', away travelling.

Grace's friendships continued with Beatrice Harraden and Lena Ashwell, both women visiting her in Holland and helping her with her work in Poland afterwards. It seems that on at least one occasion Harraden was considering travelling to Holland with Grace's sister Violet Vulliamy but synchronizing dates was awkward. She wrote to Grace at Rotterdam saying

> Just a line to thank you for your card. I should love to come but don't think I can manage to do so before August 24th. Probably your sister won't want to wait so I should have to come alone. We've been telephoning. Of course it would be very jolly if she and I could come together. But do send me a line when you get this to say whether August 24th would be too late for you please. The papers found the letter you sent too late for insertion. Every interval seems to pass with frightening speed. I've not yet found a place so I am still here until Sep. 29th. But I'm in a .... houselet ... Blenheim Road.'

There are indications that their network extended to women involved in medical work who were serving in Egypt. Harraden continued 'DO send a card to Sister Barrett ...Cook & Son, Alexandra, Egypt. So far she is all right.'

[280] See Flowchart, Chapter 5.

YMCA, Red Cross and Dutch Medical Service

When officer prisoners began to be exchanged Grace Vulliamy was asked by the YMCA to work with them but she needed to know what these responsibilities would entail. Baroness de Brienen cabled Miss Vulliamy saying that the work would consist in organising clubs, workshops and entertainments for released prisoners with the YMCA's representative and to cooperate with the executive committee. In July, Mr Carbutt also contacted her to find out if she was officially asked, would she act as British Red Cross representative in Holland. Grace said she would be glad to do it. She must have known she was taking on a lot although she was giving up the work for the Friends and for the civilians in the camps. In fact, she discovered her decision meant she was tied to the office desk too much. However, she was still able to meet all the exchanged prisoners at the frontier, and her presence there was no surprise to the Dutch who had refused permission to the Red Cross and YMCA personnel to meet the prisoners. In each case she took the prisoners' names and cabled them home, thus avoiding considerable delay and difficulties. Evidently the lists of prisoners and their details, like Miss Vulliamy herself were much appreciated. For example, Major Tweddie wanted a list and Adelaide Livingstone asked Grace Vulliamy if she could send her one: 'I know what a hectic time you must be having but the list would be of the greatest use to me and if possible, I do hope you will send it to me.' Mr Carbutt wrote:

> 're the lists which you so kindly provided of the civilian prisoners that were repatriated. These you always used to let us have when the Prisoners came to Gravesend or Tilbury and were of immense use and there was great competition to get a copy of them. Do you think you would be able to manage these lists again when the exchange is made at Boston I know that it will be very difficult for you if they send as many men as they suggest that if you could possibly help us in this way it would be of great use.'

The YMCA was responsible to military authority for the 'lodgement, general care and good behavior of the Lena Ashwell parties' who travelled to France and Holland to boost troop morale by providing entertainment. As representative of the YMCA, Grace was involved in this responsibility.

At that time Miss Vulliamy was attached to the Dutch medical service so that her medical knowledge might be used to assist and advise in the arrangements which were being made for the hospital treatment of British Prisoners of War to be interned in Holland and because of her knowledge of the Dutch language. 'Her services were of great value. She organised various hospitals and herself nursed some of the most serious cases.'

'Almost every party of British prisoners was met by Miss Vulliamy who collected the names of each individual. She arranged to which hospital invalids should be sent in the case of those who were destined for internment[281] and in the case of those for repatriation she, together with a representative of the Rotterdam Lloyd Company, decided as to which ship and which part of the ship each individual should be allocated. She supervised the drafting of the lists of prisoners which accompany every transport. In addition, Miss Vulliamy made out Instructions for Listing so that in the event of her absence others knew exactly what information was to be passed and to whom. For example, complete lists were to be sent to Sir John Hanbury Williams, the War Office, the Legation, the Consulate and to Miss Vulliamy herself. Other lists went to the Central Charities Committee, the Red Cross, Mrs Livingstone and others. This would have necessitated a great deal of work – either many carbon copies, or many re-types.

In August 1917 she was asked by the British Red Cross in London if, in the event of The Hague Agreement with regard to official exchanges of prisoners of war between England and Germany being ratified, she would represent them in Holland. She replied that she would be very glad to do so and did so until the end of October when further representatives had to come out while she met trains from the frontier.

So Grace now acted as Red Cross and YMCA representative in Holland.[282] These organisations both wanted her to work exclusively with each of them but she preferred to be independent and to help wherever most needed.

Offices and Organisers

During September 1917 Miss Vulliamy left the Quakers and working under the War Office concentrated on the wounded and special exchange prisoners from Germany who were to be interned in Holland. At this stage the British workers did not have suitable premises for offices. On 25 August Arthur Stanley of the Joint War Committee asked her if she would 'look out for any buildings, workshops and so on, near the camps' in Holland but not to commit herself to them at this stage. He also asked her to consult with Sir Walter Townley about the Red Cross having a working committee in Holland and to suggest a few names of appropriate people. Consequently in mid-September she went with the General to find somewhere for their offices, but it was extremely difficult to find anywhere suitable. At last he decided on a place over a theatre, with a rent of about

281 *Times.* 3.1.1918
282 IWM. Prisoners 17/1

£300 a year, which concerned Grace as rather high. The General was willing to pay £150, but the YMCA only wanted one room which left three for the Red Cross

Additional expenses such as for light, telephone, and taxes would come to another £50 a year for each body, but a decision needed to be made quickly or they would lose the place. In England Sir Arthur Yapp of the YMCA Headquarters in London had been appointed Director of Food Economy under the Food Controller, now Lord Rhondda, and this placed a burden on him which was more than one man could carry, so he decided to give four days to his new work and keep three for the YMCA. Hanbury Williams now acted as head of the Red Cross and a working committee of about 20 people was wanted. Grace was asked for suggestions and agreed she would let Stanley know. Organising comparatively few prisoners did not need a large amount of administration, but the numbers now to come through were a different matter. A Red Cross representative was urgently needed to sign a contract for land seen by Lord Sandwich, (representing the British Red Cross and the Order of St John) and offered by the town with rent one florin per year, and drainage, fencing etc at the expense of the tenant. The YMCA agreed to share land that was suitable for workshops etc. But office furniture must be paid per month and was needed immediately.[283] This work included going on board ships to ensure everything was as Grace wanted for the prisoners so Consul-General Maxse wrote a letter of authorization saying that, with the sanction of the Right Honourable the Viscount Grey, she was charged with the meeting and transport of British returned civilians from Germany to the United Kingdom on his behalf and seeking permission for her to visit and board any British ship lying in the harbour at Rotterdam as his representative.[284] He asked that this courtesy should be extended to her especially in connection with leaving the boat and returning to it for the purposes of looking after invalid and mental cases.

However, the YMCA needed permanent male organizers. Mr H A Dennis, a 'rattling good chap,' went out on 27 October 1917 to work in Holland accompanied by Mr Clapperton whose experience and knowledge of YMCA work would make him invaluable as Mr Dennis's colleague. Dennis had opened the YMCA work at the Vickers factory in England so he had useful experience. Grace had suggested that Mr Faulkner, another helper, could use her house as a temporary office and on 24 August Arthur Yapp in London wrote saying he was happy to agree to Grace's suggestion

---

[283] 7.11.1917. Cable from Grace to Sir Arthur Stanley, British Red Cross, London.
[284] 15 July 1916. 4 October 1917

about the payment of expenses but Faulkner was having difficulty getting his passport, so the temporary arrangement might last longer than originally planned. Dennis and Clapperton were to cross by the first Admiralty boat.

Plate 10.4 The Hague. YMCA Officers' Sitting Room

However, once the male prisoners were in Holland they would need some kind of occupation and in order to provide this the men needed classifying according to their fitness for any kind of work as far as their health was concerned. Then their various qualifications needed to be taken into account and once these things were organised, the way that accommodation had been allotted might also have to be changed.

General Hanbury Williams was appointed by the British government to represent the interests of the British prisoners in Holland; General Onnen was doing the same job on behalf of the Dutch. Grace had seen General Onnen who said he had not yet been officially informed that the British Red Cross was taking up the question of employment and education. She asked Sir John to tell him so officially but feared that Onnen had made some plans of his own, thinking that the British government would pay. Grace's role as representative of the Red Cross involved her in all this. She wrote, pointing out that in this instance the British could learn from the Germans:

> **Employment.** It is extremely bad for the men to be living in enforced idleness which is the case with about two thirds of the total number. The Dutch can give them practically no employment as they have plenty of unemployed themselves. The German Government

has arranged that every German should be employed. Raw materials, such as leather, wood, etc. are sent from Germany and made up by the interned in Holland; there is also an artificial limb factory, a shoe factory: complete suites of furniture are made and shipped back to Germany, and all this gives employment not only to the men but also to the officers and NCOs who have the supervision of the work. Employment is also found in this way for German civilians.[285]

Plate 10.5 YMCA Picnic

The British War Prisoners Department in Holland had accommodation ready for as many officers as were likely to arrive for some time and also one large hotel for NCOs. These two groups were the only ones included in the arrangements for internment in Holland. Uniforms were being sent out from England for the men to wear.[286] But these were at first only officers and NCOs; privates were ignored until Grace started urging their immediate release.[287]

Red Cross - Housing

---

[285] CAB 24/57/84 Note of Statements and Suggestions made by Miss Vulliamy.

[286] *The Times*. 19.11.1917

[287] Vulliamy Box 1 Notes. Returned Civilians. *Star* (Jo'burg, S.Africa) 11.5.24 She it was who insisted on our Gov arranging to bring the British from German prisons to Holland. They said it was impossible; she said it was not. Newton reported against.

A company, the National Grondbezit Company Ltd, established at The Hague in October 1917, was formed to deal with accommodation and a formal Agreement was drawn up between that company and the Dutch Ministry of Foreign Affairs. This was checked by A K C de Brauw, who concluded that it was 'highly profitable for National Grondbezit', but admitted he did not know whether it would be possible to get an agreement on better terms. Miss Vulliamy's Report on Conditions in Holland shows that the agreement was not adhered to by the Dutch. Grace was not happy with the conditions in which the men were now required to live and she took steps to let the authorities know what was actually happening on the ground.[288] She wrote:

> CONDITIONS IN HOLLAND
>
> (note: I should much appreciate that the source of the following information be kept confidential as I am still working in Holland in connection with the Dutch government)
>
> Food. The food conditions are very bad. The British government have made a contract with the company who are not honourably carrying out that contract. The amount given by the Government of Fl 3.25 a day is sufficient, even under the present food conditions in Holland, to cover reasonable diet. The food is however so often badly prepared that it is uneatable and it is always insufficient. The men come from Germany in an ill nourished condition needing good food, and they themselves state that they are worse off with the food in Holland than in Germany because they are not allowed to receive parcels and the diet is so poor that they really are suffering ... cases of exhaustion due to insufficient food...

The New Year of 1918 approached. Under the authority of the British Prisoners of War Department at The Hague, the British Red Cross Committee for Holland that Miss Vulliamy had been asked to organize,[289] was formed under the presidency of Lady Susan Townley. Members were colleagues with whom Miss Vulliamy had worked and included Grace Vulliamy herself who carried out the administration and practical work in connection with the prisoners. The first Committee meeting was held on Tuesday, 27 November 1917. Mr Voules spoke of the splendid contribution of Baroness Brienen in offering Clngendaal as a Hospital for officers suffering from various nervous disorders including barbed wire disease. This was the name given to the complaints arising from boredom,

---

[288] CAB 24/57/84 (Note of Statements and Suggestions made by Miss Vulliamy.

[289] See Chapter 9.3, page 6

never being alone, or able to get away from people with unpleasant habits such as noisy eating, as well as those requiring special treatment. Men who were prisoners longer than 18 months suffered from this disease and most civilians had been prisoners over 3½ years. The hospitals were ready. All that was needed now was for the prisoners to arrive.

Clingendaal

Baroness de Brienen offered the use of Clingendaal, her home near The Hague, to the Dutch Red Cross but this offer needed to be transferred to the British Red Cross. Therefore she needed to see Sir Arthur Stanley about this, and waited at home in England three weeks for his return, by which time she was in bed, suffering with bronchitis. As a young man in the early 1890s Stanley had suffered an acute attack of rheumatic fever which left him permanently disabled and frequently in pain. His lameness forced him to use crutches, or at best two sticks, and in later life confined him to an invalid chair.[290] In his mid-forties now, he could not manage the stairs, so she suggested that his 'understudy' could come instead. She wanted Clingendaal used by all British medical people, including staff, doctors, nurses, and VADs. The British paid all its expenses, running it as an officers' hospital with the Baroness in charge. They wanted to put 'maison démontables' in the grounds, like the huts built for homeless Belgian refugees which gave extra accommodation in Holland until the end of the war, when it was planned to dismantle and transport them to Belgium to be used there. Working from The Hague, Grace Vulliamy wrote to the Baroness de Brienen in mid-September that the greater part of the medical staff would have to be Dutch and if the Baroness wanted helpers in Holland, Grace warned that this should be dealt with quickly as people were already offering their services to the hotels and houses being opened for the prisoners from Germany who were also coming to be interned in Holland. While most were genuine, this provided an opportunity for some spies to get information to pass to the Germans. One such opportunist claimed to have been engaged to an officer in the Royal Flying Corps who was killed on the day they were due to be married. Grace answered her letter but noted on it she was a 'British girl spying for the Germans.' How she came to this conclusion is not explained. In speech an American accent often betrayed the person, but it would not happen in this instance. This might be one of those occasions where she 'just had a feeling.'

---

[290] Dictionary of National Biography. b. 18.11.1869 http://www.oxforddnb.com/search/results/contributors.jsp?contributorId=43031. 16/02/2017 13:08

In November a meeting was held by the Red Cross in London at which the Baroness Brienen was asked to write to Grace to see if she could procure items needed for Clingendaal, which was to start as a forty bed hospital. First wanted were twenty beds, a hundred sheets, ten bedpans and 160 towels. However, the opening of the Clingendaal hospital was dependent on the date of the delivery of the fuel which was being arranged in London. Clingendaal was 'for officers needing a rest cure, more of a home than a hospital. Hospital huts were to be constructed later. Seven medical inpatients were already being treated and those needing operations had been sent to the Dutch military hospital. Neglect of teeth while they were prisoners meant that a dental Department needed to be started by the Red Cross.'[291]

The Baroness suggested that Grace Vulliamy tell Mr Dennis to secure some premises as an NCO club in The Hague and as no one could use a motor in that town she suggested hiring a motor shop and garage as a club and gave an example of one which would be splendid if it could be had at a reasonable price. She wanted Mrs Chilton to suggest two cooks saying they would be wanted between 15 December and 1 January.

So Grace Vulliamy organised the first temporary Hospital for sick and wounded PoWS, the first batch arriving on 29 December 1917. On 6 December Grace told Baroness de Brienen that the hospital staff had been engaged and consisted of a matron, two nurses and three VADs. Orderlies were to be engaged when the Baroness arrived. The hospital was to be arranged as a comfortable home with carpets and curtains, not as a regular hospital. Mrs Chilton had organised things with the Prince de Ligne and two good Cooks found, so the wages needed to be decided. Mrs Chilton wrote an undated note to Grace saying that the Princess de Ligne asked if she would say when and time she came to the The Hague and she would give the Princess the message. Further, Mdme Reyntiens had left 40 florins for her with thanks and goodbye. She added that she hoped Grace was not 'absolutely done by your trip over and back. It was such an angelic thing to do.' She ended 'much love' and signed her name.

The British government was providing things necessary for their prisoners of war so Major General Onnen thought that a similar quantity paid for by the Dutch should be imported on behalf of the German prisoners. It was suggested that a special steamer should be put into service under British control to import all articles for the prisoners. Onnen approved British nurses and doctors being sent out for special cases and promised every

---

[291] February 5, 1918 *British News.*

assistance to relatives and friends of interned prisoners who came to visit. It was a matter of common knowledge that the Dutch would be subjected during the winter to certain privations. In fact, the winter of 1916 - 1917 was so bad it became known as the 'Turnip or Hunger Winter,' when for three to four months in large parts of Europe there was nothing to eat except turnips. Civilians in particular suffered because troops were given preference to what food was available. People were still experiencing the effects of this under-nourishment two years later. It was also bitterly cold that winter and the workers in Holland were able to take advantage of the fact that rivers froze and went skating whenever possible. On 23 January 1917, Donald Harkness recorded that the weather was 'Colder still. The bath is now all ice and thus the foam on the beach is all frozen. Thousands of people skating.' [292]

Grace Vulliamy was becoming extremely well known as the troops returned home and began to talk about the various ways in which she had helped them, collectively and individually. A letter dated 28 December 1917 from a lady in Leicester is an example. The mother of a prisoner, she had been in touch with the Baroness de Pallandt and had mentioned that Grace Vulliamy was interesting herself in the released prisoners who might go to England. She was hoping that her son, Philip Gale Linnell would be amongst those to come from Ruhleben. She begged that Grace would do what she could for him and to wire her of her son's arrival. Another parent sent a postal order with which Grace could obtain money to buy some things for her prisoner son when he arrived. Yet another letter from J Stanford, an ex-prisoner, gives 'my very best thanks' from a hotel in London where he stayed with his mother and sister having been enabled to travel home with them through Grace's 'good offices.' To his surprise and amusement he found he was running across friends made in Germany and Holland, like himself, ex-prisoners who had been exchanged. He hoped Grace would soon be able to come home and invited her to stay with his mother.

Meeting between British and Germans at The Hague

The question of the internment in a Neutral Country of Prisoners of War who had been in captivity for not less than 18 months, was fully discussed at a meeting between British and German delegates at The Hague on June 24, 1917 and again in July. The British government delegates who arrived at The Hague were Lord Newton, Lieutenant-General Sir Herbert Belfield and Sir Robert Younger, Judge of the High Court. Grace had dealings with

---

[292] Harkness. 382

all these men and is understood to have had behind-the-scenes discussions with them at this time. They intended to discuss with the German government delegates solely questions connected with prisoners of war, among them parcels, camps, sites of camps, reprisals and matters connected with the exchange of interned prisoners over military age and disabled prisoners. There were three German delegates and one representing the Netherlands.

As usual Grace was attending to individual's problems as well as the political issues and at that time Grace had been asked to arrange to send a child of 8 to England. The Mother was German married to an Englishman, she had been doing intelligence work for the Germans, and using the child as a decoy. When the Commission left Grace took the child by night to the Hook of Holland and asked Lord Blanesborough to take it over. 'What!' he said, 'you are asking me, a judge – to assist you in kidnapping?' but he did it!'

In August, a War Office report stated that 'according to Lord Newton the chief German delegate admitted quite candidly that the treatment of German prisoners in Britain was distinctly superior to what it was in any other country. The German authorities would not release Prisoners of War from whom work could be enforced under The Hague Convention of 1907, viz: those whose permanent rank was below that of full Corporal. It was consequently possible to reach an Agreement only as regards Officers and NCOs, from whom no work could be exacted. Lance Corporals and Privates therefore did not fall within the terms of the Agreement.'[293]

Grace was greatly concerned about these lower-rank prisoners and took further steps to try to change the situation including approaching Lord Blanesborough, formerly Robert Younger who had been included on the Commission to arrange the prisoner exchange.

He replied:

> Dear Lady…
>
> I have heard from General Belfield and he recalls to my mind was I never forget – how hard we fought at The Hague to have the Men included in the Neutral Country arrangements, and how we entirely failed. It was a case of taking the NCOs or nothing below officers, and we felt we could not in justice to the NCOs refuse

[293] Copy of War Office Print: 1 August 1917

> them the privilege open. General Belfield has sent me a print of the answer on this subject which the War Office now makes to all enquiries.

A further message implies they had kept in contact and said:

> Perhaps as we are both so much preoccupied it will be better to leave your report till we meet next week.... We shall want it as an authentic record of the past. Shall we say dinner at 8.15 on Thursday next. That date suits Mrs Bromley Davenport and also the Duchess of Bedford, another of your devoted ladies. Yours sincerely.

However, Grace's friends were also able to help in this fight for justice for the lower rank soldiers. Beatrice Harraden had shown her humanitarianism by her work with Grace Vulliamy in the refugee camps in Holland, with the Americans' Committee for Relief in Belgium and various other ways. Her writing skills were invaluable for publicity purposes. On 20 May 1918 Grace wrote to Miss Harraden from The Hague:

> My chief object in writing to you is to lay before you the case of the British private soldiers who are still in Germany as prisoners of war. You will doubtless have realised that here in Holland we have quite exceptional opportunities of hearing from private soldiers themselves exact details of the appalling conditions under which they have to live. One cannot help feeling that those at home have not the same opportunities in this respect as we have here for two reasons:
>
> 1. We can meet and talk with many hundreds of NCOs and soldiers whose statements only reach home in the shape of formal evidence.
>
> 2. As regards those prisoners who are repatriated we see them before they have had time to have the vividness of their impressions dulled by the warmth of their reception on arrival in England.
>
> When one knows, as I do, the almost unbelievable misery of their conditions and the savage brutality to which they are continually subjected, one is compelled to conclude that the authorities at home are at any rate partially ignorant of the true state of affairs: it is inconceivable that men in their position should only have attained the present results for ameliorating the lot of the privates were they in possession of the full facts of the case. Consequently I feel that it is of prime importance that the whole truth, regarding

> the conditions under which our private soldiers exist in Germany, should be as widely known as possible, in order to avoid any possibility of the evil continued through lack of the necessary information reaching competent authorities.
>
> I fear that in England although the vast majority of people admit the truth of the allegations made regarding the German excesses in 1914 and 1915, there are an enormous number who believe that, since that time, the conditions under which our men live have improved steadily. It is of the utmost importance that this erroneous impression be removed at once …

Although trying to help the troops *en masse,* Grace was never too busy to help individuals who wrote for help, some directly but others referred to her in letters to a third party. For example, a Mr Garrard was expecting to see his brother arrive from Germany, but he was afraid it might not be possible to see him since he understood that in many cases the prisoners went straight from the train to the boat. He wrote 'I believe that there is a certain Miss Vulliamy who is greatly concerned with these matters.'

Examples of the small tasks that Grace undertook which meant so much to the prisoners include when one correspondent asked on 30 April 'So grateful if you could buy butter and eggs for me.' A few days later, on 6 May a wife writing from Kimberley on behalf of her husband, a Private in the First South African infantry who was at present a PoW, directed her request 'to Miss Vulliamy at the Society of Friends in Holland.' He had asked the wife to forward money to Grace to make him a parcel of sweets and chocolates and a few odds and ends. She enclosed a 10 shilling postal order as a way of covering the cost. Mrs Wolfe, a British subject, though German born, was married to an Englishman interned in Ruhleben. She was living in the Netherlands and wanted to stay there till her husband was released but she had no money so the Legation were obliged to send her to England. But there was money owing to her. Grace needed to write to Miss Alice Davies, of 14 Bellhaven Terrace, Glasgow, perhaps a relative, asking her to arrange with Mr Duff, a solicitor, to send £25 a month to their London office, who would then pay her the same amount in the Netherlands.[294] This request seems complicated enough but in addition required investigation into who Mr Duff was and his credentials. It also was necessary to decide how much money should be sent and as this was wartime to make sure the

[294] 21.4.17

money got through to the right people.[295] Many people she had helped like this kept in touch for quite some time.

Plate 10.6 First Military Exchange. 29 December 1917. Grace Vulliamy standing middle front

Fanny Vulliamy

However, while she was working in Holland, dealing with all the problems of the prisoners-of-war themselves and the difficulties this created for members of their families, Grace was also closely in touch with members of her own family. On 29 December 1917 her sister Fanny wrote to her from Torquay. This seaside town has a mild climate. Many people who had been living abroad used it when on leave or to recuperate from illness, as did Fanny now. This letter shows that daughters of the family were in touch with each other and at this time of the year sent each other gifts. From it we learn much more about Grace and in particular how much she was supporting Fanny at this difficult time. Fanny had formerly been a missionary in China and was 12 years older than Grace. She is believed by the family to have been the first woman missionary to go to China but this is unverified.[296] Now she was in very poor health and had not felt able to write before. She had a swelling of the left arm and foot and a painful bony growth in her shoulder so she was resting in bed for a few days. On

---

[295] Reply from Duff, 10th May 1917.

[296] Letter from Poppy to Daniel dated 27.10.1989

Christmas Day sickness began and was rather bad the next day. She then wrote: 'this is too much about myself' and changed the subject. After discussing the vagaries and delays of the postal system she thanked Grace for the generous gift she gave each month which Fanny felt was too much and if she got better she would have all she needed and mustn't accept so much.

> 'But oh it means so much to have a little fund like it to help me. Now I have so much else to thank you for – that lovely little cloth done in Holland, the book case and yet another to come that your Secretary is getting for me ... I mislaid this letter and had to send on to Violet – hence the delay. I so hope that she will take my small gift heavy with grateful love... you will know that is Chinese - it is the fanciful character for happiness - and the bodice Nellie made me a long time ago and I have kept it for best ... I always need such warm ones I do hope it will be of use to you I know Nellie will not think me ungrateful. When I get tired I get so drowsy so I have left your nice letter to answer to the last. I am sure I used not to make you feel ashamed about not writing for I **do** think it good of you when you have so much always on hand. Yes I should love to see your new home and I'm so glad you were able to get it. Certainly we are well off compared to you though we are feeling the need now as never before.

From this it seems that Grace was subsidising her sister's living costs and medical expenses, one of which was probably for an operation.

> ... I do not know what I should do just now without Miss Legge. My maid too is very willing - her mother has the same trouble and feels in the future she may have to have the same operation. One cannot help wishing for oneself that Our Lord will come and so all pain over for ever and no death but I ... dread more pain. But ... I cannot tell you what all you have done has meant to me. Thank you so much for Mr Macaulay's letter I am glad you were able to send the music he wanted ... I saw Miss Macaulay and she said how different his letters were now - so much brighter... my Christmas Gifts from Lionel and Nellie, stamps and a lovely box of his aunt's potted turkey. You gave us our nice Christmas dinner – a pheasant, it was so nice and is nearly all being kept for me as I have to be so careful what I eat – also a tin of Ovaltine. It would not be much good to you because of lack of milk. Mother gave me £1 for shoes which then I needed very much... They are so expensive now... please forgive this very untidy letter. With very much grateful love,
>
> Your ever loving sister Fanny Vulliamy.

In fact, Fanny did not have to wait long for all her pain to be over; she died on 10 February 1918 and is buried in Torquay churchyard.

CHAPTER 11

1918. ARRIVAL IN ENGLAND

Plate 11.1 *Herring Hill, the Wash, when the tide is out.*[297]

From now on, different categories of prisoners, military and civilian, were passing through Rotterdam on an almost daily basis *en route* to or from Boston. One day there were expected to be about 360 civilians – amongst them a number of the Boston fishermen interned since the beginning of the war. The town was not very well prepared to care for prisoners when they arrived in Boston, Lincolnshire

The English ports at which troops landed did not include Boston until agreements were made with Germany in January 1918 about exchange of prisoners. Boston's lack of significance in the air war was used to advantage by the British government in making arrangements with Germany for the exchange of prisoners. It was suggested that the route taken should be through Holland to Rotterdam and then to Hull; this route was unacceptable to the German Government as Hull was still a target for Zeppelin air raids. It had been bombed by a zeppelin in June 1915, and

[297]*http://www.geograph.org.uk/photo/1453218*
http://www.geograph.org.uk/photo/1494200.
Downloaded 7.1.2011. TF 4036. 1453218. 63c3bd22

again in March 1916 when Miss Vulliamy collected several photographs of the damage.

The British Admiralty then suggested Boston, Lincolnshire for prisoner exchange which was accepted by the German authorities.[298] However, Boston was less accessible to ships because it was on the Wash so it was not an easy choice.

The Wash, which is about 16 miles by 20 miles, was approached by channels known as the Boston Deeps. Plate 11.2 shows the Wash when the tide is out. Large vessels cannot go up to Boston at any time, but have to moor six miles down the river, so tenders had to be got ready to transfer the men. These needed to be able to take stretcher cases, mental cases and walking men. On Friday 4 January, military, naval and Home Office officials began arriving in Boston to see to the 'proper reception' of the 700 or 800 returned men.

Plate 11.2 Queen Street, Hull. March 6, 1916. After a Zeppelin raid.

because Boston was a difficult port for ships to get to. An ex-prisoner wrote to Miss Vulliamy on 10 November 1918 from his home at Ardour, Argyllshire saying that his 'first note to Holland must be to her' and describing the journey:

> We got away before daylight that night and had an uneventful passage, anchored somewhere off Cromer for the next night and

[298] Storr. *Home Front, Lincolnshire. Ch. 7. Fishing.*

> reached Boston about 4 p.m. A long trip, 1½ hrs in the tug up a sort of canal, during which time the VADs and women's papers were vised (sic) and we got our money changed ... No trouble at all about baggage at Boston no one took the least interest in it, and all ours, except the crate of furniture which they said they really had no room for on the train, was carried to town and dumped before next morning into the Prince of Wales' Hospital (Great Central Hotel). We ran though very slowly in a hospital train, ...after some trouble were allowed to buy tickets for our VAD wives and take them on the same train. Arrived in town about ½ an hour after midnight. My two sisters were on the platform, and Dame Adelaide and other people also met us. . .. Muriel and I were lucky and stayed at Kensington Palace with my Colonel in Chief, Princess Louise, who sat up to give us some supper at 2 am.... There was such a fuss at Boston about our wives that we nearly as possible lost them. The arrangements there are very bad indeed.

On 6 January 1918 the hospital ships *Koeningen Regentes, Sindoro,* and *Zeeland*, arrived at Boston. It was the occasion of the National Day of Prayer and a church parade was held at St Botolph's Church, known as the Stump, its apparently cut off or incomplete tower without a spire giving it this name.[299]

The next day, the prisoners returned. The Press was denied facilities to witness events, or even talk to the men. Grace had experienced how intrusive they were in Holland and had taken steps to limit the number of journalists who could approach the men. This time the authorities had done the job for her. There were 230 soldiers and 370 civilians. They were transferred to four tenders, which went down the river from Boston Dock to the Clay Hole on the evening tide on Sunday and lay alongside the hospital ships until day break. This could be seen from the vantage point down the river. By mid-day all the men had disembarked and refreshments and cigarettes given out. There was cheering from the waiting people and much bunting flying. Fishermen met their wives, usually accompanied by their children who, in some cases were born in their father's absence. Outside the Seamen's Institute, where there were 16 Boston men, Ivy Parker greeted her father, Capt. Wm. Henry Parker, a skipper captured in 1914, sent to Sennelager and badly treated. Then he was transferred to Ruhleben, where there was better treatment, but the food poor, and they relied on parcels. Another man was Frank Gale, chief engineer of the *Marney*. There were 28 cot cases.

---

[299] *The Times. 7* January.

Plate 11.3 St Botolph's Church, Boston, Lincolnshire
© David Budgen. 2007

During January, Major General Sir John Hanbury Williams sent a telegram for the information of Miss Vulliamy, forwarding information from Mr Maxse, Consul General at Rotterdam, showing the numbers of men involved in the expected transports and indicating the amount of work that Miss Vulliamy and her helpers were going to need to do.

> Prisoners of War ships due to leave Rotterdam 8 am January 16. Due to arrive Boston first tide Sunday 20 Jan.
> *Ss 'Sindoro'* 12 officers including one stretcher case. 50 soldiers, stretchers cases, 16 insane, remainder walking, including two civilians who remained in Holland after last exchange. Total 170
> *Ss 'Zeeland'* eight stretcher cases, remainder walking, total 101
>
> *Ss 'Koningen Regentes'*. All walkers. Total 63. Total in all 334. Vessels of last sailing were not detained for reason of completing list of names but would not leave on a Friday and as a matter of fact arrived at Harks lightship on schedule time. Signed Maxse

The fact that the *Koningen Regentes* would not leave on Friday shows how superstitious sailors were – Friday being considered an unlucky day on which to sail. This fear might have been intensified due to mines and submarines and the fact that the type of 'insanity' of the passengers seen in this war was unprecedented – sometimes the soldier merely seemed dazed, but some were unable to walk or talk and many shook uncontrollably. Would such symptoms bring bad luck? The British Army tried to differentiate between those whose symptoms followed explosive exposure from others, to justify the name 'shellshock' but the people dealing with these men on their journey to safety needed to know in advance what they were dealing with – were they suicidal or otherwise dangerous? Mistakes sometimes occurred. Annie Barnes, Acting Secretary of The Central Charities Committee, wrote to Grace Vulliamy:

> There is just one point I want to clear up before the next party. In your letter of 15 November 1917, you gave a 'code' to be followed in regard to telegraphing the description of cases – 'mental' was to convey 'violent and suicidal'. In your telegram of 4 January 1918 regarding the last party is stated '17 mental' but only eight of them were certified on arrival and the remainder were only slight nerve cases. Our workers appreciated the situation and cared for the comparatively well men of the 17 accordingly but you will understand that it is very necessary that we should know exactly what the words used in telegrams signify. Picture if our workers at Boston had firmly declined to deal with the eight on the ground that they were 'violent and suicidal' and must immediately be taken to the lunatic asylum! With kind regards, yours sincerely ...

On 16 February Miss Vulliamy travelled in the train from Maastricht to Rotterdam with 141 severely wounded British officers and men including five cases of mental derangement. They were due for repatriation and arrived from Aix la Chapelle in the hospital train. Exchanges continued and four more batches arrived before the end of May 1918.[300] Men were also being returned to Germany, therefore travelling in the opposite direction. Three trainloads of Germans being repatriated arrived in Boston on 9 January and the remainder arrived the following day. The prisoners included military officers and men, and naval officers and lower ratings who were quickly transferred to the tenders, which took them to the waiting steamers in the Boston Deeps and then set sail for Rotterdam. Grace wrote:

> There is also strong feeling against the NCOs as these men say they have been deserted by the NCOs who availed themselves of the opportunity of internment in Holland and already they have not failed to express the sentiments.

---

[300] *Ibid.*

I think the bitter feelings of these men could be moderated greatly by making much of them on return. I would suggest that on arrival in England they should be met by a military band, be provided with a good hot meal with beer et cetera and that a great welcome should be arranged at which special and allusion should be made to the services of the 1914 and 1915 men. Also that a message from the king should be sent which could be delivered to them immediately on arrival in Holland at Rotterdam.

I also think that it would be greatly appreciated were free telegrams to be sent to the relatives of these men in case they should be delayed at Rotterdam more than a day. I also consider that the British colony in Holland should be used as far as possible to welcome them and so help to dispel this bitterness as rapidly as possible. Yours sincerely,
GC Vulliamy

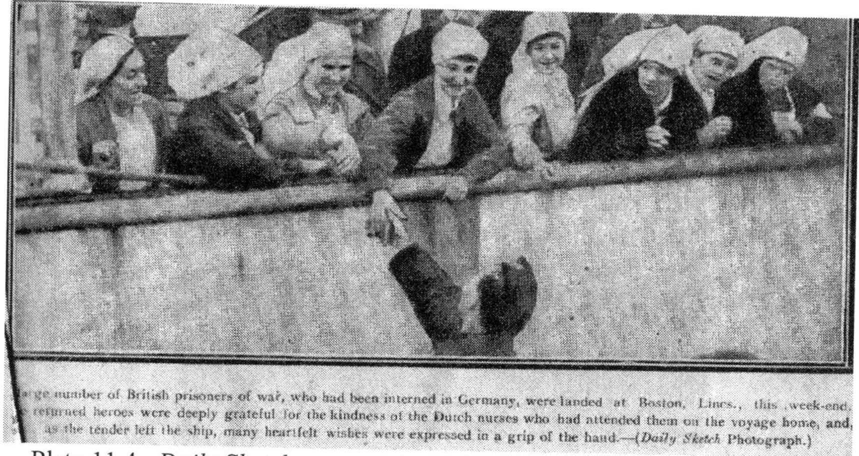

...rge number of British prisoners of war, who had been interned in Germany, were landed at Boston, Lincs., this week-end. ... returned heroes were deeply grateful for the kindness of the Dutch nurses who had attended them on the voyage home, and, as the tender left the ship, many heartfelt wishes were expressed in a grip of the hand.—(*Daily Sketch* Photograph.)

Plate 11.4 *Daily Sketch* some of the 230 soldiers and 370 civilians saying goodbye to the Dutch nurses as the *Sindoro* landed at Boston on 16 January 1918. Miss Vulliamy met these men at the Dutch frontier on 12 January

Thoughtful suggestions like these made all the difference to the returning men.

This was a time when voluntary societies were indispensable, exactly as they had been on the outbreak of war. One was the Invalid Comforts Fund for Prisoners of War with Mrs Bromley Davenport as its guiding light and with whom Miss Vulliamy had many dealings including investigating prisoner of war camps in Germany after the Armistice. Another such lady was Annie E Barnes under the auspices of the Social Welfare Association for London. She wrote to Miss Vulliamy on 18 January 1918:

> We are just beginning to breathe again after the 370 and are thankful that no more are coming this week.
>
> I cannot tell you how grateful I am to you for telegraphing direct to me last time. Of course, I made arrangements with the office to have my telegrams opened if they came after office hours and telephoned through to my house, and I received yours long before the Foreign Office gave me any information.

Honours

On 8 January 1918 Adelaide Livingstone was awarded the DBE. Grace Vulliamy was not so honoured at this time although she was asked to recommend other people - which seems somewhat offensive and is a problem of the Honours system. However, an unsigned letter from Ottery St Mary, Devon, dated 10.2.18 but marked in Grace's writing 'answered 5.3.18' is intriguing because of the fact it leaves the reader with various uncertainties. The writer sent:

> 'Congratulations on the 'Order' – it is at any rate a recognition; but it would take a great many orders to cover all that you have done for the P.o.W.s ... reminds me of a journey down from Rotterdam and your magic bag – perhaps [the lost letter] got lost in that... That is an awfully fine idea of yours for benefiting those who have suffered mentally at the front... But you want to take a really good holiday before embarking on it. For it is, to use an Americanism, a big proposition.'

We know nothing about the 'magic bag' and details of her idea for helping men who had suffered mentally might be lost in it.[301] However there is a Scheme for International Work Amongst Prisoners of War which will be found in the Appendix. Like so much about Grace, it remains a mystery. Perhaps the writer of the letter got the year wrong! This often happened when letters were handwritten or typed on a typewriter - people forgot to update the year.

---

[301] See Chapter 12 where this is mentioned as being in Save the Children file [EJ.187] Poland II/BCR/1: British Committee for Relief

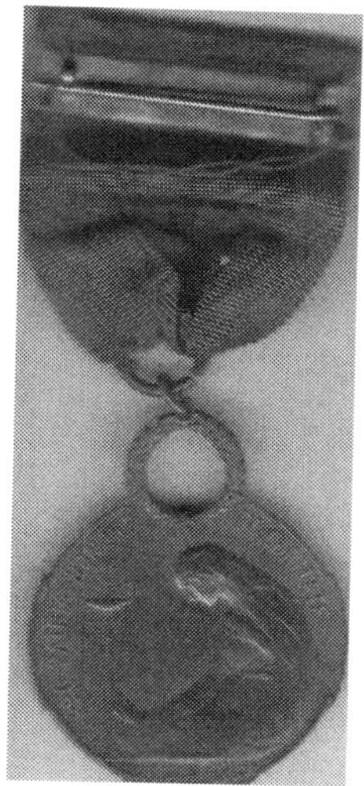

Plate 11.5 Left: Obverse of Grace Vulliamy's *Medaille de la Reine Elisabeth*
Right: Reverse of the Medaille

The Belgian Queen Elisabeth medal was instituted on 15 September 1915 and awarded to Belgian and foreign women who had personally dedicated themselves to the relief of Belgian civilians and soldiers in connection with the war by providing financial, material or medical assistance from 1914-19. The medal's reverse depicted a seated woman bearing an oil lamp, an allegorical female figure personifying the spirit of service and sacrifice, and a reference to the religious nature of nurses' training at that time. The base of the medal was inscribed '1918-1918' with 'Pro Patria Honore Et Caritate' along the rim (i.e. 'for the country, honour and charity).

Germany, Grace and Spying

Until 1918, the Germans did not realise Grace Vulliamy was English. Once they did, they no longer allowed her to travel on the train with the wounded.[302] 'The German wireless stated that on no account was she to proceed to the Dutch Border to take over the exchanged prisoners of war.'[303] It seems they suspected her of spying and Berlin had made representations to the Dutch authorities objecting to her presence. These events are reminiscent of her work in the early days of the war when she helped weed out undesirable refugees at Gravesend. Now she was filtering returning 'British' PoWs 'to weed out any German spies, a rather different

[302] Vulliamy papers. Rotterdam, 30 May

[303] Unattributed newspaper cutting. 'Miss Grace Vulliamy. Invested with C.B.E. by the King.'

emphasis from helping pass information secretly back to the UK.'[304] Spies could often be detected by an American twang in their speech because they were often talk to speak English that way. Alternatively, they might use the identity of someone who was in fact dead or perhaps know nothing about the place in England from which they were supposed to come. However, on 29 May when seven officers and a hundred and four men, all severely wounded, arrived from Germany in Rotterdam for repatriation she was not allowed to travel on the hospital train. This was the first time she had been unable to welcome the British subjects on their arrival at the frontier. Instead she waited for the prisoners in the Red Cross sheds in Rotterdam. It was undoubtedly a disappointment and made the task of listing their names, addresses and other details more difficult to do. Some prisoners were too ill to travel to England immediately but on 27 June 1918 the first party of British prisoners interned in Holland were passed by the Dutch Medical Board for repatriation to England. The party consisted of four officers, four NCOs and two civilians and left for England in the charge of Miss Grace Vulliamy

Companies often donated some of their goods to the troops and to refugees. This was seen as patriotic but was also a good way of advertising their wares ready for future peace. On 20 February 1918 The Vittoria Egyptian Cigarette Company sent 500 boxes of cigarettes to Miss Vulliamy and they asked her to be good enough to distribute them among the next contingent of prisoners which was expected on Saturday. On 6 March 1918 another 500 boxes were sent and on 24 May 1918 a further 5000 cigarettes sent. This gave her another task to organise.

Prisoners Still in Captivity – Royal Interviews

Nevertheless, at the same time Grace was still dealing with the problems of the prisoners in Germany who were not being released and continued to take steps to set them free, for example, interned British civilians over 45. On 7 March 1918 Viscount Devonport asked a question in the House of Lords about them because it was stated that there was a British military objection to their release. Was this the case? On 14 November she prepared a letter to an unknown recipient which showed she was very aware of the

[304] E-mail to writer from Daniel Vulliamy. 12.4.18. From 'a note from Poppy, my father's other sister, which emphasised Grace's role as filtering returning 'British' POWs to weed out any German spies, a rather different emphasis from helping pass information secretly back to the UK.'

political consequences of keeping men in captivity because they were of low rank. This was a social class issue of which the authorities at home seemed unaware. She wrote:

> I have seen and talked with those released prisoners of war who have already arrived from Germany at Rotterdam. Most of them were private soldiers and many captured in 1914, many in 1915 and some later. Practically all of them, though especially those captured in 1914, are very bitter and hostile towards the authorities at home for having allowed them to remain so long not only in captivity but under such bad conditions.
>
> The sentiments of these men may perhaps best be gathered from remarks made by many of them to the effect that 'if England has another war she won't find me ready again as she did in 1914.'

Eva Vulliamy explained 'So through the influence of a friend, she obtained an interview with Princess Helena Victoria. Through further channels she obtained an audience with King George V and Queen Mary to ask their help in 'getting our prisoners brought out to some neutral Country, naturally in exchange for the same number of Germans from England.'[1] She did not explain how she achieved this audience, but it might have been through Netterville Barron, mentioned earlier, or more likely with the help of Lena Ashwell who was married to Dr Henry Simson, the royal gynaecologist. She said that Lloyd George began to listen to her proposals when she told him that the enfranchised prisoners-of-war hated him and would never again vote for him!'[305] Grace wrote:

> so it was my privilege to approach the King and Queen and to ask their help in getting our prisoners brought out to some neutral Country, naturally in exchange for the same number of Germans from England. It was His Majesty himself who arranged that I should have a personal interview with Lloyd George, who wished for a detailed report and finally an agreement was made with Germany.

---

[305] Vulliamy papers. Woman of Action, p.3

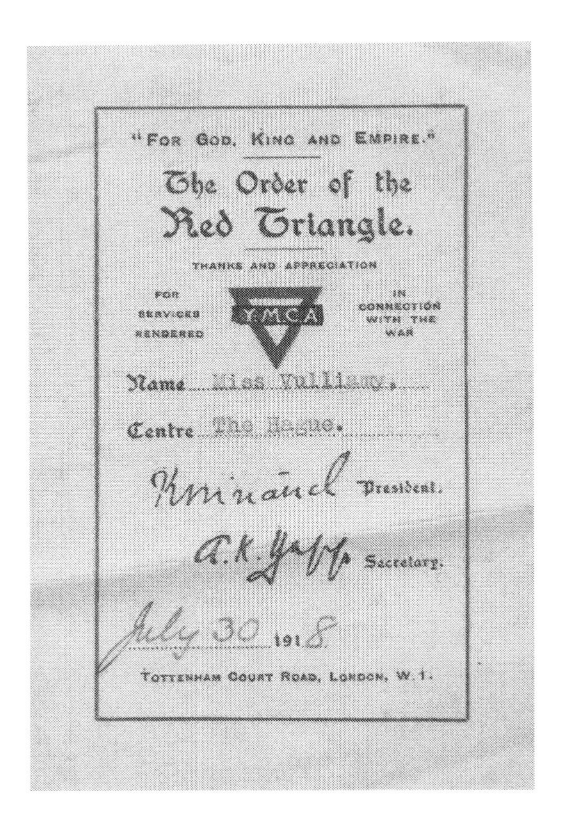

"FOR GOD, KING AND EMPIRE."

The Order of the Red Triangle.

THANKS AND APPRECIATION

FOR SERVICES RENDERED

Y.M.C.A

IN CONNECTION WITH THE WAR

Name Miss Vulliamy.

Centre The Hague.

Kinnaird President.

A.K. Yapp Secretary.

July 30 1918

TOTTENHAM COURT ROAD, LONDON, W.1.

Plate 11.6 The Order of the Red Triangle from the YMCA awarded on 30 July 1918

Grace's records show these interviews took place in July 1918. On 9 July 1918 the Prime Minister left her a telephone message 'could Miss Vulliamy come to 10 Downing Street at 4.30 instead of 3.30 please confirm by telephone.' On July 15 or 18, (date is unclear) 1918 a further telephone message was left for her saying 'The king and queen would like to see Miss Vulliamy at Buckingham Palace at 10.30 a.m. Friday - please write and confirm to Lord Stamfordham, (the King's private secretary).' So it remains confusing.

Adelaide Livingstone, writing on printed notepaper from the Government Committee on The Treatment by The Enemy of British Prisoners of War at the Houses of Parliament, wrote to Grace on July 24, 1918:

> I wish to heartily congratulate you on the great success you have had over here and I am delighted to hear you have been to see the King and Mr Lloyd George. I am sure you will have assisted our

prisoners even more than you have heretofore although that would be difficult. I do not wish you to slip away without seeing you. Would you come to lunch with me on Thursday at 1.30. Ring me up and tell me if that would suit you. Would you come to my club 29 Dover Street and we can talk over everything. Yours sincerely Adelaide Livingstone. Hon Sec.

On 6 August Grace wrote to Francis Aveling of the British Legation at The Hague, telling him about the honour she had received by being summoned to Buckingham Palace. She told him that His Majesty had asked many questions about the prisoners still in Germany, enquiring about their welfare and general condition. He had said that he and the Queen both hoped that the British prisoners in Germany did not think they were forgotten by the government and those at home. He wanted a message sent to them saying that never a day went by that he and the Queen did not think about them. Miss Vulliamy wondered whether there was any possibility of this message being conveyed to the prisoners because she felt it would 'cheer the hearts' for all those still in Germany.

Nonetheless, it appears that not everyone was so delighted with Grace Vulliamy's audience with the King and Queen. Mr Carbutt of the Red Cross sent a letter on 6 August saying that Mr Stanley was upset that she had discussed the Red Cross with Their Majesties. Grace replied by telegram on 28 August asking him to inform Mr Stanley that he she did not discuss the Red Cross with the King, Queen, and Prime Minister. The only views expressed about the Red Cross were those in a statement she had shown to Lord Sandwich. This rather nasty episode was probably a gender issue, Stanley assuming that as a woman she could not be trusted and was probably also a matter of hierarchy. Was this woman perhaps getting above herself? With signs of the war drawing to a close, women would be expected to return to their subservient roles. This would not suit Grace.

Grace's Pay

In contrast, some people were taking steps to ensure that Grace was at last properly remunerated for her work. On 17 September 1918 Arnold Robertson at The Hague wrote to the former Prime Minister, now Foreign Secretary, AJ Balfour, about her pay. He asked for consideration to be given to the question of the salary being granted to Miss Vulliamy who owing to the increasing cost of living and other reasons found herself in a financial position which would mean she would need to relinquish her work. He wrote:

Prior to the Hague Agreement of 1917 Miss Vulliamy was employed by the Society of Friends in Holland from whom she received a living allowance of £250 per annum in addition to which she was paid through HM Consul General at Rotterdam the sum of pounds 365 per annum by HM government as the official charged with the care and reception of British civilians arriving in Holland from Germany and Belgium.

Since the prisoners arrived Miss Vulliamy has laboured untiringly in their interests and has given most invaluable help in the organisation of the various hospitals and has herself nursed some of the most serious cases. For these services she is paid £300 per annum which the Netherland Government cannot well increase without causing friction amongst other members of staff who are paid at a fixed rate. On her taking up this appointment Mr Maxse felt that he was no longer justified in paying Miss Vulliamy a salary in view of the fact that such other services as she might in future undertake would be done on behalf of the Prisoners of War Department of the Legation. Her salary was therefore discontinued by Mr Maxse as also that formerly granted by the Society of Friends. It is in connection with the work which Miss Vulliamy has performed on behalf of the Legation that I beg to draw your special attention. Almost every party of British prisoners which has arrived at the frontier has been met by Miss Vulliamy, who has collected the names of each individual and arranged to which hospital invalids should be sent in the case of those for internment, and in the case of those for repatriation she has, together with a representative of the Rotterdam Lloyd Company, decided as to which ship and which part of the ship each individual should be allocated. She has supervised the drafting of the name lists of prisoners which accompany every transport. She has met and assisted civilians over 45 years of age and invalid civilians who have been repatriated and has personally obtained the necessary undertakings to refund the cost of the passage. She made herself responsible for the care of the party of British women and children who arrived from Belgium on the 12th instant, seeing that they were fed and assisted at Roosendaal and given every possible comfort while awaiting their departure in the sheds at Rotterdam. I would add that Miss Vulliamy has at all times willingly offered her services to the Legation in matters relating to prisoners of war. In view of the foregoing and of the fact that, in spite of the increased cost of living her income has been reduced by over 50%, I earnestly begged that you will authorise me, without delay, to pay her the difference between her past and present salaries, that is approximately 3600 florins per annum.

I have the honour to be with the highest respect Sir, etc
(signed) Arnold Robertson

How did this compare with the pay for a male member of the commission? A letter sanctioning part-time retention by the Commission of the services of Mr Bertram Fox for three months, shows that he had a salary of £500 per annum.[306] However he was only required to devote three days a week to the Commission. Miss Vulliamy's salary was therefore considerably less. Gender bias remained firmly established.

Armistice
People were beginning to sense the War was nearly at an end and at the Armistice in November 1918, Miss Vulliamy was asked by the War Office to stay in Holland, to help the repatriation of all British PoWs, until March 1919. The saddest time Grace Vulliamy had was after peace was proclaimed in 1918 when those who had been prisoners in Germany came pouring into Holland many of them victims of the 1918 flu and she spent three weeks visiting men dying of it and writing letters to their friends and family for them. This was her greatest task after the cessation of hostilities. When the Armistice came, thousands of prisoners of war without awaiting instructions just fled to the borders this was during the great flu epidemic and many, many died on the road but thousands entered Holland ragged emaciated and covered with lice. She took a leading part in the relief work in this connection.[307]

Prisoner-of-War Camps in Germany
Just after the Armistice in November 1918 it was arranged for Miss Vulliamy and Mrs Bromley Davenport to go into Germany and visit the prisoner of war camps. Sick men were distributed in all the centres to be visited and decisions needed to be made about moving them. Grace Vulliamy was provided with a letter of authorisation to proceed to any concentration camp and frontier post and hospital where British soldiers might be in order to visit the NCO's and then 'every facility should be given to Miss Vulliamy to enable her to move freely among the NCO's. After which she reports direct to the repatriation commission.'[308] There were about 17 camps and she had many photos of this investigation in her collection. These centres varied from splendid accommodation in the

---

[306] Numbered 48861, dated 1 January 1919 from Robert Chalmers to the Secretary, Commission Internationale de Ravitaillement
[307] Vulliamy Papers. A Woman of Action
[308] 19 December 1918.

casino at Venlo where the sick men were cared for by an Austrian doctor who was thought to be anti-English, to the worst at Gennep where the bedding was very dirty, there was no heating and no hospital equipment. This photo (Plate 11.8) of the prison camp at Chemnitz was taken for German propaganda purposes early in the war. In contrast Plate 11.7 shows the prisoners' typhus cemetery at Wittenburg camp.

Grace had worked with Mrs Bromley Davenport, the Honorary Secretary of the Invalid Comforts Fund for Prisoners of War, Hove, for some time and recently she had written thanking Grace for the time she gave at The Hague which had 'given me more understanding and grasp of the outlook of the prisoners. It has made me feel rather sad as I hate to think that they are bitter and they think their sacrifices are not understood at home.' She was also concerned about Grace's health and finished 'Do take a little care of yourself as you really have got a horrid cough and look tired. Muriel B D'. Both women were concerned about the apparent lack of concern for the sick by the military authorities. Mrs Bromley Davenport, who was told Grace that she had written a letter to *The Times* because it was 'only right that the public should know that no systematic effort has been made for the collection of the sick.' She hoped her letter would bring pressure to bear on Sir Edward Worthington, and perhaps there would be pressure also by the public.[309]

Mrs Bromley Davenport wrote a four-page letter on 28 December in case by some chance Miss Vulliamy was unable to get her on the telephone. She felt her presence and 'driving force' would help to clinch matters with the War Office. Immediately on her return from Holland she had reported the serious condition in Germany two weeks ago about the sick prisoners in Germany and how stretcher cases had not come through. All the men passing through Holland alleged that the bad cases were left in the Lazarettes; in many cases without any doctor to look after them and no medical supplies. These men would be left there until some arrangement could be made for their evacuation and transport supplied for them. Efforts she had made had been useless because information had not been passed to the appropriate people at the War Office. However her report strongly indicates lack of interest and commitment on the part of those in Adastral House, including Sir Edward Worthington. It was undoubtedly this kind of bureaucracy that led Grace to keep a poem entitled *Gods of Whitehall* in her collection of papers.[310] Three stanzas are:

[309] Letter from Mrs H R Bromley Davenport 6.1.1919
[310] See Appendix

I sent a remarkably civil enquiry
(I noted the date, April 1, in my diary)
To the Gods in Whitehall …

Then I waited a week, and no answer received;
Up till then I had firmly and simply believed
You were gods in Whitehall. …

….

At last your reply was brought in by my minion
"The Minister cannot express an opinion."
Damn the gods of Whitehall.

Plate 11.7 Typhus cemetary at Wittenburg camp

Influenza Epidemic

Mrs Bromley Davenport asked Miss Vulliamy to go to all the people she mentioned in her letter and point out that every day meant loss of life due to the Spanish fever, the filthy insanitary condition of the camps and overcrowding. She continued 'I cannot tell you how glad I am to feel you are in England, as I know you have a way of getting things put through and this has been a terrible struggle. The trouble has not been with the Central Committee or with the Inter-Departmental Committee but with the War Office.' She finished by inviting Miss Vulliamy to lunch in Sloane Street on Wednesday and said she wanted to give her a Burberry as a "small Christmas present in memory of the very happy time which I had with you in Holland." She signed the letter Yours affectionately, Muriel Bromley Davenport.

Plate 11.8 Prisoners Behind the Wire Fence at Havelberg Camp

Mrs Bromley Davenport also referred Miss Vulliamy to the *Times* report on 8 January 1919 concerning influenza in Copenhagen brought from Germany. Colonel Miller, consulting physician to Second Army home on leave had twice been sent to Germany due to epidemics at Meschede and Kassel in the Rhine area. He wrote that the conditions 'are too terrible at Meschede – evacuated all in 60 hours. Kassel not so bad but nine days taken.' Mrs Bromley Davenport thought that 'if French women are going into Germany there is no reason why English women should not go. .... The unfortunate thing is that these people (Redman, Sir Edward Worthington, Col Pollock) do not know you, and all British Officers have a rooted objection to the idea of English women going into Germany. What we now call sexism continued unabated.

Grace was still in touch with members of the Local Government Board, 18 Victoria Street, London, in early December sending New Year wishes for 1919 to Christopher Roundell. He replied on 31 December thanking her for good wishes 'which I reciprocate most heartily'. They discussed what was likely to happen in the future, he quoted from the Bible that there is to be 'a new heaven and a new earth' adding 'Heaven send that the corollary will also come to pass – that there will be no more war.' He thought that women and doctors were to be 'to the fore.' He continued 'your reputation for wonderful work ought to be enough to get you a hearing for whatever may be going – do remember me when you are set in high places,' adding more seriously 'Of course if ever I have the remotest opportunity of saying a word for you I will do so.' This changed future looked possible particularly when Viscount Knutsford, who had wanted nurses to be nothing more than the faithful carriers out of doctors' orders, sent her a note saying 'Could you conveniently call here Wednesday at 10. I have heard from Captain Christie Miller about your help to prisoners. I have to do with shellshock cases amongst officers. (signed) Knutsford.' Christie Miller was an officer in the Coldstream Guards and had briefly been a prisoner of war in 1914.

Plate 11.9 Prison camp at Chemnitz

Major General Hanbury Williams wrote to her on 30th December 1918 saying he had heard her work in Holland with prisoners of war and repatriation was coming to an end. There is a hint that he recognised women's work was under-valued. He said:

> I hear your work in Holland in connection with prisoners of war and their repatriation is coming to an end. I trust your organising and administration administrative abilities capabilities will find you some acceptable employment in reconstruction work or otherwise. No one knows better than I do what splendid work you accomplished and how your untiring energy accomplished work that few men could have done. All ranks of the Imperial forces whom you helped owe you a deep debt of gratitude, and I trust that if my name or recommendation can help at any time you will use it freely. I am yours sincerely

Awards

On 16 June 1917 it was reported in the *British Journal of Nursing* that the Dutch Red Cross Order had been presented to Grace Vulliamy by the Prince Consort of Holland as President of the Dutch Red Cross (the first English woman to be so honoured). This was the first of her several . The next was the YMCA Red Triangle on 30 July 1918. Then came the *Medaille de la Reine Elisabeth,* the medal that had been specially instituted for service to Belgian prisoners of war and refugees in the Netherlands. The actual medal was sent to her on 31 October 1919, because 'owing to your departure from the Netherlands His Majesty's Chargé d'affaires was unable to present it personally'. In addition, she had the Belgian King's permission to wear the Medal without restriction. Amongst her documents is one from the British King George announcing his decision to 'nominate and appoint her as a Commander of the Civil Division of the Order of the British Empire' in the New Year Honours, dated 1 January 1919. This Order was instituted by King George V on 4 June 1917 so that recognition could be given to civilians for their service in wartime. Grace's award was announced in *The Times* on 9 January 1919 with the citation that it was for assistance to British civilians and prisoners of war in Holland. The CBE investiture was on the 14 November 1919 and she was the only woman to be so honoured at that particular investiture.[311]

There is in Grace's documents a letter dated 17 January 1919 from someone at the British Legation in The Hague; it is not known who sent it because the final page is missing but it is highly significant nonetheless. Possible writers include Townley and Aveling.

> I want to put on paper what you know I have felt concerning your 'honour.' No one knows better than I of your work in Holland of your untiring consideration and exertions on behalf of all sorts kinds and conditions of people. It's been wonderful and I can't tell you how it has been appreciated by hundreds including myself. The one thing I think that has struck me most has been the fact that nothing has been too big or too small for you to take up. In your element with a lunatic on one arm and a consumptive on the other you have still managed to assist any other wretched fellow on crutches or a woman who has lost her baby and her temper. When you have been worried out of your life you have always done and said small things which most people would have avoided doing and saying but which have meant such an infinite lot to those concerned

[311] *The Times.* 9 January 1919, p.2. For assistance to British Civilians and Prisoners of War in Holland.

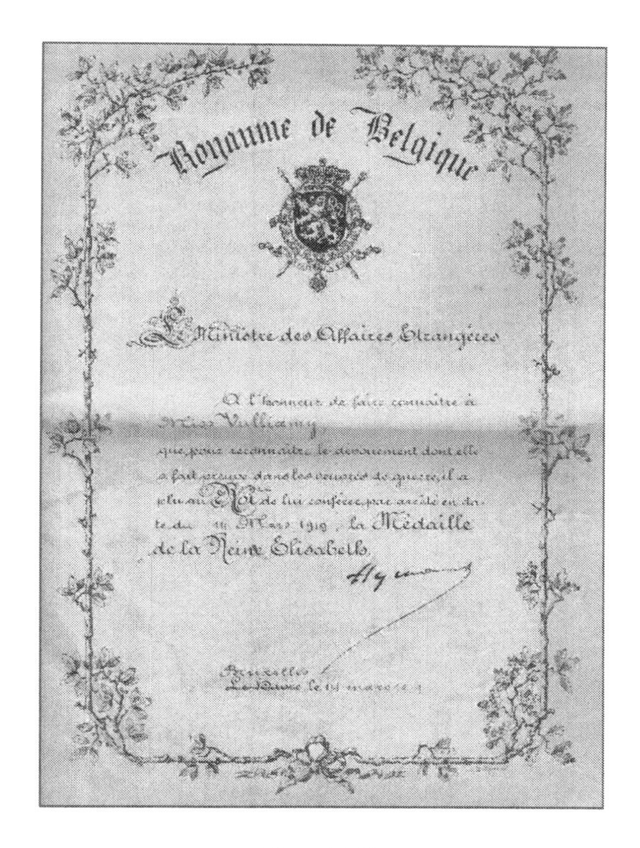

Royaume de Belgique

Le Ministre des Affaires Etrangères

A l'honneur de faire connaître à Miss Villiamy que, pour reconnaître le dévouement dont elle a fait preuve dans les oeuvres de guerre, il a plu au Roi de lui conférer, par arrêté en date du 14 Mars 1919, la Médaille de la Reine Elisabeth.

[illegible]

Bruxelles
~~Le Havre~~, le 14 mars [illegible]

<u>Plate 11.10</u>
<u>The Certificate accompanying her</u> <u>*Medaille de la Reine Elisabeth*</u>

Thank you so very much for all the help you have always given me and 1000 congratulations on your 'recognition' by the powers that be. Any nonsense about your refusing it must stop at once!! And all are well bestowed is shared by all so that's that.

Plate 11.11 Grace Vulliamy after receiving the CBE accompanied by her guests, her nephew Tom Vulliamy Collard and her sister Violet
Courtesy Mark Vulliamy

CHAPTER 12

POST-WAR WORK, SOUTH AFRICA & END OF LIFE

Lady Paget's Mission

Grace Vulliamy was still based in the Netherlands at the Armistice, which is barely mentioned in her papers except for the fact she was asked to stay on for a few months until March 1919 to help with repatriation. However, prior to the Armistice she arranged a period of work in Czechoslovakia. Lady Muriel Paget, an aristocratic relief worker, had worked on Russian relief but was now in the Czechoslovak Republic. She needed someone to be in control while she went away for a few months. On 13 April 1918 Lady Paget signed a document authorising Miss Vulliamy to enter into any provisional agreements on her behalf with reference to her responsibilities toward the Czechoslovak government.[312] She wrote 'owing to my absence .... I shall be quite satisfied if it covers any responsibilities I may have towards the Czechoslovak government but as Dr Osusky, the Czechoslovak Chargé d'Affaires, is not in London, I cannot delegate such power [to him]. A further letter of 13 April 1918 stated that:

> Miss Vulliamy, Miss MacInnes and Miss Ward are proceeding to Prague, in order to make arrangements for the arrival of the Mission of hospital and social workers that I hope to bring out to Czechoslovakia in May. Miss Vulliamy will be my assistant commissioner and Miss MacInnes Matron-in-Chief. Miss Vulliamy is authorized to enter into any ..... arrangements on my behalf and I feel sure that both Miss Vulliamy and Miss MacInnes will receive the same co-operation and sincere kindness that was given me by many friends in Czechoslovakia.
>
> Miss Vulliamy has had .... experience in organization of relief during the war and we are extremely fortunate in obtaining her help and advice.
>
> (Signed) Muriel Paget'

In the early months of 1919 Grace joined Lady Muriel Paget's Mission to Czechoslovakia, which she was in charge of for six months. Here Grace carried out one of the most important aspects of that Mission, training local

[312] 9 Grosvenor Place, SW1. 13 April 1918. This has a big black smudge down the left side, obscuring many words.

paediatric nurses and social workers.[313] The Mission, partly funded by money from New Zealand and later the Save the Children Fund, organized child welfare and relief work in Estonia, Latvia, and Lithuania, where there were many Russian refugee children as well as local children needing help.

Plate 12.1 This photograph from the Vulliamy collection is believed to be of Lady Paget's Mission to Czechoslovakia

In August 1921 the League of Nations appointed Dr Fridtjof Nansen, delegate for Norway, as High Commissioner for Russian and Armenian Refugees whose existence was central to the League's attempt to define 'refugee' and to begin to provide aid.[314] In 1922 when Save the Children withdrew financial support from the Paget Missions, Nansen agreed with Lady Muriel's complaint that they favoured short-term feeding instead of long-term constructive work, affecting aid to Russia where she had been invited to help train child welfare workers. Lady Paget was a dynamic woman who expressed her views without deference to gender expectations. From Versailles, where the Great Powers were discussing the terms of the Treaty to be presented to Germany, Harold Nicolson[315] wrote to his wife Vita Sackville-West: 'her energy is terrifying. She sends Prime Ministers scuttling at her behests.' Lord Weardale, a member of the Fight the Famine

[313] Oldfield: *Women Humanitarians,* 2001. Continuum. 162

[314] Storr, *Excluded.* 134

[315] Nicolson, Nigel 1973. *Portrait of a Marriage*. Weidenfeld & Nicolson. 133

Council who became President of the Save the Children Fund[316] complained: 'Lady Muriel Paget ... makes commitments about which she has never consulted anybody'. Four members of the Mission, including Grace, went on a tour of orphanages, hospitals, and homes in April 1919. Grace included in her papers a report made by one of these colleagues, noting the size and cleanliness of the accommodation and the nationality of the people, particularly recording the number of Jews and commenting on their financial position. This was probably for practical purposes such as diet and the necessity for fund-raising among other Jews who traditionally took responsibility for their co-religionists.

Fight the Famine and Save the Children

During the period of Armistice before the signing of the Treaty on 28 June 1919, efforts were made by various pressure groups to influence the course of decisions made by the statesmen responsible for making the Peace Treaties of which the League of Nations was a part. One such Committee was 'Fight the Famine'. The sisters Dorothy Buxton and Eglantyne Jebb gathered some friends to form the Fight the Famine Council to exert political pressure and educate the public about the need for a European economic system that would abolish hunger.[317] Its first public meeting was held on 1 January where a provisional committee was elected, with Lord Parmoor as Chair.[318] The provisional Committee included the Quakers Ruth Fry, with whom Grace had worked in the civilian internment camps in Holland, and Marian Ellis who had helped Ruth Fry with women victims of the Boer War.[319] On 15 April 1919, at the Fight The Famine Council Executive meeting Dorothy Buxton proposed that a special sub-committee be appointed to raise a relief fund for children.[320] Nonetheless, Eglantyne Jebb is always credited with founding the Save the Children Fund (SCF) and, while the latter was devoted to raising funds for relief work carried out by other relief organisations, the Fight the Famine Council also aimed at studying the general economic situation in Europe and helping to form an enlightened public opinion.[321]

Save the Children was launched at the Royal Albert Hall in May 1919. That year SCF sought Miss Vulliamy's advice on finding a suitable person in

---

[316] from the end of 1919 until 1925 when the Duke of Atholl took his place
[317] Wilson. *Rebel Daughter.* 173
[318] S.C.F. Archive Paper 7.
[319] Oldfield. *Women Humanitarians.* 66
[320] Wilson 1967: 174
[321] Mary Sheepshanks7/yyy8

whose name an appeal might go out, because the writer of the letter and Miss Jebb were not well-known enough.[322] This implies that Grace was much more famous at that time – although the situation is now completely reversed. Her fame meant that many high-ranking people of various nationalities approached her for help. For example, on 27 August 1920 a letter from the British Legation (signature unclear) informed her that Prince Sapieha of Poland wanted to discuss with her 'how to arrange housing for the prisoners who have been captured on the Eastern front'.

There is much new information and photographs about Grace's work with Save the Children which cannot be fully explored at the present time. Indeed, it is thought that Grace's work contributed to the formation of Eglantyne Jebb's charity which she thought would be short lived, but it is, of course, still working a hundred years later. On 12 October 1920 Grace wrote to Mr Maudesley (no address) asking him if it was possible for her to have Mr Salin as Transport Officer. This was probably Algernon Maudslay of the War Refugees Committee in London, who had been elected to the Serbian Relief Fund Committee on 18 September 1918, had an interview with the recently formed Save the Children Fund[323] and received £2,500 with promises of more.[324] She told him the Save the Children Famine Fund were sending goods out to her the following week and it was essential for her to get someone 'out there' by the end of the week; they were also sending her £250 for administration purposes and workers' expenses. She and her helpers had raised about another £300 but it was necessary to have £1000 in the bank to enable them to carry on work free from financial worries. He had promised her a typewriter and she asked if he could get it sent to her home at Ware. Grace's connection with Save the Children administration is further indicated by a photograph of a SCF Conference in her collection but she was unsure of the date, writing '? 1923' on the back. (Plate 12.1) Grace wrote to Miss Jebb on 2 October 1921 about beginning their work in Warsaw and on 12 October 1922 to Mr Maudsley (sic) of the Save The Children Famine Fund (sic) which indicates that Fund's early support of Grace Vulliamy's work in Poland; indeed, they were sending out goods and a further £250 the following week. Miss Ashwell in London was simultaneously forming the Committee for Grace's charity, the British Committee for Relief in Poland. The Red Cross promised to help and gave food and clothes. An ex-prisoner of war sent her 100 suits and money. The Admiralty undertook to ship these

[322] [EJ.187] Poland II/BCR/1: British Committee for Relief.
[323] See Storr, *Excluded.* Chapter 8. An End to the War to End all Wars? Wars, Famines, Revolutions and Blockades. *The War in Russia and Poland.*
[324] See Storr, *Excluded.* Chapter 7. Serbia.

things with her to Poland. The YMCA and Save the Children also helped her in different ways.[325]

Grace Vulliamy met Dr Katharine MacPhail who was one of the people helped by Save the Children. She was described as a slightly-built, courageous Scotswoman who had served in medical units all through the war. Since most women doctors were suffragists, it is also probable that Katharine was one. There are informal photographs of MacPhail with the Queen of Yugoslavia in Grace Vulliamy's collection, and of patients lying in their beds outside buildings – being in fresh air was a treatment for TB. By 1934, when MacPhail was nearly 50, 170,000 children had been treated in her hospital and many girls given nursing training. The hospital was then handed over to the Yugoslav government, and with the money raised she built a specialist home for children with TB of the joints and bones. Save the Children, which had special concern for refugee children, continued to aid her children's hospital until the country was invaded early in World War Two. Despite the fact her work was among children, MacPhail was sometimes denigrated by the British for working for foreigners. Save the Children itself was not immediately accepted by sections of the British public because it was working for foreign children.

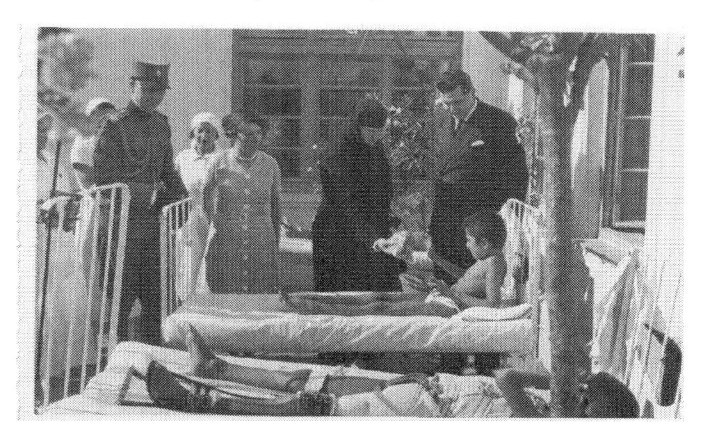

Plate 12.2 Dr MacPhail with the Queen of Yugoslavia visiting one of MacPhail's hospitals for children.

Civilian suffering

At the Armistice millions of people were displaced. There were, for example, Serbian refugees in the Loire and in Corsica; and more than 1 ½

[325] Vulliamy Papers. Amalia Close (du Plessis), Cape Town

million Russians were to be found throughout Europe.[326] There were Belgian refugees in Britain, France and Holland. Millions of people from Poland and the Baltic had been forcibly evacuated to Russia and Siberia. Some refugees streamed back half-starved and diseased to where their homes had been and where there was little or no medical aid. In spring 1920, 50,000 war prisoners were still cut off in prison camps in Siberia, Caucasus and Turkestan, unable to get home although officially free.

In reality the war had not ended, since 'some eighteen wars [were] still in progress.'[327] Some were civil wars, but others were manifestations of Britain's war now being fought against bolshevism. Plate 12.2 is of a Russian girl dressed in men's clothing who fought with the White Russian Army. The prolongation of the blockade and of 'small' wars meant continued suffering as did boundary changes determined by the Great Powers at Versailles that created thousands of displaced people. Poland, which was then part of Russia, did not benefit, as England did, from the November Armistice; its war and suffering continued as a result of the Russian revolution and boundary changes. There was 'a desolation only to be seen elsewhere in the devastated areas of France and Belgium'[328] and there was famine. The Russian famine was one not only of food but of everything including clothes and soap, exacerbated by a shortage of water. Miss Vulliamy visited refugee and internment camps and was horrified by the conditions. It was during this time that as she put it, Grace was adopted by a little Russian boy, Misha Sychoff, who became her legally adopted son and lived with her in England and later in South Africa. Part of his story given below is in his own words. He changed the way in which he referred to Grace, calling her Miss Vulliamy and more familiarly Ma, and uses the initials GCV which she often signed herself by.

Misha's story

> It was the time of the Russian revolution. My parents were quite ordinary folk. My father was a lieutenant in the White Army (pro Czar) and my mother a school teacher. There was defeat by the Bolshevicks so they made their way to Poland. At that time, the wives joined their kin and made their way to refuge ... with the men-folk (soldiary). Grace Vulliamy had her HQ in Warsaw, from there she established orphanages. I can recall about four. These needed a lot of financial

[326] Nansen, 1923. 1

[327] Charles Roden Buxton and Dorothy Frances Buxton. *The World After The War.* George Allen & Unwin Ltd., London, 1920. 10

[328] SCF.EJ73

support and staff so Ma would commute back to England, campaigning for money, giving speeches and lectures, meeting influential folk and generally keeping the orphanages running. She would recruit voluntary staff from England, who she trained and in such a way they bonded with her and gave all their energies. As for delegating responsibility she did this readily and in no time each orphanage had its own staff.

Money was the problem for food clothes and medicine. ... The SoF appreciated her effort and gave their whole-hearted support. Ma at times had to interview the Prime Minister, also the Royal Family, all of whom she persuaded to help with the cause.

Plate 12.3 A Russian girl who fought with the White Russian Army

As the armies retreated my mother who was pregnant with another child - to simplify things an abortion was made. In no way could a baby be brought into the world they thought in those conditions, and sadly this went wrong and she died. My memory still ... very vague impressions .... Being lifted to kiss a corpse in a coffin ... walking, very tired towards lamps on tall fencing glowing in the dusk. This must have been some refugee camp. Some hazy memories of soldiers being very kind and laughing a lot, giving me lap rides and singing.

My father was sick somewhere and died of TB due to the privations he been through. His best friend Doctor Taratsoff and wife he asked to look after me. I lived with them in one room in a timbered barrack-like area. They quarrelled a lot, not unkind to me, but I was terrified of Dr Taratsoff – bad temper. The room was about 10 x 12 ft. with beds in the corner. There was a communal bath like a small swimming pool, gloriously warm, shared by many others together. Bars of soap. Queuing up with other children being fitted out with new clothes smelling of moth balls. Forever wanting to have a wee, and forever wet trousers. Not knowing where to go or who to ask. Being bundled into railway carriages, climbing up what seemed huge heights to get in. Then some ladies walking about giving out oranges. I had one clutched in my hand but didn't know what to do with it. I think an elder child took it eventually.

Plate 12.4 Lydia, Valya and Misha, aboard ship in the Baltic, en route to the U.K.

I find myself at last in a very pleasant orphanage outside Danzig called Hoybuda. Dormitories in the main building and the dining area was a barrack. About 100 of us age from 4 to15. Here at Hoybuda I met Lydia and Valya (who came to England).

Now the children bathed in the Baltic, enjoyed playing in the sand, and with an orphanage dog called Bally given by Grace for the children's benefit and everyone loved it. Another amenity was the gramophone.... Nursery records would be played – 10 little nigger boys. Winter was an ordeal, always cold and shivery. I was sick most of the time with bronchitis. I remember lying in bed – usually wet, too cold to get out into the lavatory – hazy and vague. The one thing that stands out is Miss Vulliamy's visits. Sweets, presents, clothes were handed out and the orphans had to give some sort of display – sports or charades.

Having a bad chest, Ma was worried about my health so she took me from the body of the orphanage to her premises nearby. I had a bed on a camp stretcher. Oh the feeling of security and warmth! ... Sleep ... I peeped above the blanket and watched Miss Vullliamy working on books and letters in the same room. I stayed there several days and to my dismay was returned to the orphanage. On her next visit of inspection it was reported to her that little Misha was far from well and basically I was pining for the love and attention I had recently experienced. So the process was repeated but after that I gather I took it for granted that Miss V would not let me return. As it was obviously too difficult for me to travel around with her, another worker, a Miss Gunter, took me over in her care. I went to another orphanage at a place called Sulewick, and was accommodated with Miss Gunter in her private room. Here my ablutions started. Nightly I would be bathed – a rubber folding one with kettles of hot and cold water. This became great fun as taps were introduced. From this period on, I was privileged as a member of the administry (sic) ... Miss V who wherever possible would give me a great deal of attention. The wonderful feeling of being able to get into bed with her and have stories and games. The other children in the orphanage treated me well, but I was no longer one of 'them.'

During this period, unbeknown to me, Mum was negotiating with Dr Taratsoff to get him to give me up to her for adoption. It was a difficult time as he had promised my father to look after me. In the end he realised my future would be more secure in the hands of GCV and he gave his consent.

When this was effected, I went to Warsaw with GCV and stayed there I think a summer and a winter. I can remember Polish Cavalry Regiments, with lanes, in the streets, also riding in the horse drawn cabs ... in the winter in sledges being whisked along in absolute silken in the snow. In this flat GCV had various dinner parties. The flat itself I thought was huge, on the second floor.

Poland

Straggling soldiers of many nationalities, accompanied by their families, retreated from the Bolsheviks, and civilians with broken health resultant from the famine and terrorism poured into newly-constructed Poland.[329] Grace Vulliamy wrote to Lena Ashwell:

[329] Florence Barrow, head of Friends Relief work in Poland.

They are in a deplorable condition and are absolutely destitute ... it is really through our bad policy they are in this plight – many are dressed in British uniforms. Children with no drop of milk.'[330]

All children were very white and lethargic, suffering from lack of nourishment and unhygienic surroundings. One boy age 10 had hidden in a cellar for two weeks.[331] Grace Vulliamy received a letter from the Commandant of the camp which said that he and:

the Polish Government wish to help these people, but it is very difficult as we have no food, clothes or boots. Soon it will be winter, very severe as it is in Poland, and we must think of clothes, food and boots. The Commandant knows the generosity of England and begs England to do all possible. He is sure England will not refuse this help, and he sends thanks from all Prisoners of War.

Signed Stefan Calli, Col, Commandant.'

Plate 12.5 On the Russian-Polish border

In November 1919, on her return journey back to England she met Count Pawlowski, ADC to Mr Paderewski, Prime Minister of Poland, who begged her to visit Dabie Camp, near Kraków with a view to obtaining help from England for the Russian refugees pouring into Poland. She was amused by the references to 'England' helping, saying that it was not England but 'only me'. This Dabie Camp contained 5,000 souls, Russians who had fled with their families from the Bolshevists, Ukrainians, Ruthenians, and others. Eighty-five percent of them had no shirts, and sixty per cent no

[330] 28.3.20. GCV To Lena

[331] Vulliamy Papers. Amalia Close.

footwear whatever. The Commandant asked her to inspect their daily ration, which consisted of a piece of bread insufficient for a meal, weak coffee made of acorns without milk or sugar, and a small bowl of dried vegetable soup full of floating maggots!

The British Committee for Relief in Poland

On her return to England Miss Vulliamy sent an appeal to the newspapers from her home at Littlehome, Herts, specifically aimed at any ex-prisoners of war whom she had 'the privilege of meeting on the Dutch Frontier and who, remembering the hour of their release may help these men with shirts and boots through the terrible winter before them.' She then established the British Committee for Relief in Poland with Lena Ashwell as Chair and Beatrice Harraden on the Committee[332] and returned to Poland for five years. It was here that, in her words, 'she was adopted by Misha, a little Russian boy'. She brought him back to England with her and brought him up as her son.

On 7 January she received a letter from General Herbert E Belfield, with whom she had worked on prisoner relief in Holland, enclosing a copy of a letter written to General Carton de Wiart, head of the British Mission in Warsaw, promising to help her work in Poland. He also offered his:

> Congratulations on the decoration which has been conferred on you. You have the satisfaction of knowing that it has been very well earned.

Grace Vulliamy began work alone in the spring of 1920 in the camp at Dabie. Now seeing Grace struggle, Sir Paul Dukes sent to her aid a Miss Cade who spoke fluent Russian. Grace was able to leave her in charge of her camp. This enabled her to start crèches elsewhere. Sir Paul Dukes had been in St Petersburg studying music on the outbreak of war and become a member of the Anglo-Russian Commission, a British propaganda organisation. In the summer of 1917 Dukes was asked by the Tsarist Secret Police to spy on the Bolshevik leaders. To do this he joined the Bolshevik Party and was in the Red Army. The British offered him a responsible post in the Secret Intelligence Service, believing that Russia would not long continue to be open to foreigners and wanting someone to remain there to keep the British Government informed of the 'march of events.' There is no clue as to how Dukes knew about Grace and her problems, but there may

---

[332] 'Grace, like Paget, politically colour-blind.' Oldfield, p.162. 'Inveterate traveller, goes straight to the top.'
She remained in Poland for five years.

be a connection with Sir John Hanbury Williams with whom Grace had worked in Holland. In addition to this work, Hanbury Williams during the First World War was head of the British military mission with the Russian Stavka, the high command of the Russian Armed Forces, with direct access to Tsar Nicholas II.

Visiting other camps meant that Grace spent six uncomfortable nights out of seven on trains, with no doors, and no upholstery to soften the seats. She had a narrow escape from being captured by the Bolsheviks by crossing a bridge over the Vistula immediately prior to it being blown up. In the camps, typhus, the hunger and dirt disease, was rampant, people emaciated, sanitary conditions indescribable. The peasants didn't realise hygiene and diet were linked with disease.[333] In one camp in June 1922, eighty-nine per cent of children had rickets and TB was rife.[334]

By 1921 there were twelve other centres, mostly in erstwhile internment camps, where help was organized from the Committee's Warsaw HQ. Assistance was given to the Committee by the British American and Norwegian Red Cross Societies and the YMCA. The Polish military authorities also helped but for many months Miss Vulliamy worked alone. After establishing crèches, maternity homes and kitchens, workrooms were opened and the refugees were taught arts and crafts of all kinds. Then Grace received another SOS from the nearby hospital where there were eighteen destitute expectant mothers with 'not a shred of clothing for the babies'. However, the Americans sent out hams wrapped in muslin and this was washed and used by the mothers to make baby clothes. Grace did her best to help such unfortunate people but made them work for what they got, thereby creating self-respect and productivity. The BCR always had two great objects in view – to give personal and direct help to those in need, and to give help, as far as possible, only in return for work done.

The Polish Government gave Grace a railway carriage and allowed her to hitch it to any train going to any destination she wanted to reach in Poland and Germany. To venture into Russia would have been suicidal. The carriage was self-contained; it had a kitchen, WC, and sleeping area and could accommodate about three or four people. There was a resident steward who prepared meals. This was 'James [who] looks after me.' Misha often slept on the train but dreaded when it was shunted and connected to other trains, usually with terrible jolts and bumps. Grace used this for transporting children to orphanages of which she had at least seven,

---

[333] Friends House Library. Box 7.2.2.
[334] Vulliamy lists and notes. In Szczypiorno,

supported financially by the new Save the Children Fund. Children came in by trains and public transports from Refugee Camps all over Europe. The first activity was always to open a children's kitchen. Parents, or the child, worked for and were paid in clothes if they were well enough. At orphanages children were encouraged to dress dolls which were then sold to help support them. When the time came to hand them in, one child had 'no doll' because she'd kissed off the nose! Grace started crèches in thirteen centres. Refugee teachers earned by teaching the children. At Danzig-Heubude Grace ran a Seaside Holiday Home where children from the camps went for three weeks' recuperation. This is reminiscent of her work as a mental nurse at Holloway Sanatorium.

Plate 12.6 Grace's train carriage

Save the Children

Grace Vulliamy's Fund for Poland seems to have been the first fund to be helped by Save the Children. Indeed, it is thought that her reports may have helped instigate its foundation by Eglantyne Jebb. Their records contain firstly, Miss Vulliamy's Correspondence and Reports from 27 November 1919 to December 1922 and correspondence about allocations and the dispatch of aid materials; detailed reports on conditions in Poland, work done and grants and materials received. They include a proposal [c 1920] by Miss Vulliamy for a scheme for international work among prisoners of war – most probably the scheme that was mentioned in Chapter 11. There is a letter written in Russian, with translation, by a child in a refugee camp; including accounts of 'adopted' (sponsored) children; detailed reports of conditions and of SCF work done, 1922. These records were not available to the writer at the time the research was being done because they were in inaccessible storage.[335] Grace Vulliamy became Life Vice-President of Save the Children Fund.

In 1923 Grace went to South Africa to raise funds to support the orphan children. By then she was also delegate for the International Save the Children Union.[336] At this period none of the great voluntary agencies except SCF and the Red Cross were in existence to share the burden. In Cape Town, a sale of work was held under the auspices of the National Council of Women. Most embroidery was in cross stitch and settings which had an exceedingly beautiful base and embroidery effects were produced in drawn thread work. In Durban the National Council of Women again supported her. Ten percent of the takings were to be given to the local Child Welfare Society. Out of this grew the Slavonic Handicrafts Depot, run by the London Committee and the National Council of Women and was not restricted to London. Grace's house in London was 42 Great Russell Street, right opposite the British Museum. Family and friends visited and sunbathed on the roof – the garden as it was called. The ground floor was devoted to the shop 'Slavonic Handicrafts' and floors 1, 2, and 3 were accommodation, some of which were let out and some Grace and Misha used.

Their shop sold handicraft made by refugees in the various camps. On occasion they also bought things brought to them by refugees such as Russians who had formerly been wealthy but now needed to sell their precious items in order to buy food and other necessities. One of the customers in the Johannesburg shop was the famous actress Sybil Thorndike. She wrote to Grace that the thing she had bought were 'positively beautiful'. They would revive her memories of Johannesburg when she looked at them in London.

One report stated that 'Civilisation was tottering and Miss Vulliamy and others were working to alleviate the sufferings of the women and children thereby keeping civilisation alive'. The adoption scheme was promoted and for £5 (five pounds) a year one could adopt a Godchild. Today this would be called sponsoring.

335 [EJ.187 & 188] Poland II/BCR 1

336 to the value of 500 Swiss francs per month. SCF and Grace now had joint offices.

Grace Charlotte Vulliamy herself is first mentioned in the Save the Children Fund Annual Report for 1924 in a section which refers to the end of the work of the British Committee for Relief in Poland due to:

> improved conditions and the breaking up of the refugee camps… the warm thanks of the Council are due to Miss Vulliamy, to whose devoted and untiring efforts in administration of their grants for Polish children they have been indebted for three years.

Plate 12.7 Save the Children Conference, Geneva, possibly 1923

She is listed as a member of the Association in 1924, and in the 1925 Annual Report she is a member of Council. In 1925 Miss Vulliamy 'enjoyed a well-earned rest' in London but also had a cottage in Beaconsfield. She remained on Council until 1930 and is listed as Vice-President in the 1930 Annual Report. This title was changed to Honorary Vice-President in the 1933 Annual Report, and she continued to be listed, with others, in this office, in subsequent annual reports into the 1950s, so it is likely that this was a life role.[337]

The *Rhodesia Herald,* published in Salisbury an article on 23 May, 1930 said that Grace Vulliamy was the 'Original organiser of the Nichevo and

[337] is-heslop@adf.bham.ac.uk to David Budgen . Fri, 4 Mar 2016

Slavonic Handcraft Industry, based at 1 New Zealand House, Cape Town, the premises having been found for her by the National Council of Women.' She was then 'staying with her sister, Sister Eva, at St Mary's House and with her, is her secretary, Miss Molchanoff, a Russian refugee.' The latter had passed through Siberia, was at school for two years under the Bolsheviks, and found her way out through China to England.

Plate 12.8 The British Committee for Relief in Poland leaflet
Courtesy Mark Vulliamy

'Retirement'

Grace 'retired' to Cape Town, South Africa, in 1937. Many years later her adopted son Misha commented:

> 'Retired' perhaps is not quite correct as she was for ever acting in some pastime that helped others. ... 'we bought' a cottage amid 12 acres of open veld. It was primitive, no electricity, we had Coleman lamps. Water came from a bore-hole in the ground, pumped up by a windmill. Cooking was done on a 'Dover' stove, burning wood or coal. Wood was plentiful and available from wattle trees on the land. Misha spent quite lot of energy chopping and sawing this up.

During the Spanish Civil War, in 1938, as an inveterate traveller and humanitarian, Miss Vulliamy with National Joint Committee money set up a canteen for wounded and worn out men in Spain. The Quaker Dr Edith Pye described it in a letter to her friend Hilda Clark as a 'Terrible tragedy here – one solid block of refugees.' Grace's nephew Daniel later wrote:

> May 1937 represented the 80th anniversary of the arrival in the UK of almost 4,000 Basque refugee children after Italian and German planes bombed Guernica and attacked Bilbao. We know that Grace was involved in advising on arrangements for the children

> to be put in tents on their arrival, before going to centres all round the country. She obviously pressed my father's sisters, Poppy and Chloe to use their language and other skills. Both Chloe and Poppy ran children's homes from May 1937. Chloe was still running one of the last homes, in Carshalton, in 1938 when she wrote a really interesting piece about making the homes self-managed by the children, now considerably older, but with some of them still traumatised by their experiences. To an extent, Chloe was continuing the development of Grace's ideas.[338]

During this period it is possible Grace was at some kind of crossroads. When this occurs people sometimes turn to esoteric disciplines to help them and between the Wars many people became interested in Theosophy. Theosophy stressed internationalism and included astrology in its teachings; there were affinities between it and Quakerism, with which Grace Vulliamy seems to have been particularly sympathetic. Dr Rotten, who was known as the Florence Nightingale of Ruhleben and with whom Grace cooperated in regard to prisoners of war, was interested in both and joined the Friends in 1931. See Chapter 8.[339] From the limited correspondence that survives between them we know that Grace worked with Dr Rotten, helping prisoners of war for at least two years. There is also a Newnham link between them. (See Chapters 1, 8 and 10)

In 1938 at Malo, Grace had her handwriting analysed by a graphologist; she also had an analysis of her astrological sun sign, which was Virgo. She was told this made her practical, discriminating, methodical, industrious and intelligent with a keen sense of justice and that she was also kind, modest and retiring. From what we have learned of Grace this would appear to be accurate but whether it was of any help to her it is impossible to know.

World War 2 parted Grace and Misha – he to Egypt and Italy while Grace stayed in the Cape where she started in very small way something that grew into a village of the poorer folk. Observing the hardships and privations of the Cape Coloureds she started off by getting a large aeroplane crate; these were available being war-time. This she converted into a shack, a games-room and set up a club for local coloured youth, the 'skollies' from the deprived Cape Coloured community where they could come and play cards, dominoes and such like. Misha wrote:

---

[338] Daniel Vulliamy to the author. 4.9.2017

[339] Friends FWVRC. Box 10, parcel 2, folder 3. (Hereafter 10:2:3) German Babies' Teats Fund. To Secretary, Ministry of Blockade. 4.1.1919. Royston. *"Let Their Lives Speak"* p.36

> Skollie means urchin and not a good one at that. Next came clothes for these specimens and they in turn had relatives so it grew and in growing committees were set up. Charities were organised and even lawyers helped voluntarily. Gradually clothes, food, and medical care was brought in and finally housing. Coffee, buns and games were provided. At first only half a dozen turned up but eventually a small village-cum-township developed. This had cottages, workshops, a school, women's health care, social work, bakery, second hand clothing and book shops and other initiatives still surviving from that work more than 60 years later. This housing was laid out on a farm. Each holding was very tiny, two or three rooms, but space for expansion. A professional warden was engaged who handled all this. The British Prime Minister of the time was Clement Attlee and his sister lent her name and considerable efforts to the cause.[340]

Attlee was Prime Minister of the United Kingdom from 1945 to 1951, so this dates Misha's experience to that period.

Misha said his 'small contribution to this was in the entertainment field'. Every Saturday night he would work a projector and show films (Wild Wests usually). Sometimes he was assaulted and had the takings 'filched' off him but usually they were returned the following morning by the culprits themselves, humbly apologising. This was not entirely voluntary though, as in the background in the bushes were the mothers, armed with heavy cudgels and sticks. 'The aged mother was the supreme law, and even a hardened criminal had to toe the line.'

After the war Grace settled in Cape Town quite near Princess Vlei. It was not long before she saw that her work of helping the helpless was not done. Together with Mary Attlee, Rachel Dick and others, whose names are commemorated by street signs in what is now Cafda Village, she started a soup kitchen in the winter months and a relief centre for those affected by floods in her own locality. Very soon a small nursery was added to care for the little children of working mothers, and out of these beginnings was born CAFDA (Cape Flats Distress Association),[341] or as Misha wrote: CAFDA by the way stands for Cape Aid for Distressed Areas.

A commission of inquiry, appointed in 1942, disclosed the shocking state of affairs in which thousands of people were living - in the most appalling conditions in the southern areas of the Cape Peninsula. People lived in hovels in conditions of poverty, disease, malnutrition and often

---

[340] Misha Vulliamy

[341] Newspaper biography. Undated. Unidentified.

experienced severe flooding of their homes in winter. The commission published its findings in 1944, and in that year, the subsequent Cape Flats Development Association CAFDA was founded to seek to address many of these problems. It acknowledges that 'In those early days the organization was known as the Cape Flats Distress Association' and that CAFDA's first Chairperson was Miss Mary Attlee, the sister of the then British Prime Minister. Mary Attlee and Grace in fact travelled out together on at least one occasion, but Grace is not mentioned on their website – one of many examples of how what occurred before WW2 is ignored, and in this instance of how Grace Vulliamy was again written out of the record.

Misha wrote:

> Ma was retired to a cottage near Cape Town and endless folk beat a path to her home, usually to get a game of bridge or decent conversation. She was very social, entertained, and went out equally as much, driving somewhat erratically though. And smoked rather a lot, most photos of her had a cigarette in her hand. She often had visitors and was loved by all. Animals surrounded her, more often strays, and she made a few pennies selling puppies and kittens. The setting of the cottage was in 8-10 acres of veldt near Cape Town, to the rear of Table Mountain and lent itself to keeping animals. Never at that period could one equate Ma to that period of being a vibrant leader and organiser that she was in her hey-day. She was simply a charming lively 'old lady' with a gorgeous sense of humour. …

At some point Miss Vulliamy underwent a serious operation but recovered very quickly. Living at Princess Vlei, (Vlei means lake in Afrikaans) she considered the locality a perfect place for recuperation, confirmed by the fact that her neighbour was a bird-scientist![342]

Nevertheless, the post-war period brought personal difficulties to Grace. On 5 September 1954 Constance wrote to her from 820 East Street, Parkville, Missouri, USA –

> I was delighted to get the translation of the article about you and will read it to Mother and Beano, I mean Gerald. … It is lovely, and I surely learned a lot about you I did not know. …I recall you telling us some of the school episodes when we were children but I always thought you made them up! I was too young when you

[342] Vulliamy Papers. Woman of Action

were here in 1914 to know what you did for us then, but I am willing to wager it was plenty. I only know that Gerald and I just adored you and I know we hung on you and made ourselves general nuisances to you all the time.

Grace Vulliamy

However, all was not well. Many places around the world saw serious flooding in 1953 and 1954, including the U.K., the Netherlands and South Africa. Connie was shocked to learn about the floods Grace had coped with; she had experience of this and knew the trauma. She was imagining Grace all alone and ill, with water coming through the roof and no one to help her. But there were more worries – Connie was further shocked to know how 'close to financial disaster you were just then (and probably now, unless the government came across).' She was writing to Grace by return mail asking her 'please to do me the big favour of telling me how much money you really need – not just to tide you over for one week, but for an appreciable length of time.' To persuade her to do this, Constance said:

> Did you ever consider all you have done for all of us all of your life, or what you have always meant to this family? Do you remember how you took care of me during all of that summer in 1935 when I was in England?... It is distinctly time that a few of us did something for you.'

Constance had already sent one cheque and wanted to send another, so she tried to convince Grace that she could afford it and was not denying herself. She continued:

> You are an amazing person and I am proud to be related to you by blood. I recall you telling us some of the school episodes when we were children but I always thought you made them up! I am distressed to learn of the stroke, slight though you say it was. I wish someone were living with you. Is it high blood pressure? If so, you should be able to keep it under control by diet et cetera without "living as an invalid" as you put it.... It would help you if you were sensible and keep from real hard stroke. You would hate it if you had a bad one like Mother and had to be nursed.

It is possible that Connie passed on her concerns to Lionel, who had visited her in Poland. There was yet a further worry which is expressed in a letter from Lionel to Grace on 26 June 1956 where they had a discussion about the price of houses. He said: 'I have a feeling that money may be tight. I rely on your promise to let me know whenever you are in any way short of money.'

Constance had already sent one cheque and wanted to send another, so she tried to convince Grace that she could afford it and was not denying herself. She continued:

> You are an amazing person and I am proud to be related to you by blood. I recall you telling us some of the school episodes when we were children but I always thought you made them up! I am distressed to learn of the stroke, slight though you say it was. I wish someone were living with you. Is it high blood pressure? If so, you should be able to keep it under control by diet et cetera without "living as an invalid" as you put it.... It would help you if you were sensible and keep from real hard stroke. You would hate it if you had a bad one like Mother and had to be nursed.

It is possible that Connie passed on her concerns to Lionel, who had visited her in Poland. There was yet a further worry which is expressed in a letter from Lionel to Grace on 26 June 1956 where they had a discussion about the price of houses. He said: 'I have a feeling that money may be tight. I rely on your promise to let me know whenever you are in any way short of money.'

This generation of the Vulliamy family had become smaller as a result of deaths. Fanny died in 1916, and Blanche died on 4 August 1923. Violet had passed away in 1942. Janet had died in Salisbury in 1949 leaving £4295.15s. 6d but her Will and Blanche's were tied together in some way, meaning that Blanche's Will could not be proved until securities in Janet's Will had been sold. This was not completed until October 1956 when Grace received £289.11s.4d. as her half share. She had already received £150 in advance so this had to be deducted first and further emphasises the financial problems that Grace was experiencing. However, Blanche had not signed her Will before she died and Lionel explained that it had been agreed by the other beneficiaries that what she left was to be divided up the way she intended. Nevertheless, Connie was giving Grace her share. Lionel considered Connie 'one of the most generous, unselfish people who ever lived.'[343]

At some point towards the end of her life when Grace understood that her death was near, she wrote a very moving letter to Misha. This not only gives rare and deeply personal insights into their relationship and what it meant to Grace, but also into her philosophy. This is expressed in the final sentence and helps understanding of her life and what drove her. She wrote:

---

[343] Caudwell House. 15.7.56 Lionel to GCV

Plate 12.9 Mary Attlee travelling out to South Africa with

Misha Darling

> You know how difficult it has always been for me to express in words my feelings, but I do want you to realise how very much you have contributed to my happiness in life. You have been a wonderful son to me and my heart is full of gratitude.
>
> I don't want you to grieve for me, but just remember how fortunate we have been to have had such a happy life together. I know you will miss me but you have nothing to regret, so no need to be unhappy. Real happiness or rather worthwhile happiness I do feel comes from helping others when one can and that is in your nature to do.

Grace died at her home Grassmere, Princess Vlei, on April 10, 1957. Her Will, which she approved on the copy in pencil writing 'all OK, GCV, 21.8.55' appointed Michael or Mischa Vulliamy as one of the executors. Constance, of

East Street Parkville was the first person named to receive a gift followed by Gerald then her relatives Chloe and Hope; also Mrs Shura Bilsby of Hampstead, London. Her maid, Annie Weitz, who lived with Grace, was left £10. Save the Children Fund of Cape Town was left her close of value. Her maid Elizabeth Caroline Parsotham of the Holy Across Convent, Retreat, was left £50, her bedstead and mattress, four blankets and four sheets. Mischa was heir to the residue of her estate.

She asked for her remains to be cremated. There was a private cremation and she asked for no flowers but donations instead to Save the Children Fund care of Mrs L Benjamin, Clandon, Southfield Road, Plumstead.

One obituary summed her up thus: 'Her compassion was not of the stodgy and over-emotional kind which merely felt sorry in the face of suffering, but .. immediately set about the most practical remedial measures …'[344]

Newspaper biography

Her specific job was to find abandoned, lost or orphaned children, to render comfort and keep them, to trace their parents and, if they were untraceable, to find alternative adequate homes for them. In this work she showed a determination, a selflessness and courage which, together with the brilliant and effective way in which she accomplished her task, earned for her the decoration she so richly merited.

At the same time she was intimately, from the beginning and through the rest of her life, connected with all causes for the uplift and the betterment of children, and more particularly was she identified with the work of the Save the Children Fund.

Her unassuming nature and the quiet way in which she set about what is probably the most productive and important task earned for her little publicity and limelight; but this pleased her for she was ever one to shun publicity. In her we have lost someone whose shining example could always be followed by others.

Epilogue

---

[344] Unattributed newspaper cutting.

Letter from Grace (only part of it) the lot of the privates in Germany has become steadily worse, until at the present time the conditions under which many of them exist are even more appalling than those which they endured in 1914. Urge immediate release.

Many years later Misha visited the cottage where he had lived with 'Ma' as he used to call Grace. He discovered that the house was very different, added to and seemed bigger. He wrote:

> Our old house is now no longer in the middle of open veldt but hidden in sub-divided plots metres apart. Eventually after much trial and error we found the place. Timidly I knocked at the door and was given a wonderful welcome. 'Come in, do!' by a Moslem lady. This was in spite of no warning or knowledge of our visit. Grace's small bedroom was still there, but empty; it was there that she passed away. Risking religious offence I told the lady that Grace's ashes were buried in the garden and I indicated the spot which was now covered by a double garage. Luckily we managed to laugh about it.

There is little doubt that Grace too would have enjoyed the joke.

There, in Cafda Village is Grace Vulliamy Street, her only lasting memorial.[345]

Plate 12.10 Grace in the grounds of her cottage at Princess Vlei

[345] Vulliamy Papers. Woman of Action.

Plate 12.11 Grace Vulliamy Street, Cafda Village, Cape Town, South Africa

APPENDIX 1

RUHLEBEN

A FEW POINTS TO DISPEL FALSE IMPRESSIONS OF THE CAMP

1	Sanitary Conditions	Disgraceful
2	Food Questions	Naturally no German food. subsist on parcels and pull through
3	Clothing	Difficulties in winter
4	Heating	Single pipes in lofts. No arrangements for drying of clothes
5	Ventilation	In summer inadequate – refuse, flies etcetera
6	Quality of interned	Every type
7	Recreation and study	All organised by interned. No help from Huns. They exploit it
8	Length of captivity and effect	Blindness, physical weakness; drunkenness (better class) hysteria, lunacy
9	Hopelessness of position	
10	Overcrowding	
11	Invalid accommodation insufficient.	Two deaths in 1918. Three deaths - master mariner between 23.12.17 to 12.3.18
12	Age of prisoners	50 between ages of 55 and 68. Largely mercantile marine.
13	Mercantile Marine.	Those at Ruhleben have received no Government grants as officers.
14	Dr Wiener's Sanatorium	Separate from Ruhleben. Patients received indifferent attention. Exploited. Affected by doses of sleeping draughts. Food insufficient . Overcrowding. Interference with patients' parcels.

15	Cost of living in hospital.	First class 20 marks per day. Second-class treatment - eight marks per day
16	Case of Otto Struckmeyer .	Melancholia misanthropist Just left public school (Sherborne) in 1914.

APPENDIX 2

MEMORANDUM ON CONDITIONS AMONGST PRISONERS OF WAR AND CIVILIANS IN GERMANY AND HOLLAND by GCV

I have had particular facilities for hearing from direct sources the conditions in Germany, having worked in Holland since 1914 and having met all prisoners, repatriated and interned. There is a strong feeling amongst the men that the privates have not been considered in the exchange this has created a feeling of extreme bitterness against the British Government. I think there is little doubt that the Germans foresaw this possibility when they would not discuss the question of exchanging privates, realising what a great source of danger these men would become to England. Many officers first considered refusing to come to Holland, then decided they could help the case of the privates more by doing so. The men themselves consider they have been deserted because they are valueless from a military point of view in this country. This applies not only to the British soldier but also to the thousands of old overseas soldiers whose attitude to the Mother country is likely to be a serious menace which is daily increasing, and large socialistic meetings are being held in many of the men's camps. Further, the privates have sent a message to say that they have decided that they cannot hold out any longer and will agree to work in German munition factories where they are offered good treatment, good food and good wages.

I should like to lay certain facts before the War Cabinet: –

A. MILITARY (Germany)

Most of these cases seem to fall into two classes: –

1. Cases of brutal treatment and arbitrary enforcement of work;
2 Cases of brutal treatment and neglect of men who were even acknowledged by the German doctors to be hospital cases

The following examples of both classes are unquestionably indicative of the general conditions amongst the NCOs and men....

Medical Treatment
Doctors from the Central Camp from which the working parties are drawn do not visit the working Commandos and small camps. The under officer

in charge of the above is often the civil contractor and it frequently occurs that he does not call in the local doctor until it is too late

Sick Exchange. For the purpose of choosing the men for the sick exchange, neutral doctors do not actually go to the camps. All cases the Germans consider suitable for exchange are sent to Aachen and there come before the neutral Medical Commission. In this way many sick men are never seen by the Commission. The reason for this is that the Germans will keep a man if he has even a few months' work left in him no matter what his condition, so valueless to them is human life except as a medium of work.

B. CIVILIAN (Germany)

Ruhleben. Since the transfer of the 400 civilian prisoners from Ruhleben to Holland , the rest of the camp who have no hope of exchange under the agreement of 1917 seems to have sunk into despair and mental inertia, due partly to the fact that practically all the leaders of the camp have been repatriated or interned in Holland. The most serious result of this has been the rapid increase of nervous diseases and insanity, especially among the younger men. Their whole moral future is being endangered by this prolonged inactivity.

C. CONDITIONS IN HOLLAND

(note: I should much appreciate that the source of the following information be kept confidential as I am still working in Holland in connection with the Dutch government)

Food
The food conditions are very bad. The British government have made a contract with the company who are not honourably carrying out that contract. The amount given by the Government of Fl 3.25 a day is sufficient, even under the present food conditions in Holland, to cover reasonable diet. The food is however so often badly prepared that it is un eatable and it is always insufficient. The men come from Germany in an ill nourished condition leading good food, and they themselves state that they are worse off the food in Holland than in Germany because they are not allowed to receive parcels and the diet is so poor that they really are suffering cases of exhaustion due to insufficient food...
Employment.

It is extremely bad for the men to be living in enforced idleness which is the case with about two thirds of the total number. The Dutch can give them practically no employment as they have plenty of unemployed themselves. The German Government has arranged that every German should be employed. Raw materials, such as leather, wood, etc. are sent from Germany and made up by the interned in Holland; there is also an artificial limb factory, a shoe factory: complete suites of furniture are made and shipped back to Germany, and all this gives employment not only to the men but also to the officers and NCOs who have the supervision of the work. Employment is also found in this way for German civilians.

With regard to our arrangements this very important department is in the hands of the Red Cross who are dependent upon the public for the funds and who therefore are not able to do things on a sufficiently large scale to meet the needs of the men. Many of our civilians are destitute and need this employment from a pecuniary point of view. In this respect they were better off in Germany because they have their parcels and relief money of 16 marks a month. Now they are receiving 10 gulden, which certainly does not go as far as 10 marks, and no parcels. The civilians are very bitter about their treatment by the British Government in Holland and this great bitterness of the prisoners (military and civilian weather in Germany or Holland) is a grave peril since these men have said that on that returning to their homes both in the British Isles and the Colonies, they will express their resentment.

<u>The need for women</u>
This need is very great. The bitterness of the men has been greatly increased by the difficulties which the Government have made in allowing their wives and relatives to visit them. The present number of women who have been allowed over from this country is only 26. German women are posing as Belgians and getting hold of the men, and there is no doubt in my mind that this is part of German propaganda.

SUGGESTIONS
the following are suggestions which I feel might be of use in considering the direct steps to be taken to remedy the conditions already described

1. That in justice to the men the rank-and-file be added in just proportion to the exchange already arranged for officers and NCOs so that the 1914 and 1915 men would automatically be released and thus give hope to the remaining prisoners.

2. That German officers should be put in raided towns in England as is done to the British officers in Germany and the regulations with regard to the Germans high rank and social position should be so formed as to ensure better treatment of our prisoners of all ranks

3. That arrangement should be made for neutral doctors to visit more frequently and have free access to base internment camps, all small camps and working Commandos.

4. That the Medical Commission should visit more camps, should choose the cases for repatriation or internment, and it should not be left to the German authorities to say who should be sent to Aachen.

5. That repatriated officers and men be used in the German camps in England to enable the government to true report of the difference of treatment in the German and British camps from these men who have had experience.

6. That much greater publicity might be given to cases of ill-treatment. Responsible and able people of whom there are many among the repatriated prisoners, would be allowed to relate their experiences; there is no doubt that this would be unpalatable to the Germans and have great effect.

7. That they should be allowed repatriation of all interned British civilians. Removal of these in Germany to Holland does not meet the case.

8. That a food expert should be sent by the government to Holland to look into the entire food situation and to examine the working of the existing contract.

9. That the British government should make themselves directly responsible for the development of industries in which all British prisoners of war in Holland could be employed. This scheme would automatically include officers.

10. That women should be sent over in greater numbers to Holland. They are badly needed and could be used for work under the YMCA, VADs, or in connection with social work among the men. Also that where men have large families they should be given leave to visit their homes and that wives who have no families should be sent to Holland and given employment under these headings.

APPENDIX 3

HOLLAND

Grace Vulliamy's Comments

SUGGESTIONS

That women should be sent over in greater numbers to Holland. They are badly needed and could be used for work under the Y.M.C.A, as V.A.D. s, or in connection with social work among the men. Also that where men have large families they should be given leave to visit their homes and that wives who have no families should be sent to Holland and given employment under these headings

(NOTE: I should much appreciate that the source of the following information should be kept confidential, as I am still working in Holland in connection with the Dutch Government.[346]

FOOD The food conditions are very bad. The British Government have made a contract with a company who are not honourably carrying out that contract. The amount given by the Government of FI. 3.25 a day is sufficient, even under the present food conditions in Holland, to cover reasonable diet. The food is however, so often badly prepared that it is uneatable, and it is always insufficient. The men come from Germany in an ill-nourished condition needing good food, and they themselves state that they are worse off for food in Holland than in Germany because they are not allowed to receive parcels and the diet is so poor that they really are suffering. Cases of exhaustion due to insufficient food.

EMPLOYMENT It is extremely bad for our men to be living in enforced idleness, which is the case with about two thirds of the total number. [For the German prisoners] materials are sent from Germany and made up by the interned in Holland; there is also an artificial limb factory, a shoe factory, complete suites of furniture are made and shipped

[346] War Cabinet, Conditions Amongst Prisoners Of War' And Civilians In Germany And Holland. (Note of Statements and Suggestions made by Miss Vulliamy.) Catalogue Reference: CAB/24/57

back to Germany, and all this gives employment not only to the men, but also to the officers who have the supervision of the work.

The Red Cross cannot deal with the problem. It is dependent on voluntary funds from the public and cannot do things on a sufficiently large scale to meet the needs of the men. Many of our civilians are destitute and need this employment from a pecuniary point of view. In this respect they were better off in Germany because they had their parcels and relief money of 16 marks a month. Now they are receiving 10 gulden, which certainly does not go any further in Holland than 10 marks in Germany, and no parcels. The civilians are very bitter about their treatment by the British Government in Holland, and this great bitterness of the prisoners (military and civilian - whether in Germany or Holland) is a grave peril, since these men had said that on returning to their homes both in the British Isles and the Colonies, they will express their resentment.

MEMORANDUM BY THE HOME SECRETARY ON MISS VULLIAMY'S STATEMENT

The statements made by Miss Vulliamy, whose admirable work in Holland among our prisoners of war is well known, carry great weight; and they are confirmed by the report of Mr Justice Younger's committee and by what I heard at The Hague.

The British Delegates at The Hague lodged formal complaints as to the treatment of British prisoners of war in some of the camps, in the mines (especially salt mines) and behind the lines; and these complaints will form part of the records of the Conference and will be available for future reference. The German Delegates while declining to admit the facts promised enquiry.

CAB\24\58 War Cabinet

With regard to Miss Vulliamy's "suggestions" I add the following remarks: –

1. It was agreed before I left the Hague that 15,000 privates on each side, as well as some of the older prisoners, should be exchanged before any officer or non-commissioned officer was repatriated I have no doubt that this provision, although not mentioned in the telegram from the Delegates, is included in the agreement. This will have the effect which Miss Vulliamy desires.

2, 3 and 4. The agreement provides for all these matters.

5. This may be right but it should be remembered (1) that the agreement has not yet been ratified and (2) that retaliation on German officers will lead to counter retaliation on the British prisoners of war in Germany.
6. This appears to be right
7. This will certainly be necessary if the prisoners are to remain in Holland.
8. I strongly urge that women should be sent to Holland in greater numbers. The present arrangement involves great hardship on the married officers and non-commissioned officers who are there.

16 July 1918

APPENDIX 4

PRIVATES LEFT IN GERMANY

The case of the privates and NCOs left in Germany, owing to their not coming under the terms of agreement with regard to being interned in a neutral country.

The officers and NCOs who have benefited by this agreement have one and all felt very much the hard lot of those left behind and in very many cases the only thing that persuaded officers and NCOs to come to Holland was the feeling that once out of Germany they could plead the men's cause, their inclinations being to remain in Germany as long as their men did, knowing as they do the men's treatment is infinitely worse than anything they themselves have experienced.

Briefly put the case of the men appears to be as follows: –

1. The delegates are known to have failed to get the men included in the internment agreement because Germany would not agree.
2. It is not known whether the delegates made any attempt to exchange men direct to England
3. It is thought that no attempt to exchange direct has been made, because the Government has laid down the principle that no sound man should be exchanged
4. Our men are by now very few of them really sound, as the German treatment undoubtedly tends and is intended to break them down:
5. The German prisoners of war are probably sound and will remain so as long as the war goes on:
6. If nothing is done the final result will be that 40 to 50,000 half broken British will be returned to England and 100,000 sound men to Germany, and surely manpower will be a very important item for the nation after the war:
7. Why not therefore try to obtain direct exchange of the men and drop the principle mentioned in 3 in their case?
8. The result, it is true, would be that some 20,000 Germans would go back to Germany fairly soon, but they would go back in batches and would be required to work in the country itself or at the front; in the former case they would not release men from the front as they would only replace prisoners of war; in the latter case it is open to question whether their fighting spirit

would be very good. And at the worst what do 20,000 represent? Only about a week's casualties in a big battle.

9. Every single British returned from Germany would form a centre of the best kind of propaganda against Germany.
10. A point also worth noticing appears to be the fact that now England has practically to feed its own prisoners of war in Germany and the Germans in England, whereas Germany only partially feeds the British prisoners of war in Germany and nowhere else.
11. If the government fails at first to obtain an agreement for direct exchange let it try, try again – and each time publish the facts and reason of the failure;
12. Finally, is the government wise in failing to plead the cause of the men in these days of democratisation?

APPENDIX 5

Ruhleben

A The official explanation of the several large moves to different camps in Germany in December 1917 was that the officers so removed were going to a concentration camp for Holland.

B. Thus the big moves from Swärmstedt, Ströhen, and (?) Augsburg to Holzminden.

C. ... During the year beginning about 1 August 1917 prisoners in the 10th Army Corps command were forbidden to have the envelopes of their letters.

D. Lord Newton's limitation of parcels caused great bitterness and, till ways of circumventing it were discovered, made many prisoners go hungry and in rags.

G. At the time when this lyric was written the British officers at Holzminden refused to go out for walks until General Carl von – Hänisch GOC 10th Hanover Army Corps withdrew his statement that the parole of a British officer was worthless. Later he shuffled out of it and walks were resumed.

H. Lord Newton was reported by English newspapers as having made a statement to this effect in the House in reply to a question regarding the disgraceful treatment at Ströhen where officers were being bayoneted and generally strafed merely because they were British. The remark caused much bitterness.

J. General von Friedrichs, O.C.Prisoners of War in Germany, a plausible knave. It is said that the British and German delegates of the first meeting at The Hague in 1917 about prisoners of war positively fraternise and actually exchanged photographs. It was generally considered in Germany among the prisoners that this contact was improper and that the British delegates had been fooled all along the line. Lord Newton was reported in the English papers as having paid tribute to the agreeable character of his relations with the Germans.

K. Also, General von Hänisch said to have shielded the Emperor in the Eulenburg scandal, removed from the Front for incompetence during the

Battle of the Somme, 1916, distinguished by his frenzied hatred of the British and the brutality and insult general in his command, the worst in Germany. [The scandal was concerned with homosexuality, similar to that of Oscar Wilde]

L. Apparently in the autumn 1917 escaped officers were actually ordered to give their parole not to speak of treatment in Germany. It was said that at one time officers who refused to do so were not allowed to cross from Holland to England.

M. The English papers reported Lord Newton as having stated that there were no complaints from prisoners in Germany and if there were any these were baseless. The remark did not make him more beloved by the prisoners.

APPENDIX 6

To the Gods in Whitehall

I sent a remarkably civil enquiry
(I noted the date, April 1, in my diary)
To the Gods in Whitehall
I waited a week then I wrote to complain
To the gods in Whitehall

Then they wrote that my case was receiving attention
Then I waited a week in a state of suspension
Oh, the gods in Whitehall!

Then I wrote a request for an early reply.
Then I waited a week, then they bade me apply
Somewhere else in Whitehall.

I redrafted my note and dispatched this new
To another Department infested by you
Little gods of Whitehall.

Then I waited a week, and no answer received;
Up till then I had firmly and simply believed
You were gods in Whitehall.

But I called at the office, was given a pass
By virtue of which I saw Lord Sparrowgrass
A God in Whitehall.

I told him my trouble, he smiled and replied
"I'm sorry the matter is not for this side.
You must traverse Whitehall."

I did: got a pass and my next interview
Took the form of a chat with a lady in blue –
Oh, you lads of Whitehall!

She listened and took an elaborate note,
Disappeared, reappeared, and then hurriedly wrote
To a God in Whitehall.

I went with her letter through nine corridors

In nine separate lists to nine separate floors.
Oh, the floors of Whitehall!

The God I required was at lunch but a cute
Sub-Director suggested a good substitute
Who was still in Whitehall.

He saw me; he got the original file
Of my correspondence and there in a pile
Were my notes to Whitehall.

There were minutes about me by X and by Y,
And a tentative draft of a final reply
From the gods of Whitehall.

I wasn't allowed to peruse it just then
For it was not initialled by Admiral Spen
OBE of Whitehall.

I went away happy, and waited a week:
I had seen in the flesh, I had even heard speak
The gods of Whitehall.

At last your reply was brought in by my minion
"the Minister cannot express an opinion."
Damn the gods of Whitehall.

E.W.F.

APPENDIX 7

SCHEME FOR INTERNATIONAL WORK AMONGST PRISONERS OF WAR

From experience gained during working in prisoner-of-war camps in Poland, I have realised the importance of an organisation to work entirely for prisoners and interned in the various countries. Prisoners have to suffer much unnecessary misery and disease simply owing to lack of supplies and assistance. In most central European countries there is a great shortage of medical relief and these countries cannot be expected to make the welfare of prisoners their first consideration. In Poland there is no ill-will towards prisoners, but an absolute lack of everything. The camp I have worked daily for three months contains 7000 interned and prisoners, mostly from Denniken's army. When I arrived the hospital was over for and many sick were accommodated in the barracks with those fit. There were four nurses for 200 patients; many lay without sheets or shirts. When leaving hospital they received no food for 48 hours, as food was issued for the camp 48 hours in advance. This was lack of organisation. When I suggested some way might be found to meet this difficulty, I was told that no-one had complained. Prior to my coming there was nobody with whom they could lodge complaints.

In many cases relations are separated in their flight and there is no organisation to trace such relatives.

There is no occupation of any description for the men, no recreation and no exercise. The demoralisation is deplorable.

There are no schools in the children and no beds or baths for the babies.

I suggest that Poland be the training ground and the first country in which to commence this work. The Polls are quite unable to care for prisoners themselves as they have so much to attend to in their country. They are, however, a humane race and are glad that their prisoners should be well treated and would certainly put no obstacles in the way of such effort. Later, when possible, a party should be sent to Russia to care in the same manner for Polish prisoners and others in the hands of the Bolsheviks, and also to other countries where the need is great. The principles of the work should be to assist all prisoners, regardless of nationality or creed, and to employ workers who have the work at heart. I would suggest that a committee be formed in England representative, if possible, of all the large welfare organisations, such as the Red Cross, YMCA, Society of Friends, et cetera. Also that appeals be sent to all countries. Social workers should be engaged on a six-months' contract, at a reasonable salary.

The Chief work should be

(1) To improve the conditions of the sick.
(2) The care of children.
(3) Employment

(Signed) G C Vulliamy

APPENDIX 8

Grace Vulliamy's account of 1914.

CHAPTER I

The first feeling that swept through the world on that never-to-be-forgotten 4th of August in 1914 was one of over-whelming horror, temporarily stunning the mind, but after the first shock of realization had passed everyone became feverishly active in the intensity of the desire to serve – to be of use to his country in its hour of desperate need. Within a few days of the declaration of War, a centre called 'The Women's Emergency Corps' was formed by (blank) …

The particular department in which I was interested was the interpreting dept. and one of the first tasks which this dept. took in hand was the handling of the Belgian Refugees as they arrived in England. …

After 3 months spent in this way, the Local Govt. Board approached the W.E.Corps for a worker with a knowledge of languages to go across to Holland and assist in the handling of the Belgian Refugees on the other side of the Channel, and the W.E.C. loaned me to the L.G.Board for this purpose, and I went over to Flushing. A very short time at Flushing convinced me that I could be more useful there than in London and, as linguists were much in demand, with some reluctance the W.E.Corps agreed to allow me to continue there. I therefore returned to London in December in order to hand over my dept. at the W.E.C., and returned to settle to the work in Holland…

They invited the homeless Belgians into their country, threw up large camps of army huts which would provide shelter [?for] those who would remain in their country, and made arrangements with one of their shipping lines for the transference to England of those who wished to go there. It will be remembered that 1500 British marines were interned at Groningen in October 1914 and an able and enthusiastic committee of Dutch immediately formed itself in Amsterdam to provide what comfort, recreation and occupation it could for these people After first providing books, sports requisites, gymnasium apparatus, laying out tennis courts and skittle alleys, etc etc the Committee organized scientific classes for those men who were desirous of employing their time in studying. Of these classes the instruction given in Deep Sea Navigation proved most popular and of great assistance to many of our interned men. Later the British Board of Trade was approached with a view to sending examiners out to Groningen so that the regular examinations might be taken and very gratifying to the excellent instructors were the results of these examinations for different branches of the Marine Service.

The first English organization to offer assistance to the Dutch Government in handling Belgian Refugees in Holland was that of the Quakers, and upon learning that the best way they could be useful was in going into the camps and supplying the 'life' in these settlements of people, provided with food and shelter certainly, but without any of the activities of normal human life. The Society of Friends offered themselves for this purpose and asked me if I would undertake the organization of this work for them.

The wife of the Belgian Consul General, Mme Goffart, was doing splendid work in employing (this line has been crossed out)

There were four large camps in existence at that time, at Gouda, Nunspeet, Ede and Uden, and it was very soon apparent that there was a great need for organised employment and recreation among the hundreds of people housed in these camps. Of these, the one at Gouda stood by itself. This was far the smallest, containing about (gap) people, and instead of specially erected wooden buildings, the Refugees were housed in empty greenhouses in which has been arranged tables and forms. It was sad to see there strong, young men, sleeping or lounging about with no occupation, and here it was a cheery thing to pick out the handy men, joiners, carpenters, smiths, etc etc and put them at work on the little wooden houses which had been approved by the Committee of the S of F for erection. That our efforts in this direction were appreciated is well shown in the following charmingly described account, written by one of our Refugee workers …

… bags full of plans and sketches, their heart full of love for humanity and Christian cheerfulness to assist their fellow men with the construction and arranging of own temporary buildings, first deed of practical altruism. And with each driven nail, with each freshly paint stroke we hear their merry laughter of inciting cheerfulness, coming direct from the heart of those three Quaker girls!"

Workshops were soon started and by August 1915 in Uden Camp alone there were some 1,800 men and women regularly employed as tailors, shoemakers, basket makers, smiths, brush-makers, lace-makers, knitters, rug-makers embroiderers etc etc and a market was found for the goods either within the camps or elsewhere, the workers being paid sometimes in 'points' to be eventually realised in coin as this became possible, sometimes in clothes, household requirements et. In many instances the Dutch Govt … ? provided materials free of all expense to the Refugees or their instructors.

As the work developed the camps became hives of industry and comparative happiness, and on a fine sunny morning it was a pleasant sight to see rows of girls at Ede camp, clad in pretty pink pinafores, seated under the avenue of trees which border the main road assign Ede camp. The view of the moors, purple with heather, and the distant wood making it strangely peaceful.

There were needs outside the camps to be met as well. At Amersfoort for instance, scattered about the town were about 4,000 women and children, the families of Belgian soldiers interned in a camp a few miles away. They had come in response to the great desire of their husbands to have them near, and were in most distressing circumstances. The money granted to them (?by the Belgian Govt) was 75 centimes for each woman and 50 for each child (per diem?) there was no provision for their lodging and prices in Holland were at that time very high. A large empty granary at Koppel, which held about 300, had been kindly lent by a Dutch merchant, but the rest of the 4000 were housed as well as could be managed. One woman with her son lived in a cupboard of a room, just the length of the bed, with no air except through the door.. When her husband returns on leave the boy sleeps on a mattress in a garret above.

Then, too, were the people from refined and sheltered homes who, arriving at Flushing en route for England, were held up there awaiting their opportunity of embarkation These people were mostly of a different type from those inhabiting the camps, and as the majority knew little or none English or Dutch, they were very much exploited by the Hotels. (This paragraph is crossed out)

In Feb 1915 owing to the German's refusing to guarantee that neutral boats would be exempted from torpedoes (crossed out) blockade the Dutch Govt were obliged to stop the service of their boats which they had kindly put at the disposal of the British for transference of Refugees to England, which resulted in the holding up of many hundreds of people at Flushing who, (p.11) in the hope of the boat service being resumed, preferred rather to remain at Flushing and starve them into one of the camps. In order, therefore, to assist these people, the Strand Hotel in Flushing was rented by the S of F and fitted up for their accommodation, and thus provision was made for them at the lowest cost to them, while they waited during the months until England was able to arrange for escorted transport for them.

Belgians in all conditions were pouring into Holland at the rate of some tens of thousands a week, and although about 1200 a week were transported to

England, many hundreds remained in Holland. Early in 1915 the lamentable state of the children in Belgium led the German Government to consent to a proposal that a number of failing children should be sent each month into Holland to be fed, clothed and cared for, for a period of four weeks. The sufferings of Belgium's children at that time may be judged by the fact that 200 came each month from then until the end of the war, each one of whom held a doctor's certificate of ill-health. Tuberculosis was the great scourge, the result of bad and insufficient food over a long period. The worst of those cases were allowed to remain indefinitely in sanatoriums in Holland.

In regard to English, Belgians and others who were passing through en route to England, towards the end of 1915 the British Government officially asked for assistance from the Dutch Government, with whom the Society of Friends were requested to co-operate, in meeting and transporting Refugees and released Interned through Holland, and from November onwards we met the regular monthly contingents which Germany sent through. We were generally advised of the number of people coming through by the special train set aside for the purpose, and among these were many sick and stretcher cases, cases of insanity, women and children, and also negroes. No arrangements for distinction as regards colour, race or sex were made on the train: some had a little money, some had none, and any money they had was German and therefore useless until exchanged. The border station was Gennep, those bound for England travelling on from there to Flushing, and so – on. I therefore arranged with a good doctor to join the train on the frontier and to see that stretchers and other medical necessaries would be in readiness at Flushing, and on the 6th December I went up to Gennep to meet the first party coming through in this connection, taking two workers with me.

The train arrived two hours late, but the railway authorities kindly allowed it to wait there another hour in order that refreshments might be given out to the travellers. Some of these came from Ruhleben, and one and all showed great appreciation of the reception prepared for them, and evinced unbounded delight at meeting English people again. We heard from them that one of their company had died on the journey and there were among them two stretcher cases and four cases of insanity. At Boxtel, en route for Flushing, we were met by Dr Merkens of Flushing, who attended to the sick as we travelled. We reached Flushing at 1 a.m. and there found another member of the Society of Friends who had hot soup and other refreshments prepared. While the food was being served, passports were being visa-ed, but this formality was not over until 6 a.m. an the boat taking the travellers over to England sailed at 7.30 a.m. Upon our arrival at Flushing, the cases of sick were dealt with immediately by the Consul and Dr Merkens, assisted by two

Red Cross nurses sent from England for the purpose and then removed by them directly to the boat. As there were a number of negroes in the party, to members of the Society of Friends were detailed to accompany the prisoners to England, in order to give their attention to these and, if necessary, to the insane. We arrived at Tilbury at 4 p.m. where the sick were taken over by the British Red Cross and the destitute by the Charity Central Committee.

Some of the cases of civilians were very hard: there was, for example, a little woman who had taught English in Germany for 18 years, and who had all her friends there as well as her connection, and no-one and nothing to go to in England. She had been expelled with so little notice that she had only been able to bring £6 with her in money, and her references had been retained by the police in Germany.

Had these unfortunate people known that the War would last for years to come, their despair would probably have weighted them down to a state of inertia, but then there was always the hope that it would soon be over, that this upset and uprooting and exile was for a short time only, and, unhappy though it was, all would soon revert to its former normal state. But the sick, homeless and destitute were to continue pouring into and through Holland for many a long weary month before return to former interests could be contemplated.

As the parties came through, we were able to obtain impressions of the conditions prevalent in Germany at the time, though the accounts varied, of course, according to the different localities from which the prisoners came, and naturally as time went on and food and clothing and other essentials of life became increasingly difficult to obtain, conditions became more distressing.

It is characteristic of the British soldier that, once freed from conditions of discomfort, pain and suffering, he comes mute upon the subject of his former misery, and in regard to the prisoner, much tactful and persistent enquiry was soon needed in order to extract from his unwilling lips any kind of detailed or comprehensive account of conditions in the prison camp from which he had been released. Owing to this innate and universal reticence, it was difficult for many to realize anything of the discomfort, wretchedness, misery, pain and suffering which thousands of our prisoners endured for many weeks, months and even years. When they reached Holland, however, their minds were still open and innocent of the seal of forgetfulness with which they so splendidly and so pathetically closed them as soon as they realised their freedom and knew that those long days of unhappiness and despair were done with for ever.

In the same spirit and believing that no good purpose can be served at this time by setting down the evidence in my possession of the indescribable and unbelievable conditions in which these men lived, tales of squalor, dirt, disease, brutality, cruelty, misery and suffering incredible of body, mind and spirit, only enough of this aspect will here be related to enable the reader to appreciate the efforts which these men made to combat the conditions in which they found themselves, and keep themselves as normal, healthy and sane as was possible in n atmosphere of abnormality, falsity and distortion.

Prisoners fell naturally under two headings, civilian and military. As is well known, Ruhleben was the centre of imprisonment for the former. Their release began in November 1915, when a few at a time were included among the prisoners sent through to Holland monthly. Owing to the blockade, however, their release was stopped after .....(?) and not resumed again until .....(1918?). in spite of great efforts to preserve their normal condition, at the end of three and a half years of captivity in the conditions imposed at Ruhleben, it became almost impossible for them to hold out any longer. As one of their number put it:- 'After over three and a half year internment there is not a man in the camp regardless of age or calling, who has not reached the end of his power of resistance. The uncertainly of the ultimate fate, anxiety as regards matters both private and public, the continual effort to keep up an appearance of cheerfulness, all this is producing an ever-increasing number of cases both of nervous collapse and insanity. Many of these cases have been caused by the apparently unreasoned picking and choosing of candidates for exchange. [written in margin at the side: Chas. F. Winger] I have known men to figure as any as seven times on the lists for exchange only to be finally disappointed. One man over sixty has been taken twice as far as the frontier, only to be brought back from there to the camp.

The following are descriptions given by various of the released prisoners, and as such, speak for themselves.

"Ruhleben, as an internment camp for British civilians in Germany first came into being in 1914. Between then and the following Xmas, fresh relays of captives were constantly brought in. [Duncan Jones]

These for the most part had already served terms of imprisonment of varying duration at the local gaols of the neighbourhoods where, either as visitors, patients or residents, they were first put under arrest. Unlike England, Germany did not permit herself to discriminate in this regard. No-one was spared internment, and by far the greater number were incarcerated either in the wire cages, so much favoured by criminal authorities in Germany, or in solitary confinement for three weeks or a month before removal to Ruhleben (Duncan Jones)

There were in the early months of the War between four and five thousand prisoners in the camp, men of all classes and vocations, as divers in character as the motives which take Englishmen over to the Continent. Here were professors and stable boys, artists and seamen, merchants and acrobats, musicians, jockeys, students, trainers, under-graduates, engineers, teachers, business men and football-professionals, flung indiscriminately together.

The case of the civilian who finds himself in an enemy country at the outbreak of war is peculiar. (Digby R Lawson) He has no status and is immediately deprived of all right civic, domestic and economic. The soldier reckons upon imprisonment as a possible factor in his career, while the Officer and N.C.O. my look forward to release after 18 months of imprisonment. Military prisoners receive treatment according to rank in ways agreed upon by an international convention. Officers and men do not cease to draw their pay. To the civilian prisoner, deprived of earning his living and thus of his claim (Digby R Lawson) to that independence which is the right of every active worker, and becoming therefore a burden to his family and friends, is thus added yet another humiliation and cause for depression. Is it because a civilian is supposed to feel his position less acutely that no provision for his release after 18 months is made?

As time went on and these prisoners saw little or no prospect of release, urgent enquiries began to be made by them as to the reason of their indefinitely prolonged captivity, and the reply from our Government was that "military reasons" made it necessary for them to remain there, as "the handful of captives at Ruhleben are the means of preventing two fresh enemy division from entering the field." The vast majority of the prisoners were always ready to offer their lives for their country, but in view of the "military" nature of the reason of their detention, one cannot help feeling that they would have been more justly treated and the impulse which sustained them to a point of protracted and courageous endurance much strengthened, had this been made clear to them for the first and their position put on a military basis. A definition of their task and status in an authoritative message from England would have given a new direction to their lives, and a fresh inspiration to their thoughts an their efforts, which were bound to grow bitter an resentful when faced for years with an indeterminate, and seemingly unnecessary, sentence of imprisonment. (F.W.Hughesdon)

(D Jones) Arrive at Ruhleben, what did we expect, what did we find? Those who had experienced the hospitality of Germany in times of peace, who had admired her careful and precise arrangements in such matters of human welfare a railway stations, restaurants and public gardens, expected at least adequate space and reasonable cleanliness. We found stables – stables with horse dung still on the floor of the horse-boxes – and above these stables lots, so dark that every movement was a menace, so low that to stand upright except in the centre was impossible. These horse-boxes were allotted as dwellings to the prisoners at the ratio of 6 men to 1 horse, six men occupying the space previously accorded to one horse. In the lofts above overcrowding was still more dense. We slept at first on the floor on straw sacks; later in iron bedsteads fixed one above the other or in beds made of wood and rope by the prisoners themselves.

In winter the camp was heated by a single steam pipe, running close under the roof, which was hot for 15 hours a week, but as there were no arrangements either for washing clothes or for drying them when washed, any heat there was in the pipe was entirely absorbed by soaking garments hanging upon it. During the winter of 1916-1917 the ceiling above the beds was daily covered with long icicles, and ice gathered on the floor round the walls of our habitation.

There was no drainage or flow of water, the sanitary arrangements were entirely primitive, and the spitting to a degree unknown and unsuspected in the freedom of ordinary life, constituted an ever-increasing menace. (C.J.Winter)

(D.Jones) Here we must sleep, eat, try in vain to shelter from the Prussian winter, write, work, in fact, live.

Such were the conditions in which we found ourselves, and realising the importance of living as normal a life as possible in the circumstances, we set to work to organise various activities. The obstructions and difficulties which had to be dealt with were sometimes well nigh insuperable. Intense old in winter and exhausting heat in summer, severe illness, melancholia and insanity, lack of proper food; lack of books and instruments; the abject nature of the material at the disposal of workers; weariness, sadness, strain; exile from our country at the moment when service was most needed; surrounded by enemies; squalor, misery, dirt; perpetual calls to fresh endeavour; the overcrowding, noise and horror of life in conditions avowedly unfit for human existence; the hard, long pressure of sorrow; this was the soil into which the seed of our efforts was cast, and none but a prisoner of war can fully comprehend how dangerous, bitter and foul that soil can be.

Yet it is ever that when life asks most, most is offered and the impossible is achieved.

That we were to become a community in the most absolute sense of the word was not then apparent, but exile, national stress, oppression and a devoted watchfulness and admiration of the superb efforts made by our army at home and in the field sustained in us the unfaltering confidence, uniting elements otherwise irreconcilable. Democracy worked spontaneously at Ruhleben. The circumstances of our lot all combined towards a realisation, within our own sphere, of the principle of unity, and on this understanding, so real that it was hardly ever referred to, was based the whole social structure that eventually came into being.

One of the first steps taken was the election of "barrack captains," who originated from the necessity of establishing intermediaries between the military authorities and their captives, many of whom could not speak German. Gradually also the direction and control of all matters not specifically related to the military command was brought about. A police force was recruited from among the prisoners, committees and societies began to be formed for the care of such interests of education, the drama, health, sport, library, kitchens and canteens, religious services, finance etc. A school was organised, and lectures were arranged in history, literature, art etc etc.

The Camp's first corporate expression came through the medium of music. Orchestral and chamber concerts were regularly given under the leadership of various conductors. The autumn and winter months were devoted to the study and performance of a large classical repertory, while in summer open-air promenade concerts were given once a week. Then followed drama, and these two forms of artistic activity soon became the most diligently practised and wisely followed of the arts. The theatre at Ruhleben soon passed out of its tentative and occasional phase, and became the most constantly functioning, the most ardently pursued, and the wealthiest organisation in the camp. For, roughly speaking, two years it was the custom to present a different play every week. The standard, both of the works presented and of their performance, was high. Indeed, the earnest intention and the careful and steadfast work done in this remote and isolated play-house, seemed almost prophetic of a revival of dramatic art in England after the war. Shakespeare, Sheridan, Goldsmith, Wilde, Shaw, Galsworthy, Maugham, and Masefield were the principal British dramatists represented, while from among continental author works were given by Ibsen, Strindberg, Maeterlinck, Robert de Flers, and de Musset.

Where music and drama meet – in opera – five operas of Gilbert and Sullivan were played, and Mozart's 'Figaro' was only cancelled by the release to Holland of the conductor and the nervous breakdown of a principal singer.

Painting, though praised by few, was remarkable in the constant contributions of a young artist, even then well known in several countries, whose genius was a constant stimulus to his fellow prisoners, manifesting in posters, portraits, landscapes, stage designs, and several schemes of decoration, notably that of the Y.M.C.A. hut.

Handicrafts provoked great enthusiasm, and some fine work was achieved. Book-binding became a passion; metal work, leather work, wood-carving, model boat-building and carpentry were all developed to a high level of excellence by a large number of the younger men.

With regard to education, the future holds the fulfilment of the efforts in this field of endeavour. The School came out with a staggering prospectus including almost every branch of human knowledge from philosophy to Diesel engines! Languages played a great part in the curriculum, French, Dutch, Italian, Russian, Spanish and German being acquired by numerous students. Arrangements were made with various bodies in England by which students in Ruhleben could enter for the following examinations: London Chamber of Commerce, matriculation, Royal Society of Arts, Doctor of Music.

Recreation was organised on a similar broad scale. Half the race course upon which the camp was placed was rented by the prisoners as a playing field, and here matches took place in football, hockey, cricket and tennis and golf, and other sports of all kinds were energetically practised here, all of which did much to maintain the physical health of the camp.

And last, but by no means least gardening was pursued with great enthusiasm by many. Flower beds sprang up all over the camp, bringing into that squalid and distressing (p.25) place a fresh, spontaneous and visible manifestation of the presence of the Kingdom of God. (D Jones)

Time has passed since these things were, and the social efforts which are being made to-day, great as they may be, are yet made in a state of freedom as compared with the conditions of the community at Ruhleben seven or eight years ago.

Sometimes one's mind turns back for an instant to look upon that scene which then seemed to be eternity itself, and only then does one realise that, whatever the present unrest, heaven has begun for the survivors of the three or four years spent at Ruhleben during the Great War.

APPENDIX 9

CHAPTER 2 BY GRACE VULLIAMY

As the parties of refugees came through we were able to obtain impressions of the conditions prevalent in Germany at the time, though the accounts varied, of course, according to the different regions from which the prisoners came and naturally, as time went on and food and clothing and other essentials of a normal life became increasingly difficult to obtain, conditions became more distressing.

It is characteristic of the British soldier that once freed from conditions of discomfort, pain and suffering, he becomes mute upon the subject of his former misery and touching the prisoner much persistent and tactful enquiry was soon needed in order to extract from his unwilling lips any kind of detailed or comprehensive account of conditions in the prison camp from which he had been released. Owing to that innate reticence it was difficult for many to realise anything of the discomfort, wretchedness, misery pain and suffering which thousands of our prisoners endure for many weeks, months and even years, but when they reached Holland their minds and the password was still open and innocent of the seal of forgetfulness with which they so splendidly and so pathetically close to as soon as they realised their freedom and knew that those long days of unhappiness were done with for ever.

In the same spirit and believing that no purpose can be served at this time by setting down the evidence in my position of the accounts of the camps however vary considerably and in April 1916 a party of somewhat stolid looking men from Ruhleben told us they had nothing to complain of with regard to the camp except that had it not been for the food sent from home they would certainly have starved. In June of the same year a man who had been captured early in the war and imprisoned at Wittenburg reported that prisoners there were suffering badly. There has been an epidemic of typhus which had killed in large numbers and he himself for trivial offences had been flogged and then tied to a tree with his hands above his head for two hours at a stretch.

In August 1917 I was unofficially asked by the British Red Cross in London if, in the event of The Hague Agreement with regard to official exchanges of prisoners of war between England and Germany being ratified, I would represent them in Holland and I replied that I should be very glad to do so. I did so until the end of October when further representatives had to come out while I met trains from the frontier.

Four Canadians try to escape from Botrop Oberhausen, Westphalia, but were caught and their punishment was that they were placed flat on the ground place under a boiler containing boiling water for four hours without food or water but with the latter before them just out of reach. In the same Russian, for refusing to work, was made to stand to attention in the snow for several hours on end for 42 consecutive days after which he was in hospital for four months.

Description of Arrival and How They Were Dealt With

We had been informed that a contingent of civilian prisoners would be sent through early in each month and after our experience with the first lot I made up my mind that I would do all in my power to ensure that adequate arrangements should be made for the reception of these people. To this end I made certain suggestions to the British Consul in Rotterdam (who transmitted them to the Foreign Office in London) and in this way we were able to arrange that food tickets should be issued for supplies on the journey from the German frontier to England. To be paid for when passengers could afford to do so and the cost of which would be borne by the British government these to be filled in and endorsed by the representative of the society of friends while travelling with them on the train so as to avoid delay and discomfort at the port or on board. We were also able to arrange the consul When issued to destitute persons. Also that… Food tickets should be issued to them at Tilbury, these to be filled in by the representative of the Society of Friends while travelling with them on the train so as to avoid delay and discomfort at the port or on board. We were also able to arrange for the Consul to meet the train in order to visas and passports while travelling and for money to be exchanged on the train at the ruling rate of exchange. And most important of all that the invalids should be separately and specially provided for and the Negroes accommodated apart from white people. We also had the assurance of the Central Charities Committee in London that with the assistance of the British Red Cross the sick and mental cases would receive the necessary care and attention upon arrival at Tilbury.

Still difficulties were not at an end. It was, of course, necessary for us to receive particulars regarding the number of prisoners coming through and the general condition et cetera in time to allow of our getting up to the station on the frontier, and there making the necessary arrangements for their reception. The delay in sending us this information, perhaps almost inevitable when it could not be sent direct, but had to go through the medium of a third party, sometimes made things somewhat difficult for us. For instance on one occasion (vide letter to Maxse 9.11.16) we received information regarding a party to be met at Gennep only half an hour before the train went by which it was necessary for us to travel in order to be at the frontier in time. Picture us flying around and rushing off to the station et cetera et cetera. And upon arrival at Gennep we found that although we had been informed that all the prisoners were sane we had to deal with two insane men.

On another occasion (vide letter to Max 9.8.16) we were advised first that nine women and children would be coming among the ...What actually happened was that... 13 women and children via Oldenzaal, many of these last without means of any sort. As we had been advised that they would come via Gennep we did not meet these poor people at Oldenzaal, who being set down there in the middle of the night, was stranded. One girl of 17 (Belgian query) for instance knowing no English or Dutch and without either money or friends was escorted to Rotterdam by a Customs Official which cost us a good deal of money – as she had then to be retrieved from there and sent on to Flushing.

The train carrying the prisoners arrived at Gennep two hours late, but the railway authorities kindly allowed it to wait there another hour in order that refreshments might be given out. The travellers, some of whom came from Ruhleben showed great appreciation of the reception prepared for them and evinced unbounded delight at meeting English people again. We heard from them that one man had died on the journey, and there were among them two stretcher cases and four cases of insanity. At Boxtel, en route for Flushing, we were met by Dr Merkens of Flushing who attended to the sick as we travelled. We reached Flushing at 1 AM and there found another member of the SoF who had hot soup and other refreshments prepared. While the food was being served, passports were visas, but this last formality was not over until 6 AM and the boat taking the travellers to England sailed at 730 upon our arrival at Flushing the cases of the sick were dealt with immediately by the Consul, assisted by two Red Cross nurses sent from England for the purpose, then removed them directly to the boat. As there were a number of Negroes in the party, two members of the SoF were detailed to accompany the prisoners to England in order to give their attention to these.

We arrived at Tilbury at 4 PM where the sick were taken over by the British Red Cross and the destitute by the Charity Central Committee.

The parties consisted generally of men from Ruhleben, Negroes, sick, insane and women and children all more or less destitute and some of the cases were very hard……

As the parties came through we gained impressions of how things were in Germany generally. The accounts regarding the state of things economic the varied a good deal according to the particular part of Germany the prisoners had been in but in May 1916 we were told that milk and butter in the Ruhleben district were then almost unobtainable and soap tickets were being issued.

In July 1916 a party of five men all from Ruhleben camp came through. As they were all well educated men their remarks were of special interest. They stated in connection with the feeding of the prisoners that in consequence of the British Government considering measures of reprisal in England with potato allowance to prisoners, withdrawn some time previously had been restored, but then German guards always went round to the dustbins each night to see if they could collect anything which might be of use to feed themselves and their families. With regard to the condition of the prisoners still at Ruhleben they said that if measures to effect their release were not……

indescribable and unbelievable conditions in which these men lived, tales of squalor, dirt, disease, brutality, cruelty, misery and suffering incredible of body, mind and spirit. Enough of this aspect will be shown to enable the readers to appreciate the efforts which these men made to combat the conditions in which they found themselves and keep themselves as normal, healthy and saying as possible in an atmosphere of abnormality and distortion.

Prisoners fell naturally under two headings, civilian and military. As is well known Ruhleben was the centre of imprisonment for the former. Their release began in November 1915, when a few at a time were included among the prisoners sent through to Holland monthly. Owing to the blockade, however, their release was stopped and not resumed again until??? 1918. In spite of great efforts to preserve their normal condition at the end of 3 ½ years of captivity in the conditions imposed at Ruhleben it became almost impossible for them to hold out any longer. (Insert page 100) the following are descriptions given by various of the released prisoners and as such, speak for themselves.

Ruhleben, as an Internment Camp for British Civilians in Germany first came into being in 1914. Between then and the following Christmas fresh relays of captives were constantly brought in these for the most part have already

As one of their number put it – after over 3 ½ years in the internment there is not a man in the camp, regardless of age or calling, who has not reached the end of his powers of resistance. The uncertainty of the ultimate fate that at that as regards matters both private and public, the continued effort to keep up an appearance of cheerfulness, all this is producing an ever-increasing number of cases both of nervous collapse and insanity. Many of these cases have been caused by the apparently… Picking and choosing of candidates for exchange. I have known men to figure as many as… Times on this for exchange only to be… Disappointed. One man over 60 has been taken twice as far as the frontier only to be brought back from there to the camp. (Charles F Winger)

… served terms of imprisonment of varying duration at the local jails of the neighbourhoods where, either as visitors, patients or residents, they were first put under arrest. Unlike England, Germany did not commit herself to discriminate in this regard. No one was spared internment, and by far the greater number were incarcerated either in the wire cages, so much favoured by criminal authorities in Germany, or in solitary confinement for three weeks or a month before removal to Ruhleben.

There were in the early months of the war between four and 5000 prisoners in the camp, men of all classes and vocations, as diverse in character as the motives which take Englishmen over to the continent. Here were professors and stable boys, artists and seamen, merchants and acrobats, musicians, jockeys, students, trainers, undergraduates, engineers, teachers, businessmen and football professionals flung indiscriminately together. (D Jones)

The case of the civilian who finds himself in an enemy country at the outbreak of war is peculiar. He has no status and is immediately deprived of all rights – civic, domestic and economic. The soldier reckons upon imprisonment as a possible factor in his career, while the Officers and NCO may look forward to release after 18 months of imprisonment. Military prisoners received treatment according to rank in ways agreed upon by an international convention. Officers and men do not cease to draw their pay. To the civilian prisoner, deprived of earning his living and thus his claim to that independence which is the right of every… And becoming therefore a burden to his family and friends, is added yet another humiliation and cause for depression. Is it because a civilian is supposed to feel his position less acutely that no provision for his release after 18 months is made? (Digby R Lawson)

As time went on and these prisoners saw little or no prospect of release urgent enquiries began to be made by the as to reason the the reason of their indefinitely prolonged captivity and the reply from our Government was that in quotes military reason" made it necessary for them to remain there as "the handful of captives at Ruhleben are the means of preventing to fresh enemy divisions from entering the field." The vast majority of the prisoners were always ready to offer their lives for their country, but in view of the "military" nature of the reason of their detention, one cannot help feeling that they would have been more justly treated (had this been made clear to them from the start and put upon a military basis. The impulse which sustained them to a point of protracted and courageous endurance much strengthened. A definition of their task and status in an authoritative message from England would have given a new direction to their lives and a fresh inspiration to their thoughts and their efforts, which were bound to grow bitter and resentful when faced for years with an indie cabinet and seemingly unnecessary sentence of imprisonment. (JW Hughes)

"Arrived at Ruhleben, what did we expect what did we find?' Those who had experienced the hospitality of Germany in times of peace, who had admired her careful and precise arrangements in such matters of human welfare at railway stations, restaurants and public gardens, expected at least adequate space and reasonable cleanliness. We found stables, stables with horse dung still on the floor of the horseboxes; and above the stables lofts, so dark that every movement was a menace; so low that to stand upright except in the centre was impossible. These horseboxes were allotted as dwellings to the prisoners at the ratio of six men to one-horse, six men occupy space previously allocated to one-horse. In the lofts above overcrowding was still more dense we slept at first on the floor on straw sacks, later in Ireland bedsteads fixed one above the other, or in beds made of wood and rope by the prisoners themselves. (Here we must sleep, eat, try in vain to shelter from the Prussian winter, right, work, in fact live.) (D Jones)

In winter the camp was heated by a single steam pipe, running close under the roof which was hot for 15 hours a week but as there were no arrangements either for washing clothes or for drying them when washed any heat there was in the pipe was entirely absorbed by soaking garments hanging upon it. During the winter of 1916 to 1917 the ceiling above the base was daily covered with long icicles, and I scan on the floor round the walls of our habitation.

The barracks were flanked by dustbins and refuse boxes and the smell as well as the flies and mosquitoes issuing from these and the neighbouring marshlands, in summer made sleep impossible.

There was no drainage or flow of water; the sanitary arrangements were entirely primitive and spitting to a degree unknown and unsuspected in the freedom of ordinary life constituted an ever – increasing menace. (Charles Winger)

such were the conditions in which we found ourselves and realising the importance of living as normal a life as possible in the circumstances we set to work to organise various activities. Note insert page 139

that we were to become a community in the most absolute sense of the word was not then apparent, but exile, national … Oppression and a devoted watchfulness and admiration of the superb efforts made by our army at home and in the field

The obstructions and difficulties which had to be dealt with were sometimes well-nigh insuperable. Intense cold in winter and exhausting heat in summer, severe illness, melancholia and insanity, lack of proper food, lack of books and instruments, the abject nature of the material at the disposal of the workers, weariness, sadness, strain; exile from our country at the moment when service was most needed, surrounded by enemies, squalor, misery, dirt, perpetual calls to fresh endeavours, the overcrowding, noise and horror of life in conditions are avowedly unfit for human existence … Pressure of sorrow – this was the soil into which the seed of our efforts was cast, and none but a prisoner of war can fully comprehend how dangerous, bitter and foul that soil can be. Yet it is ever that when life lacks most, most is offered, and the impossible is achieved.

… Democracy worked spontaneously at Ruhleben. The circumstances of our lot all combined towards a realisation, within our own sphere, of the principle of unity and on this understanding – so real that it was hardly ever referred to – was based the whole social structure that eventually came into being.

One of the first steps taken was the election of "barrack captains" which originated from the necessity of establishing intermediaries between the military authorities and their captives many of whom could not speak German. Gradually also the direction and control of all matters not specifically related to the military command was brought about. A police force was recruited from among the prisoners – committees and societies began to be formed for the case of such interests as education; drama, health, sport, libraries, kitchens and canteens, religious services, finance etc. A school was organised and lectures were arranged in history, literature, art, etc etc.

The standard, both of the works presented and of their performance, was high. Indeed the earnest intention and careful and steadfast work done in this remote and isolated playhouse, seemed almost prophetic of revival of dramatic Art in England after the war. Shakespeare, Sheridan, Goldsmith, Wilde, Shaw, Galsworthy, Maugham, and Masefield were the principal British dramatists represented while from among continental authors works were given by Ibsen, Strindberg, Metternich [the latter was an organizer of the Congress of Vienna that devised the settlement of Europe after the Napoleonic wars].

Music and drama meet in Opera. Five operas of Gilbert and Sullivan were played and Mozart's Figaro was only cancelled by the release to Holland of the conductor and the nervous breakdown of a principal singer.

Painting, though practised by few, was remarkable in the constant contributions of a young artist, even then well known in several countries, whose genius was a constant stimulus to his fellow prisoners, manifesting in posters, portraits, landscapes, stage designs and several schemes of decoration notably that of the YMCA hut.

Handicrafts provoked great enthusiasm and some fine work was achieved. Bookbinding became a passion, metalwork leatherwork, wood carving, model boat building and carpentry were all developed to a high level of excellence by a large number of the younger men.

With regard to education, the future holds the fulfilment of the efforts in this field of endeavour. The School came out with a staggering prospectus including almost every branch of human knowledge from Philosophy to Diesel Engines! Languages played a large part in the curriculum: French, Dutch, Italian, Russian, Spanish and German being acquired by numerous students. Arrangements were made with various bodies in England by which students in Ruhleben could enter for the following exams – matriculation London Chamber of Commerce; Royal Society of Arts, Doctor of Music.

Recreation was organised on a similar broad scale. Half the racecourse on which the camp was placed was rented by the prisoners at the playing field and here matches took place in football, hockey, cricket, and tennis and golf, and other sports of all kinds were energetically practised here, all of which did much to maintain the physical health of the camp. (D Jones)

And last, but by no means least, gardening was pursued with great enthusiasm by many. Flowerbeds sprang up all over the camp, bringing into that squalid and distressing place a fresh, spontaneous and visible manifestation of the presence of the Kingdom of God. (D Jones)

... time has passed since these things were, and the social efforts which are being made today, great as they may be, are yet made in a state of freedom as compared with the conditions of the community at Ruhleben seven or eight years ago. Sometimes one's mind turned back for an instant to look upon that scene which then seemed to be eternity itself, and only then does one realise that, whatever the present unrest, heaven has begun for the survivors of the three or four years spent at Ruhleben in the Great War.

*   *   *

Index

37497473R00171

Printed in Great Britain
by Amazon